SACRED FOUNDATIONS

D1714832

Sacred Foundations

THE RELIGIOUS AND MEDIEVAL ROOTS OF THE EUROPEAN STATE

Anna Grzymała-Busse

PRINCETON UNIVERSITY PRESS

PRINCETON & OXFORD

Published by Princeton University Press
41 William Street, Princeton, New Jersey 08540
99 Banbury Road, Oxford OX2 6JX

press.princeton.edu

ISBN 9780691245072
ISBN (pbk.) 9780691245089
ISBN (e-book) 9780691245133

British Library Cataloging-in-Publication Data is available

Editorial: Bridget Flannery-McCoy and Alena Chekanov
Production Editorial: Mark Bellis
Cover Design: Simran Rohira
Production: Lauren Reese
Publicity: Kate Hensley and Charlotte Coyne

Cover Credit: Detail of the bottom border of the folio with a bas-de-page scene of a messenger delivering a letter to a man seated at a desk from *Calendarium, Decretals of Gregory IX with glossa ordinaria (the Smithfield Decretals)*. Edited by Raymund of Peñafort, with gloss of Bernard of Parma. Last quarter of the 13th century or 1st quarter of the 14th century. The British Library, Royal 10 E IV f. 3v.

This book has been composed in Miller

10 9 8 7 6 5 4 3 2 1

To Josh

CONTENTS

LIST OF FIGURES

ACKNOWLEDGMENTS

THE FIRST DRAFT of this book somehow was written during the surreal pandemic year of 2020–21. Writing became a refuge and a challenge, and I am so fortunate that I could indulge in both.

My first thanks go to Peter Brown and William Chester Jordan, two giants of late antiquity and medieval history. Their college lectures were enthralling, and their passion was contagious. I caught the bug, even if it took a long time to incubate.

I am grateful to so many colleagues and friends. At Stanford, special thanks go to Lisa Blaydes, Gary Cox, Rowan Dorin, Dan Edelstein, David Laitin, and Walter Scheidel for wonderfully illuminating conversations. Dan Carpenter, Dan Edelstein, and Padraic Rohan read critical parts of the manuscript and gave brilliant comments. I am also grateful for the research assistance of Olivia Ames, Advait Arun, Madigan Brodsky, Alex Durham, Juan Fueyo-Gomez, Emily Gray, and Nathalie Kirsznowski. Above all, huge thanks go to Hans Lueders, data herder and visualizer extraordinaire, who undertook the data management for this project with his usual cheerful expertise (and patience).

Several superb scholars gave this book their precious time and attention. Scott Abramson, Lisa Blaydes, Rowan Dorin, Jørgen Møller, and David Stasavage came together to give astute comments and brilliant suggestions that vastly improved the manuscript. Sheri Berman, Didi Kuo, Noam Lupu, Dan Slater, and Sue Stokes took a break from our usual fun conversations about the state of modern democracy to critique the state of this book manuscript. My academic sisters—Jenna Bednar, Mary Gallagher, and Pauline Jones—generously shared their wise comments and criticisms. I cannot thank them enough for their keen insights, our shared political outrage, all the texts, and the wine congress.

I am grateful for the opportunity to present various versions of the argument at workshops and seminars at the University of British Columbia; University of California, Berkeley; Boston University; University of California, Los Angeles; Duke University; Griffith University; Harvard University; Johns Hopkins University; Massachusetts Institute of Technology; The Ohio State University; Princeton University; University of Southern California; Stanford University; Texas A&M University; and University of Wisconsin–Madison. At these and other venues, David Art, Giovanni Cappocia, Peter Hall, Michael Mann, Grigo Pop-Eleches, Emma Rosenberg, Jared Rubin, and Daniel Ziblatt all gave very thoughtful and helpful comments.

The John Simon Guggenheim Foundation generously supported my research and writing. The Center for Advanced Study in the Behavioral Sciences (CASBS) and its amazing director, Margaret Levi, nurtured both this analysis and the well-being of so many fellows. I am very lucky to count Margaret as a mentor, intellectual hero, and friend. At CASBS, big thanks to Alejandro, Cristian, Hakeem, Paolo, and especially Katia for their sharp insights and continuing interest in medieval equine portraiture and imperial anointments.

At Princeton University Press, Bridget Flannery-McCoy was a wonderful editor. Mark Bellis and Alena Chekanov did a superb job of shepherding the manuscript through production. I am grateful to Gillian Steinberg, who made me think about writing in a whole new way, and to Kathryn Sargent, who made this manuscript far more readable. Hans Lueders and Bill Nelson drew beautiful maps and made medieval Europe as visually legible as it can be.

Family provided the kind of constant and happy distraction that makes book writing difficult and everything else wonderful. My parents and brothers nurtured a lifelong interest in religion: I am always grateful for their love, support, and skepticism. Conrad, Casimir, and Julian are beloved, energetic obstacles to getting anything done. They have all had books dedicated to them. This one goes to my husband, Josh Berke, my partner in thinking, laughing, and shenanigans. It is most definitely his turn. He came up with the title, after all.

SACRED FOUNDATIONS

Introduction

RELIGION IS NOT AN OBVIOUS ally of the secular state. Religious authorities often appear hidebound and orthodox, careful to preserve existing traditions and focused on esoteric theology. Their demands often seem designed to stifle secular ambitions of reform and innovation.

Yet nearly a thousand years ago, the Roman Catholic Church was a transformative force in Europe. It freed itself from the control of kings and emperors, created new offices at the papal court, transformed the European legal order, and invented concepts that made political representation and rule by consent possible. Kings adopted these templates and gained both new authority and institutional capacity.

The emergence of the European state has launched a flotilla of books and analyses, most of which explore the early modern period (1500–1800) and the intense wars between fragmented states. These incessant conflicts led ambitious monarchs to invest in institutions like taxation and parliaments so they could spend and negotiate their way to victory. This highly conflictual age also emphasized science, reason, and learning, thus spurring the apparently secular development of states and economic growth.

Yet several puzzles remain unsolved. Why was territorial fragmentation so uneven, and why did it persist for so long in some areas, with Germany and Italy unifying into states only in the nineteenth century? Why were the European institutions of taxation, courts, and parliaments in place long before early modern war supposedly necessitated them? Why did the rule of law and a culture of learning develop long before the Enlightenment, with hundreds of universities already dotting the landscape? Why were early European parliaments, unlike most other councils or assemblies, capable of both representation and consent?

I argue that the medieval Roman Catholic Church holds the keys to these fundamental questions. The church heavily influenced European *state formation*: the process by which rulers amass and assert their authority over populations and territories. The church[1] was a fierce rival to secular rulers, and fragmented medieval Europe into an archipelago of states. Just as importantly, monarchs adopted the distinctive administrative solutions and conceptual innovations of the popes. As a result, critical state institutions emerged when the church was at its most politically powerful, in the Middle Ages.[2] Thus, while there are many ways to build states, the European state has "sacred foundations," profoundly shaped by the deep involvement of religious authorities.

The Powerful Church

The medieval church was so powerful because, first, it held vast amounts of wealth. The medieval church was the single biggest landowner in Europe, controlling about 20 percent of land in 1200 (Morris 1989, 393). The papacy controlled a large portion of central Italy, known as the Papal States.[3] By the time of the Reformation, more than half the land in Germany was in ecclesiastical hands (Goody 1983, 131), and in Scandinavia as much as 40 percent (Orrman 2003, 453). In the period just before Henry VIII dissolved the monasteries in 1536–41, the English church held 25 percent of English land, while the crown had only 6 percent.[4] In some areas, the share of land held by the church actually *increased* in the fifteenth and sixteenth centuries.[5]

1. The "church" here is a broader institution that comprises the hierarchy (popes, cardinals, bishops, lay priests), canon chapters, the religious orders, and the administrative apparatus of laws, courts, institutions, and councils. I refer to the specific actors involved when possible. This is a narrower category than "religion," which, as Cammett and Jones (2022) remind us, comprises both doctrine and infrastructure.

2. Throughout this book, I refer to the Middle Ages as the period from 1000 to 1350 CE and the early modern period as 1500 to 1800 CE. The peak of papal power lasted from around 1075 to 1302, although well into the sixteenth century, popes were wealthier and more educated than the monarchs they faced. This periodization differentiates the medieval period of peak papal influence from the early modern period as analyzed by bellicist and bargaining theorists, who argue that the sixteenth and seventeenth centuries were critical to state formation. Tests for structural breaks substantiate this periodization (see the appendix).

3. The Papal States were territories in central Italy, occupying land donated by Pepin the Short in 756 and then by Otto I in 962, where the pope served as a temporal lord after the eleventh century and de facto controlled even earlier (Carocci 2016). They formed the second largest state in the Italian peninsula (after the Kingdom of Sicily-Naples) for six centuries from 1270 to 1870. Thirteenth-century canonists also referred to the Donation of Constantine, a forged document that granted the papacy the western swath of the Roman Empire, but it was the earlier Carolingian donations that were widely recognized.

4. English monasteries owned about 15 percent of the land, the rest of the church 10 percent. The total income of the 825 English monasteries in 1530 was 175,000 pounds, or 75 percent more than the crown received at the time. These figures switched after the Reformation: by 1560, the Swedish church held no land at all, while the crown had 28 percent (Cipolla 1993, 46–8).

5. For example, church holdings around Florence grew from an average 13 percent of land in 1427 to 25 percent in 1508–12 (Cipolla 1993, 46–7).

These enormous land holdings resulted from earlier accumulation, in the seventh through tenth centuries, of voluntary offerings, property transfers, and bequests. The church retained these with its family law: for example, children born to clerics were, by definition, illegitimate and could not inherit, leaving property in church hands.

The church taxed the laity and clergy alike. Secular rulers were supposed to support the church financially. Numerous monarchs paid the census, a per-capita tax, starting in the eleventh and twelfth centuries (Robinson 2004b, 350). Monasteries made direct payments to the pope, and clergy made direct subsidies for specific causes, such as the Crusades. Popes also appointed bishops and then taxed them. The papacy removed such vast amounts from England through clerical taxes under the reign of the three Edwards (1272–1377) that precious metals became scarce, prompting accusations of papal abuse (Ergang 1971, 167). The pope could tax royal subjects directly for a certain number of years (Gilchrist 1969, 28). Tithing entitled the church to collect a 10-percent tax on all income, generating huge revenues even if the church rarely collected the full tenth (Morris 1989, 388). Given this wealth, "one can hardly overestimate the importance of the Church as an economic entity in preindustrial Europe" (Cipolla 1993, 45).

Taxation required both authority and administrative capacity, and the church exploited its relative administrative strength, especially where secular authority was tenuous. Medieval popes sent emissaries from Rome to ensure that the full measure of taxes would be collected from reluctant clergy, and they repeatedly asserted their right to tax the clergy. The papacy divided Europe into an efficient system of districts staffed by collectors and sub-collectors of papal taxes, and punished those who resisted. By the early thirteenth century, an "elaborate system of clerical taxation" funneled resources to the papal administration (Riley-Smith 2005, 150).[6]

Second, the church was so powerful because of its human capital—literate clerks, expert jurists, experienced administrators—committed to argumentation and written culture. Bishops were especially important, serving popes as spiritual emissaries and kings as high administrators and judges. They governed as local lords and sat in the national assemblies that provided justice, legitimated the monarchs, and granted consent to important legislation. Clergy served in the royal administrations as legal experts, imperial emissaries, local judges, chancellors, and clerks. They wrote letters, answered petitions, and kept records. Closer to home, clergy enforced local contracts; collected taxes; and recorded births, deaths, and wills in cathedral records. The church interpreted law and provided legal arbitration for both clerics and lay people: "the

---

6. The taxes included caritative subsidies (voluntary donations), *annates* (taxes on the first year's income from a new holder of a benefice), *servitia* (taxes paid by bishops on their nomination and confirmation), and intercalary fruits (income from vacant clerical offices) beyond the regular taxes waged on the clergy (Riley-Smith 2005, 264).

Church made laws, had its own courts, and exercised a jurisdiction parallel and often superior to secular authority" (Gilchrist 1969, 9). The development of both lay and church administration thus came down to a "small group of people who shared a craft literacy—the clergy" (Cheyette 1973, 150).

Beyond its wealth and human capital, the medieval church's power derived from its spiritual and moral authority. Popes and priests anointed emperors, baptized children, buried the dead, forgave sins, and condemned entire communities to damnation. The church was ever-present and all-encompassing: "the tentacles of this institution reached into the life of every court, every manor, every village, every town of Europe . . . this was the only authoritative interaction network that spread so extensively while also penetrating intensively into everyday life" (Mann 1986, 380). Monasteries, cathedrals, and bishoprics spread across the European landscape, making the church omnipresent. The church "governed birth, marriage, and death, sex, and eating, made the rules for law and medicine, gave philosophy and scholarship their subject matter. Membership in the Church was mandatory: expulsion was tantamount to a social death. Even cooking instructions called for boiling an egg 'for the time it takes to say the Miserere'" (Tuchman 1978, 32).

Above all, the church offered salvation—the promise of eternal life and divine mercy that no secular ruler could possibly match. This monopoly meant that "the church was surely the best claimant to legitimacy and coercive control. It will simply not do to dismiss the power of the Pope as depending on moral authority and influence. After all, the fear of the hereafter is potentially the most potent form of coercive control" (Davies 2003, 291). The church's "unity and cohesiveness as an institution . . . together with its power of appeal to the *apostolica auctoritas* and the possession of the sentence of excommunication as an effective means for enforcing its will, far surpassed any comparable secular institution in the Middle Ages" (Gilchrist 1969, 9).

In short, the wealth, human capital, administrative capacity, and spiritual authority of the medieval church far outweighed those of any king or prince. When medieval rulers exercised and tried to expand their authority, they continually confronted this superior power.

Fear and Envy in State Formation

Through the twin mechanisms of rivalry and emulation, of secular fear and envy, the church shaped state formation. Eager to establish autonomy for the church, medieval popes deliberately clashed with some rulers and fragmented their territorial authority. The papacy fought hostile secular rulers with both spiritual weapons and military alliances. Popes and rulers tried to undermine each other's authority, gleefully produced legal arguments and documents dug up from the archives (some forged, as with the Donation of Constantine), denounced and deposed each other, and formed alliances. These attacks and coalitions fragmented some royal authorities (Germany) and enabled others to consolidate (England). The stubborn insistence of popes on their moral and political authority stoked the ambitions of temporal rulers. As both the church and secular rulers expanded their authority, "copious conflicts" erupted over church autonomy, jurisdiction, and taxation (Watts 2009, 52). This rivalry resulted in the persistent fragmentation of territorial authority in areas targeted by the papacy, aided the rise of independent communes, and helped to elaborate both distinctions between religious and secular authorities and concepts of secular sovereignty.

Rulers also *emulated* the church. The church was an essential source of legal, administrative, and conciliar innovations, transmitted through bishops, canon lawyers, and clergy who served at royal courts. The church showed rulers how to collect direct taxes more efficiently, request and answer a flood of petitions, keep records and accounts, interpret the law, and hold councils that could provide valuable consent. Many ecclesiastical administrative templates, such as the petitioning system or church synods, influenced the organization of royal courts. Medieval jurists rediscovered Roman law and systematized church law, and the new demand for legal training prompted huge university growth, with the first law school established in Bologna in 1088. Concepts such as representation, binding consent, and even majority rules relied on ecclesiastical precedents. These ideas justified national assemblies where consent would be given to raising revenue and new kings would be legitimated, beginning with the *Cortes* of León in 1188.

Rivalry and emulation help to explain variation in the timing and pattern of medieval European state formation. Where the papacy saw rulers as hostile and powerful, as in the Holy Roman Empire, popes targeted these rulers with ideology, legal arguments, maledictions, and wars by proxy. The resulting fragmentation greatly weakened the formation of central state institutions. Where the state was already relatively powerful, and the papacy needed the king's acquiescence, if not support, as in England, state development unfolded with relatively little church interference. Where the rulers posed little threat to the papacy, either because they focused on consolidating local power (as in the Spanish territories or France until the end of the thirteenth century) or because they were weak and distant (as in Scandinavia or East Central Europe), the church had less interest in fragmenting authority, and its institutional models could be more easily adopted.

Bishops were particularly effective in transmitting ecclesiastical innovations. They traveled to Rome, were trained in church law and theology, and spoke Latin, the *lingua franca* of the church. Sent as legates (papal emissaries) from Rome, bishops brought with them the administrative innovations of the papal court. Bishops regularly sat in the royal councils and national assemblies, and they served as judges, chancellors, and other high officials. The crown also relied on bishops "because they were powerful landowners who possessed the same influence as important secular lords and because they had equal responsibility to ensure that peace existed in the territories which fell within their authority" (Dodd 2014, 222). Frequently highborn and even related to the kings they served, bishops were embedded in powerful political networks that enabled them to spread ideas and practices.

This secular borrowing was often unintentional: kings chose bishops as chancellors because they were the most trusted officials, not because they were self-consciously emulating the papal administration. Rulers rejected some templates entirely: the papacy preferred electoral monarchy, but powerful nobles rather than popes forced elections on kings, as in the Holy Roman Empire, Hungary, and Poland. There were limits to church influence: papal requests for funds and norms of chastity were both flouted regularly. And yet, since the church was so powerful and so capable, it was a natural source of institutional models, human capital, and conceptual innovations. Would rulers have adopted the same solutions without the church? The plethora of other institutional solutions found across the world, whether in Asia, the Middle East or Byzantium, suggests that this is not the case (see Blaydes 2017; Dincecco and Wang 2018; Huang and Kang 2022). Other rulers did not have to contend with a powerful, autonomous, religious hierarchy that both competed with and nourished nascent states in Europe.

A Reversal of Fortune: The State Triumphant

The ideas, resources, and institutions developed by the church took on a life of their own. They were adopted enthusiastically and adapted opportunistically by secular rulers, and were then deployed against the church. Secular rulers grew to resent the papacy's interventions and wealth, and the ways in which these undermined secular authority. Conran and Thelen identify "institutional conversion" as occurring when rules and practices developed for one purpose are used for another (Conran and Thelen 2016, 65). The processes described here are more like "institutional subversion," where secular authorities adopted ideas developed by the church and used them to subvert both the church and its aims. By the late fourteenth century, long before the triumph of the Protestant Reformation, monarchs could assert supremacy over the church.

Thanks to their struggle with and mimicry of the church, late medieval monarchs expanded their capacity to govern, to raise revenue, and to assert their sovereignty. These kings learned "much from the institutional organization of the medieval church. They had built up organized bureaucracies with networks of local administrators and centralized departments to oversee justice and finances. They were relying more and more on paid mercenary troops in place of the old feudal levies. They had begun to legislate sporadically and to tax systematically. Several of them had called into existence national representative assemblies in which the support of all classes could be mobilized"

(Tierney 1964, 160). Canon lawyers and rulers both championed early notions of sovereignty. Even the notorious advocate of papal supremacy, Pope Innocent III, confirmed in 1202 "that the king of France admitted no superior in temporal matters" (Genet 1992, 124). Medieval jurists articulated the concept of a state as an abstract entity, distinct from the ruler or the people (Canning 1983, 23; Bagge 2019, 94). Territorial borders emerged, and customs offices attempted to control the flows of people and goods.[7]

The church gradually made itself obsolete as a source of human capital and institutional models. The steady flow of clerical experts strengthened both law and administration but also made clergy less necessary, as lay clerks acquired similar expertise and skills. The secular state apparatus expanded even further in the fourteenth century (Rigaudiere 1995, 34; Watts 2009, 206). Kings used the church's taxation techniques to share proceeds with their magnates, rather than with popes, strengthening the royal position. New legal frameworks "dramatically reinvigorated older conceptions of the king and the kingdom" (Watts 2009, 74), justifying the centralization of royal power and stimulating huge new judicial and legal activity. The very law the church had helped to revive would now keep the church in its place.

As the state grew more autonomous, the church was able to extract less revenue from increasingly reluctant rulers. To fill its coffers, the church turned to the sale of offices and indulgences, in effect selling salvation, which weakened its moral authority and justified the ever-greater autonomy of the state from the church. Internal discord (the fourteenth century saw a string of dueling popes and anti-popes) belied its claims of being the one true church. Popes turned to the earthly business of finances and diplomacy rather than saving souls and preaching God's word. Viewed from this perspective, the Protestant Reformation was less a revolution than a culmination of protracted processes of internal church division and growing secular authority.

Explaining the State

Existing explanations for the rise of the state, in contrast, focus on very different actors and mechanisms. "Bellicist" and "bargaining" theories both focus on the early modern period (1500–1800) and on secular rulers. They view war and contracts, respectively, as critical to state formation. "Neo-medievalists" analyze the Middle Ages but often neglect religious authorities as a force in state formation—and when they do focus on religion, it is often to emphasize its deleterious effects.

---

7. From the ninth to the eleventh centuries, clearly understood boundaries coexisted with more common marches, porous areas where adjoining powers broadcast power but did not monopolize it. By the twelfth and thirteenth centuries, borders became more defined as rulers consolidated their rule (see Fischer 1992, 439–40).

EXPENSIVE WAR

The best-known set of explanations for state formation is the bellicist tradition. Charles Tilly's summary is as succinct as it is canonical: "war made the
state and the state made war" (Tilly 1975, 42). Violent rivalry among states led
them to tax their populations to extract resources. Rulers who succeeded in
building up the extractive and military apparatus of war went on to consolidate their territorial gains and ensure the survival of their states.

Bellicist explanations share three perspectives: first, they view the peak of
state building as occurring in the early modern era, from the sixteenth to the end
of the eighteenth century. Second, they emphasize that nascent secular states
were the main actors in the violent conflicts that drove state formation. Third,
they argue that these wars consolidated larger, more viable states.

In these accounts, "the state" was invented as a corporate entity only in
early modern Europe. Other practices of rulemaking and enforcement may
have existed, but the idea of the state before this time period is anachronistic
(Anderson 2018; Skinner 2018). Scholars from Otto Hintze to Charles Tilly
date the rise of both domestic state administrations and external sovereignty to
the early modern era, from the mid-sixteenth to the mid-seventeenth century
(Tilly 1975, 170; Ertman 2017, 54; Spruyt 2017, 81). In this conventional periodization, the Treaties of Augsburg (1555) and Westphalia (1648) helped to
establish the principle of sovereignty in international relations.[8] Others argue
that the *practice* of sovereignty (marked by a formal monopoly of authority
over a distinct territory) arose much later, in the early nineteenth century
(Teschke 2003; Gorski and Sharma 2017, 103).

The starting point for the bellicist accounts is the territorial fragmentation
of Europe. The collapse of the Roman empire in the late fifth century and that of
the Carolingian empire in the late ninth left in their wake a raft of small principalities and statelets (Mitterauer 2010; Wickham 2016; Ertman 2017, 63; Gorski and Sharma 2017, 99). Subsequent medieval governance was a disjointed
system of local authority and incomplete territorial control. No empire arose
in Europe that could compare to the Roman one: it was simply too difficult to
sustain (Scheidel 2019).

This fragmentation of both authority and territory is the setting for the
constant warfare that characterized European state making. Repeated invasions and wars eliminated weaker states and led to vigorous new efforts to
extract resources. Hintze's earlier work emphasized that the threat of war led

---

8. See Morgenthau (1985), Watson (1992), Held (1995), and Philpott (2001). Others dispute the idea that Westphalia marked the rise of state sovereignty (see Krasner 1993; Osiander 2001; Teschke 2003). Augsburg established the principle of *cuius regio, eius religio*—a
ruler's right to choose the religious denomination for his people. As De Carvalho, Leira, and
Hobson (2011) note, this principle was retracted at Westphalia.

to the ratcheting consolidation and centralization of European states.[9] Following in his footsteps, scholars such as Bean (1973), McNeill ([1982] 2013), Mann (1988), Tilly (1992), Downing (1992), Porter (1994), and Parker (1996) emphasized the fierce pressures of military competition in the early modern era.[10] Warfare was constant, both because rulers poured enormous amounts of money into conflict and because defeat did not depose princes or kings (Hoffman 2015, 26–7).

War winnowed out and consolidated states, with as many as 500 independent states in Europe in the year 1500 reduced to 30 four centuries later (Tilly 1992, 45–6; see also Bean 1973, 204). Winners had to develop more powerful governments to govern the numerous losers, which in turn promoted peace and economic development (Morris 2014, but see Abramson 2017). Larger states also lowered their per-capita defense costs. Those states that could gain the wealth and manpower necessary to wage war would survive, while "those that did not would be crushed on the battlefield and absorbed into others" (Mann 1988, 109). The threat of war also led to urbanization, as people sought refuge behind city walls. Economic activity then increased and human capital accumulated, leading to local self-governance, trade, and property rights protections (Dincecco and Onorato 2016, 2018).

Warfare led to the incidental formation of state institutions. Early modern war was costly and required the extraction of resources. Tilly (1976, 1992) argues that pressures of war led to state formation when rulers combined moderate levels of capital accumulation with sufficient coercive capabilities.[11] War thus led rulers to develop taxation (Mann 1986, 486; Herbst 2000, 120). The collection of these taxes required surveillance, which then prompted the growth of state administrations (Tilly 1992, 87). As a result, familiar modern state institutions such as bureaucracy, the treasury, courts, and parliaments are simply the "more or less inadvertent by-products" of preparations for war

9. Thomas Ertman differentiates Hintze's earlier work, with its emphasis on the geopolitical context and war, from his later scholarship, which emphasized uneven state development, with rulers in the core of the former Carolingian empire building bureaucratic administrative institutions starting in the twelfth century. The periphery developed strong local governments and lords that could either accompany a powerful monarch (as in England) or dominate weak ones (as in Poland, Hungary, or Bohemia) (Ertman 2017, 63–5).

10. Scholars debated the periodization: for Bean, the critical period was between 1400 and 1600; for Strayer, after 1300; and for Tilly, definitely after 1500 and especially after 1600 (Strayer [1970] 1998; Bean 1973; Tilly 1975, 25–6).

11. Tilly emphasizes that economic starting conditions meant different trajectories of war- and state making. In "capitalized coercion," scarce resources lead rulers to the incorporation of capital and capitalists through a centralized administrative apparatus. England and France are two examples. Other state organizations, such as city-states or empires, were capital- and coercion-intensive, respectively. These could not develop the same capacities as national states and eventually disappeared (Tilly 1992, 30).

(Tilly 1992, 26).[12] In more nuanced bellicist accounts, the timing and context of war shaped institutional development: in Thomas Ertman's (1997) analysis, early military competition led to patrimonial administrations, and relatively weak local governance led to absolutist regimes. Brian Downing (1992) argues that in geopolitically exposed areas such as France and Russia, massive mobilization of men and money abolished medieval constitutionalism in favor of militarized absolutism (see also Bean 1973). In all these accounts, state institutions arise in response to the exigencies of war.

In short, states emerged in Europe because of warfare, the competition for land and people it entailed, and the mobilization of resources that war demanded. In these accounts, initial fragmentation was incidental and state institutions were functional necessities. The vicious wars of the early modern period, with their expensive military technology and large armies, led to the transformation of Europe from a multitude of fragmented jurisdictions to fewer, larger, and more institutionalized states.

These powerful accounts of European state formation traveled far abroad. A slew of prominent analyses of state formation in Africa, Latin America,[13] and Asia exported bellicist insights (Herbst 2000; Centeno 2002; Doner, Ritchie, and Slater 2005; Thies 2005; Tin-Bor Hui 2005; Taylor and Botea 2008; Dincecco and Wang 2018; Mazzuca 2021). These scholars mostly found that outside of Europe, war either did not take place or it did not build the state. Yet bellicist theories remain a central reference point for accounts of both European and non-European state formation.

PEACEFUL BARGAINING

A different narrative of state building shares the emphasis on the early modern period but does not emphasize war. Where the bellicists see institutions as fortuitous byproducts of war, this approach argues that institutions are the result of intensive *bargaining* between rulers and society. The resulting agreements exchanged the protection of individual and property rights for steady revenue for the state (North 1981). The balance of domestic power influenced which institutions were built. Where nobles could threaten to withhold arms, men, and wealth from the monarchy, they could constrain rulers and obtain property rights (Bates and Lien 1985; Levi 1988; Kiser and Barzel 1991; Hoffman

12. Historians working in this tradition focused on the fiscal state, analyzing the early modern regimes of taxation, extraction, and war-making (Brewer 1989; Stone 1994; Bonney 1999; Glete 2002; Storrs 2009).

13. Latin America is one region where the colonial project of the sixteenth century could have brought religious influence on state formation, but that was not the case. By that point, the colonist states had already developed their own administrations. The church sponsored numerous religious missions in Latin America, but it did not shape the state directly as it did in Europe.

and Rosenthal 1997; Barzel and Kiser 2002; Blaydes and Chaney 2013). More broadly, the medieval balance between nobles and monarchs is seen as critical to the divergence between early modern absolutist and constitutional regimes (Kiernan 1965, 24; Anderson [1974] 2013; Duby 1978; Poggi 1990, 42; Downing 1992; Ertman 1997).

Where parliaments constrained powerful predatory rulers, as in North and Weingast's (1989) account of the English Glorious Revolution of 1688, property rights and public investment were protected against rapacious rulers. Scholars have questioned the timing and impact of such reform.[14] Perhaps most pointedly, Boucoyannis (2021) argues that a powerful executive was necessary to the rise of national assemblies by *compelling* nobles to attend. Nonetheless, an entire generation of economic historians has followed North and Thomas (1973) in arguing that these institutions constrained the arbitrary rule of monarchs and were critical to economic development.

As a result, competition need not be violent: Konrad and Skaperdas (2012) argue that early states competed to provide markets for security, a desirable public good. Economic expansion and competition also led to demand for governance. Where rulers overlapped, their marginal revenues dropped—and so rulers cooperated to agree on borders (Acharya and Lee 2018). Hendrik Spruyt (1994) argues that the rise of trade produced new political actors, and the coalitions between these actors and rulers produced distinct states. The national state, in which the political community and administrative reach overlap, arose as the dominant form because it could better standardize tolls and taxes, secure borders, and define its jurisdiction—and such states viewed each other as more reliable partners, copied these commitments, and thus reified each other.

Indeed, war can hinder the processes of state making. It leads rulers to postpone structural reform, solve problems on an ad hoc basis, and sacrifice efficiency for immediate results (Strayer [1970] 1998, 60). War ended intensive growth in both ancient Greece and medieval northern Italy (Ober 2015; Fouquet and Broadberry 2015). It spread disease and depleted the labor supply (Voigtländer and Voth 2013; Saylor and Wheeler 2017). The early onset

---

14. Clark (1996) argues that property rights protections, executive constraint, and the credibility of financial policy began before the Glorious Revolution. Sussman and Yafeh (2006) argue that institutional reforms did not have the expected effects: interest rates remained high and volatile. Cox (2012) shows that parliamentary rights, rather than property rights protections, were what changed. Pincus and Robinson (2011) argue that what mattered was the *de facto* shift in power between king and parliament, rather than *de jure* changes. The one clear formal innovation, the exclusion of Catholics from the throne, had no real consequences. In contrast, Carruthers (1990, 697) argues that it was King James II's support for Catholicism that turned Parliament against him. The rise of the Whigs and Tories, with the Whiggish Bank of England opposed to the king, accelerated the development of public finance and capital markets.

of military competition translated into a primitive and patrimonial administration, while later military rivalries made it possible to establish a more efficient bureaucracy with the new administrative techniques developed in the interim (Ertman 1997). The lengthy and costly wars of the fourteenth and fifteenth centuries impeded state building even as the basic structures survived (Strayer [1970] 1998, 60–1; Marx 2003, 83; see also Kaeuper 2001).[15] Wars produced crises: *ancien regime* France was exhausted by its military ventures, as was eighteenth-century Poland, so that "precapitalist states made war and war unmade these states" (Teschke 2017, 45).

GOING MEDIEVAL

The main argument of this book, that the medieval church fundamentally shaped state formation in Europe, builds most directly on scholarship that emphasizes the medieval roots of the modern state.

Recent literature emphasizes the deep history of the European state (Grzymala-Busse 2020). The Crusades, which began in 1096, facilitated the rise of the modern state through the institution of crusade taxes, sales of feudal land to finance the expeditions, the reintegration of Europe into global trade networks, and the elimination of rivals to ruling monarchs (Blaydes and Paik 2016). In a seminal series of works, Møller finds the institutional roots of the democratic state in medieval communalism and the rule of law in papal reforms (Møller 2015, 2017a, 2018, 2021). As legal systems developed, they set the stage for Europe's political and economic development (Cantoni and Yuchtman 2014, 828; Spruyt 2002, 132). Cities and communes arose (Abramson 2017; Møller 2018), along with urban self-government and interdependence (Bosker, Buringh, and Van Zanden 2013; Doucette and Møller 2021). Representative assemblies also date back to the Middle Ages, as does broader constitutionalism (Marongiu 1968; Downing 1989; Blockmans 1998; Stasavage 2010; Abramson and Boix 2019; Boucoyannis 2021). These assemblies grew along with cities (Van Zanden, Buringh, and Bosker 2012; Abramson and Boix 2019; Doucette and Møller 2021). Primogeniture (the inheritance of all land and office by the oldest son) and other changes in family law stabilized landholding and monarchical rule (Goody 1983; Konrad and Skaperdas 2007; Brundage 2009; Kokkonen and Sundell 2014; Sharma 2015; Acharya and Lee 2019; Henrich 2020).

The role of religious actors has been often neglected in these accounts of individual institutional formation, sometimes deliberately so.[16] Some scholars

---

15. Other medievalists argue that war produced medieval fiscal and representative innovations (Harriss 1975). Genet (1992) argues that the modern state was born between 1280 and 1360, thanks to the pressures of war, as feudal lords began to vie for state positions and privileges. He, too, emphasizes conflict with the church as critical to state formation.

16. In Van Zanden, Buringh, and Bosker's (2012) account, for example, the presence of archbishops is the single most powerful correlate of city growth, yet is left unexplored (see

have noted the religious and medieval aspects of some institutions, especially the rule of law (Poggi 1990; Fukuyama 2011; Møller 2017a) and the legitimation of medieval rulers (Bendix 1978, 7; Fischer 1992; Rubin 2017). Joseph Strayer stressed ecclesiastical influence during the period of relative medieval peace as a force in building the state (Strayer [1970] 1998; see also Genet 1992).[17] Notably, Møller and Doucette (2021) analyze how the church shaped the European state system by diffusing urban self-government, which they argue led to both the rise of representative assemblies and a polycentric state system.[18]

Much of this scholarship emphasizes the foundational split between religious and secular authority (see Fukuyama 2011 and Møller 2019). Social scientists who have examined the role of the church focus on the separation of church and state, and the conflict between popes and kings that led to it (Kiernan 1965, 34; Ergang 1971; Bendix 1978, 35; Poggi 1978, 120; Reinhard 1996, 7; de Mesquita 2000, 2022; Fukuyama 2011, 266ff; see also Kuran 2011). In these accounts, the church becomes important for its differentiation and withdrawal, rather than for the active contributions of religious authority to state formation.

Many economic historians also remain skeptical. They view the church as a rent-seeking economic firm that monopolized salvation (Ekelund et al. 1989, 1996) and hindered institutions that would have promoted growth (de Mesquita 2000, 2022; Weingast 2021). As Weingast notes, Adam Smith already argued in the *Wealth of Nations* (1776) that the church impeded economic growth.[19] Specifically, the church stymied the secular provision of public goods and property rights as a threat to its monopoly on both salvation and rents.[20] Bruce Bueno de Mesquita (2000, 2022) argues that an agreement signed in 1122, the Concordat of Worms, was a singular inflection point that set into

---

table 1, 856). Boucoyannis explicitly excludes the church from her analysis of parliamentary development as "historically important but not theoretically central" (Boucoyannis 2021, 24). More generally, the role of religion is often overlooked in accounts of political development (Grzymala-Busse 2015.)

17. Anglo-Saxon historians focused on church influence on royal governance (see, for example, Brooke [1931] 1981 and 1938; Post 1943, 196; Chrimes 1952; and Ullmann [1955] 1965), but this literature gave way to emphases on more localized studies of violence, lordship, bishops, and law.

18. Møller and Doucette focus on the monastic reform program, and its impact on both the local and supranational levels. Our analyses are complementary: this book focuses on the impact of the papacy on mid-level institutions such as court administrations, law and justice, universities, and parliaments.

19. In Weingast's interpretation, the church brokered a deal with the secular lords. The church would pacify the masses, but if the lords tried to expropriate the church, it would turn the masses on the lords. To maintain this equilibrium, the church had to prevent economic growth, which would have given the masses wealth and power.

20. Some scholars point to the ban on usury as a growth-hampering institution. The ban was reaffirmed at the Third and Fourth Lateran Councils, but theology was far stricter than legal practice. Both canon law and Roman civil law carved out extensive exceptions, tolerating moderate interest rates and punishing only "notorious" cases (Dorin 2015, 25–6).

motion distinct pro- and anti-growth trajectories by empowering secular rulers—and where the church got its way, it hampered growth.

Yet the church also fostered human capital, the rule of law, the protection of property rights, and notions of binding consent and representation, all historically critical to growth (see for example, North and Thomas 1973; North 1981; Greif 2006; Nunn 2009; Acemoglu and Robinson 2012; Johnson and Koyama 2017; Mokyr 2017).[21] And, as we will see, there was no single decisive episode: rather, the rivalry and transferal of resources from church to state took centuries, strengthening the state gradually and in ways often unanticipated and unintended by both lay and ecclesiastical authorities.

Taking Tilly to Church

This book builds on and challenges these important insights, acknowledging that state formation is necessarily complex and shaped by numerous forces, war and bargaining among them. The analysis here reassesses the foundational period for European state formation, the kind of rivalry involved, and the mechanisms of state building. It argues that many European state institutions and concepts developed in the Middle Ages, that the church was both a critical rival and resource, and that mimicry mattered as much as rivalry did.

Focusing on the church sheds new light on persistent puzzles. First, bellicists view fragmentation as incidental and do not explain how the fragmentation of authority persisted. Yet contrary to bellicist accounts, European fragmentation was deliberate, and it survived the period of intense early modern warfare. The medieval church holds the answer: papal conflict, whether waged through excommunications, crusades, or wars by proxy, first fragmented large swaths of Europe. Once these tactics empowered cities and barons vis-à-vis kings and emperors, the fragmentation became self-sustaining even as papal power waned.

As a result, *religious* rivalry was central to both state fragmentation and consolidation. For its part, interstate conflict was neither necessary nor sufficient for state formation (Spruyt 2017, 74ff). It was not necessary, because some states, including Switzerland, the Dutch Republic, and England, could forgo large standing armies and the extraction they necessitated (Downing 1992). Other states, among them Denmark, the Netherlands, and Sweden, developed high capacity *after* they abandoned military competition (Spruyt 2017, 88). War was not sufficient to form states: despite centuries of constant warfare, the German and Italian territories never consolidated into larger states, nor were they winnowed out. Instead, small principalities and autonomous city republics survived the pressures of war.

21. The church also "created reserves of capital, encouraged changes in land-owning, inaugurated the system of deposits, credit, and banking, proclaimed the wise doctrine of a stable coinage and took part in large commercial enterprises" (Gilchrist 1969, 69).

Another puzzle is the precocious rise of state institutions. Many familiar state institutions, whether courts, taxes, or parliaments, already functioned in the medieval era, long before the costly warfare and elite negotiations of the early modern period. By the early twelfth century, chanceries and secretariats were growing, as were the ranks of judges, revenue officers, royal clerks, and notaries. Legal innovations in the late eleventh century replaced possession with private property, oral agreements with written contracts, and ordeals with formal court procedures. Medieval parliaments had their own golden age from 1250 to 1450, centuries before the Glorious Revolution.

If these state institutions arose in the Middle Ages, early modern warfare or bargaining could not have produced them. More broadly, as North (1991) argued, competition alone is not enough to spur institutional evolution. Institutions build on extant models and personnel. In an environment of uncertainty, where rulers are concerned with legitimation, institutional isomorphism—the adoption and diffusion of similar institutional solutions—is a far likelier path (DiMaggio and Powell 1983).

Rather than inventing institutions *ab novo*, then, secular rulers in medieval Europe often adopted ecclesiastical precedents. The church was the crucial source of institutional models, conceptual innovations, and administrative solutions.[22] It also provided human capital, the learned bishops, literate clerks, and expert canonists who staffed royal courts, regional administrations, and universities alike. This emulation of the church also helps to explain why medieval institutions took the forms they did, such as the distinguishing parliamentary features of representation and binding consent.

The influence of the church thus serves to explain the persistence of fragmentation, the timing of the rise of state institutions, and some of their fundamental characteristics. In contrast to arguments about the deleterious effects of the church, these institutions fostered growth, representation, and effective administration. The irony is that by adopting these ecclesiastical innovations, nascent states grew in capacity, developed their own human capital and resources—and eventually subordinated the church.

Conceptualizing the Medieval State

State formation entailed gaining control over a given people and territory free from internal rivals or external influence, differentiating rulers from other potential authorities,[23] and establishing more effective mechanisms of

---

22. For accounts of *secular* mimicry in state formation, see Spruyt (1994) and Huang and Kang (2022).

23. Authority itself is the hierarchical assertion of legitimate rule that does not rely on coercion or persuasion (Arendt 1958, 82–3). Legitimacy, or the taking for granted of an actor's authority, even if one disagrees with the process or outcome, is central to governance, as it lowers the costs of governing and increases compliance (Levi 1988).

governance to maintain law and order, adjudicate disputes, raise revenue, and coordinate with other social actors.[24]

Medieval states thus formed in two senses. First, rulers needed to assert sovereignty or supreme authority within a territory and be recognized as having equal standing to other states, brooking no religious or imperial superiors. This is state formation as many scholars of international relations understand it. Second, and the focus of this book, is the process of institution building and legitimation, domestic state formation as much of comparative politics sees it. Rulers needed to build an administrative apparatus to back their claims of authority by answering petitions, administering justice, raising revenue—and keeping track of all these activities. The development of law provided a set of predictable rules, promoting societal order and economic growth. It was also a set of arguments, wielded in conflict with other political actors. Finally, national assemblies arose out of royal councils and, at least initially, served to administer justice and legitimate the ruler rather than represent society or legislate new laws. These processes took place from the late eleventh to the fourteenth century, reinforcing each other. In short, the "state" here is a work in progress rather than a finished edifice. The analytical focus of this book is on the elite builders: popes and kings, bishops and princes, chancellors and judges.[25]

The construction site, the early medieval polity, was distinct. There were no crisply defined "states," "bureaucracies," or "administrations." No ruler held a monopoly over the legitimate use of violence. Instead, forms of authority, whether imperial, spiritual, local, or customary, coexisted, and "grace was the characteristic medium through which personal authority was expressed . . . flexible justice, mercy and anger, gifts, bribes and comprises, rewards . . . in expectation of future service, or present advantage" (Watts 2009, 32). Kings were itinerant and ruled by consultation, cajoling, and councils rather than by coercion or an impersonal bureaucracy (Wickham 1984, 26; Davies 2003, 291; Stollberg-Rilinger 2018, 17). Kingship derived its power from symbolic legitimation and the loyalty of magnates rather than an impersonal administration.

24. Tilly identifies four aspects of "stateness": formal autonomy, differentiation from non-governmental organizations, centralization, and internal coordination (Tilly 1975, 34). A "national state" is "a relatively centralized, differentiated organization the officials of which more or less successfully claim control over the chief concentrated means of violence within a population inhabiting a large, contiguous territory" (Tilly 1985, 170). Subsequently, Tilly defines the state as "coercion-wielding organizations that are distinct from households and kingship groups and exercise clear priority in some respects over all other organizations within substantial territories" and specifically excludes the church as such (Tilly 1992, 1–2).

25. I focus far less on the lives of the populations of these lands, made up of peasants, merchants, families, monks and nuns, knights and sheriffs. This poses a danger of reifying the state, but has the advantage of imposing some constraint and discipline on an otherwise infinitely textured story.

The medieval state was not fully differentiated in its functions, nor did it have a clear hierarchy. The divisions between office and individual were only nascent. The boundaries between office and property, the qualifications necessary, and even the type of remuneration all differed from contemporary norms.[26] Institutional functions were at best imperfectly coordinated, and state power was limited (see Ergang 1971, 27; Kiernan 1980, 10–11). Few states were stable entities, as "dynastic strategies and accidents often united or separated territories" (Blockmans 1998, 35).

The boundaries between "church" and "state" were also often unclear, with overlap in both roles and personnel: "papal sovereignty was defined according to rules derived from civil law, and imperial elections were conducted according to rules derived from canon law" (Tierney 1982, 10). Magnates and leading churchmen formed the same governing class (Harriss 1993, 33). Elite clergy filled high state offices, and in turn, clerks at royal courts were rewarded with bishoprics. The same noble families provided both royal counselors and bishops, kings were anointed by bishops, and there was no "clear area of separate governmental responsibilities that could be termed secular" (Morris 1989, 18; see also Cantor 1958, 290). Nor does early modern state formation become "secular": throughout the period, European state formation was shot through with religion. In the Middle Ages, the papacy acted as a powerful authority, while in the early modern era, monarchs used religion both to bolster their own domestic control and to justify conflict with other rulers (Gorski 2003; Nexon 2009).

As a result, some argue that the lines between the religious and the political were blurred (if not entirely fused) prior to the seventeenth century (Anderson 2014; Cavanaugh 2009). As Liah Greenfeld argues, "the problem of Church and State did not exist in the Middle Ages because the State did not exist" (Greenfeld 1996, 175). After all, for most of European history, kingship and priesthood would have been more legible categories than church and state (Nelson 2006, 31). Yet this argument conflates the divine *source* of legitimate authority (the same for kings and popes) with the *exercise* of that authority (where the actors' interests differed). For those who were competing to rule and exercise authority, the distinctions between the religious and the secular were not only clear but served to motivate conflict.

The papacy sought autonomy from secular rulers and kings, and by the twelfth century, "whatever the church's political pretensions or success in political power, it remained structurally and organizationally completely separate from the state" (Smith 1970, 272–3). Functional distinctions between the *sacerdotium* (spiritual authority) and the *regnum* (royal power) were clear, especially

26. Medieval bishops serving in the royal administration, for example, did not get a salary but instead were vested with a benefice (a bishopric with lands and tenants attached) from which they made a living.

regarding questions of power, privilege, and political authority (Blumenthal 1988, 37; Eire 2016, 23). The goals of popes and rulers also differed. The papacy wanted autonomy—the ability to name its own officials, extract its own resources, and run its own enterprise of soul-saving without secular interference. Popes also wanted to exercise greater control over the church in the face of fractious clergy, papal schisms, and bishops sometimes reluctant to implement papal decrees. Rulers wanted more capacity—the ability to enforce their decisions, to gain monopoly of rule within and control of territory without.

Does it make sense, then, to talk of the medieval state? The very notions of medieval statehood, political authority, and sovereignty have been debated extensively (Friedrichs 2001; Little and Buzan 2002; Costa Lopez 2020). Some see medieval authority as private, overlapping, and lacking the conception of modern sovereignty (Hall and Kratochwil 1993; Ruggie 1998). The limited remit of government has led some scholars to argue that there was no such thing as the medieval "state" (Magdalino 1984; see Davies 2003). The term itself is an anachronism in an age when "lordship" would have been far more familiar. Others argue that medieval governance was increasingly centralized and formalized in ways that allow us to speak of states even if their subjects and rulers would not have called them such, and that the "state" serves as a useful analytical category (Southern 1970; Reynolds 1997, 32; Nederman 2009; McKee 2010, 8; Canning 2011; Latham 2012; Blaydes and Paik 2016; Wickham 2016, 12). It is increasingly clear that "feudal anarchy" was not the dominant political order and that interpersonal bonds were not the only cement of governance (Davies 2003, 281). Much of medieval authority was already public, and as early as 1200, some rulers already asserted sovereignty.[27] Centralized administrative institutions started to emerge in twelfth-century England, even if they never fully developed in the Holy Roman Empire.

I sidestep these debates and focus on state formation. There is no clear point at which the "state began." That said, there were state practices and institutions, if different from our own, that enabled rulers to exercise authority and to adjudicate disputes, extract resources, invest in human capital, obtain consent, and promote growth. The concept of a "state" still usefully captures the structures of power relations, and it is used here as synecdoche, a partial representation of rule, governance, administration, and the institutions that comprise it. My goal is not to make the medieval period "modern," imposing a false equivalence between medieval ruling practices and modern state institutions, but to show how state formation began long before the early modern period.

---

27. See Costa Lopez (2020) for an exposition of the different ways in which authority was constituted and contested in medieval Europe. Following Accursius, a thirteenth-century glossator, Costa Lopez defines *jurisdictio* as "a power publicly introduced with responsibility for pronouncing the law and establishing equity" (Costa Lopez 2020, 231).

Sources and Approach

This book argues that state institutions and governing concepts arose in the Middle Ages, before early modern war or elite bargaining. The church played a key role, and the effects were long-lasting: rivalry with the church and the emulation of church templates strengthened the state and led to its lasting triumph over the church.

To test whether and how this is the case, I rely on the vast historiography of medieval Europe, especially the period from 1000 to the Reformation. Wherever possible, I emphasize the historical consensus where it exists and note the historical debates where it does not (Lustick 1996). I also cite the work of historians rather than subsequent scholarly interpretations of that history to avoid confirmation bias, and use newer analyses where possible (Møller 2021).

To compare medieval and early modern state building, I collected data on the spatial distribution of both state and church institutions in western Christian Europe, from Portugal to Poland, and from Norway to Sicily. A critical case is the post-Carolingian German empire, where we find both the tightest fusion between clerical and lay governance and the most bitter rivalry. I collected original data on excommunications, the distribution of monasteries and universities, and the role of popes both in conflict with rulers and in the founding of universities. These complement existing data sources on cities (Bairoch, Batou, and Pierre 1988), crusades (Blaydes and Paik 2016), sites of conflict (Dincecco and Onorato 2016), primogeniture (Kokkonen and Sundell 2014), and parliaments (Van Zanden, Buringh, and Bosker 2012). The data include more than 30,000 city-year observations from 900 to 1850: from the collapse of the Carolingian empire to the modern era, although the analysis focuses on 1000 to 1350 and 1500 to 1800. The appendix documents the data sets used in this book.

Three caveats apply: first, the further back in time, the scarcer the data and the less definitive the analyses. Moreover, observational data preclude a pristine causal identification.[28] To establish credible explanations, I rely on close readings of history and analyses of primary documents, and the broader regularities that corroborate these. Second, the arguments here do not imply a linear progression or institutional teleology (never mind a Whig version of history).[29] Parliaments came and went and reappeared; legal concepts were

---

28. Partial remedies include instrumental variable analyses, but see Lal et al. (2021) on the perils of using instrumental variables with historical data. I chose not to use IV designs because almost any historical geographical IV will fail the exclusion restriction: e.g., rainfall and soil quality may be exogenous, but they are correlated with multiple variables, rather than working exclusively through the religious factors of interest in this book.

29. Chris Wickham also warns against the conventional framing of the Middle Ages as a reformist development from political weakness to state building that peaked in the

lost, rediscovered, and reinterpreted. Savvy and efficient administrations became lax and vulnerable (as in Naples), and already unclear state borders shifted thanks to dynasties dying out, war sweeping across the continent, and simple bad luck. Cities, monasteries, universities, institutions, and state borders appeared, changed, and disappeared (in some cases to return later). Third, the arguments here do not imply a religious determinism or monocausality—that the only thing that mattered was the church. State formation, like any complex historical phenomenon, does not have a single cause.

Roadmap

The European state was born in the Middle Ages. It is not simply a child of early modern warfare and taxes but the offspring of medieval contestation and emulation of the church.

The medieval church was so influential because it was armed with superior organizational reach, human capital, and spiritual authority. Chapter 1 introduces the medieval setting in which the church marshalled these resources, and how its relations with secular rulers changed over the course of the Middle Ages. Chapter 2 argues that once the church sought to liberate itself, the ensuing conflict between popes and kings led to the lasting fragmentation of territorial authority, the differentiation of religious and secular rule, and to early concepts of sovereignty.

In addition to competing with the church, rulers emulated it. Chapter 3 documents how medieval rulers took advantage of church institutional templates, investing in justice, taxation, and record keeping. Chapter 4 demonstrates that the church also fostered new legal interpretations and institutions that went hand in hand with a culture of learning: popes actively promoted universities and legal expertise. Finally, representative assemblies owe a great deal to the medieval church. Chapter 5 shows that conceptual innovations such as the rule of law, consent, binding representation, and even majority decision rules all originate in early church councils and medieval legal reinterpretations.

The church was a critical catalyst of medieval state formation. It provided the motive: the conflict over authority and jurisdiction. It also provided the means: the trained, literate personnel and the administrative solutions that were critical to building the state. The church had an immense impact through the institutions, laws, and conceptual innovations it bequeathed to the state. Each of these legacies is examined in the rest of this book.

---

twelfth century, only to "wane" with plague, war, schism, and cultural insecurity in the fourteenth (Wickham 2016, 2). See also Bagge 1997.

CHAPTER ONE

The Medieval Setting

HOW DID RULERS and popes become rivals? And why was the church so influential? This chapter outlines the relationship between popes and rulers in the Middle Ages, and the considerable organizational and material advantages of the church.

We can roughly divide this relationship into three periods. In the first, the late eleventh to the early twelfth century, the church largely freed itself from secular control. Direct church power and institutional influence peaked in the second period, from the early twelfth century to the late thirteenth. This was a time of intense consolidation of royal authority as well, aided by the institutional patterns and personnel of the church. In the third period, from the fourteenth century to the sixteenth, the papacy challenged rulers who had grown much stronger—and the sacred had to concede to the secular.

Medieval state formation and church authority coevolved, through both rivalry and emulation. The church fought to gain autonomy and authority, and it would clash with secular rulers to maintain these. At the same time, its vast stores of human capital, institutional innovations and learning meant that it could also influence state formation through more peaceful means.

Setting the Stage: Europe 888–1054

The church's influence was not a foregone conclusion. Prior to the mid-eleventh century, the papacy in Europe was not the powerful political player it would later become. The church was neither autonomous nor centralized. There was no clear separation of spiritual authority from royal power, no jurisdictional network of ecclesiastical courts and laws, and no clear hierarchy that ran from popes to bishops to the lower clergy.

Instead, lay rulers exercised authority over the church. Kings endowed bishops with the symbols of both their ecclesiastical and temporal authority, and they treated the church as part of their domain. Many churches and monasteries were "proprietary" (*eigenkirchen*), founded and run by local nobles and kings.[1] Local lords and kings alike controlled benefices (clerical offices), naming priests and bishops and selling off church offices while siphoning off resources from "their" churches. As the vicars of Christ, kings controlled the investiture (appointment) of bishops and awarded positions, called and presided over ecclesiastical synods, and governed church and society alike (Cowdrey 2004, 233). In Rome, many popes were nominal local leaders who rarely asserted their authority outside of the city (Brooke 1978, 7; Morris 1989, 33).[2] Popes were routinely appointed by secular powers, whether Roman aristocrats or emperors. For example, the German ruler Henry III appointed five loyalists as popes in rapid succession: in 1046 at Sutri he even forced a pope to resign and appointed his own pope in order to crown him successor (Wickham 2016, 113). Even the spiritual authority of the church was limited: the lands of Scandinavia and East Central Europe did not convert to Christianity until the mid-tenth century or later.[3] The Muslim lands of Al-Andalus expanded from the Iberian Peninsula in the eighth century as far as the Italian alpine passes in the ninth and tenth centuries.

The German empire, or the Holy Roman Empire as it became known,[4] became the biggest rival to the church. It was a successor to Charlemagne's empire, which dated to the coronation of Charlemagne as emperor in Rome by Pope Leo III in 800.[5] The Carolingian empire collapsed in 888. In its western territories, in what became France, barons and local warlords gained power. In 987, they decided to elect Hugh Capet, a descendant of Charlemagne, king.

1. In the German system of proprietary churches, first developed in the ninth century, most churches and bishoprics were held by secular lords who exploited "their revenues for personal and profane ends" (Zema 1944, 156).

2. Rome was not the center of the church until the eighth century (instead, five patriarchs oversaw the church: Antioch, Alexandria, Constantinople, Jerusalem, and Rome). The papacy's power and importance increased in the seventh to eighth centuries, as both a force in religious disputes and a rich landowner in southern Italy and Sicily (Wickham 2016, 49).

3. Europe Christianized gradually, beginning with Ireland in the fifth and sixth centuries; England and Germany in the seventh; Bulgaria, Croatia, and Moravia in the ninth; and Scandinavia and the rest of Europe in the tenth and eleventh centuries (Lithuania only converted in the fourteenth century).

4. In Voltaire's famous *bon mot*, the Holy Roman Empire (800–1806) was none of those things. The empire became "Holy" under Barbarossa in the mid-twelfth century, when his supporters sought to place him on equal footing with the pope (Stollberg-Rilinger 2018, 13–4; Sulovsky 2019, 1). It became "Roman" a century later, in 1254, and "of the German Nation" in the fifteenth century. I use "Holy Roman Empire" to refer to the German empire throughout.

5. The empire itself "was built by military conquest and held together by ephemeral fealty and by the centripetal effects of external threat from Islam" (Downing 1989, 215). The 843 Treaty of Verdun split Charlemagne's empire into three parts, corresponding roughly to eastern France, western France through Italy (Lotharingia), and Germany.

Three uninterrupted centuries of a father-son dynasty followed, with the Capetian line ruling France until 1848. Yet Capetian authority was initially confined to the tiny territory of the Île de France: the rest of what is now France was ruled by powerful regional barons, who entrenched themselves in their castles in the violent eleventh century and resisted central authority (Bloch 1961; Bisson 1994; Wickham 2016, 106).

In the east, the idea of the Roman empire was revived in 962 when the German king Otto claimed imperial authority and was crowned emperor by Pope John XII. These German imperial coronations were "a symbolic act [that] allowed German emperors to claim political authority over all Christians and precedence over all other European rulers" (Stollberg-Rilinger 2018, 11). Otto restored the empire by vanquishing the Magyars in central Europe and governed through a network of local officials (*ministeriales*) and pairs of itinerant administrators (*missi*), of whom one was a cleric.

The empire exerted great control over the church from the late ninth to the mid-eleventh century, and imperial authority commingled with papal. German kings alone were crowned emperors by the pope. The emperor was a *Christus Domini,* expected to oversee and strengthen the Christian religion. Under both the Ottonian (919–1024) and Salian (1024–1125) dynasties, kingship and regnality were even more "ritually tied into the Church" (Fried 2015, 104) by means of anointment and coronation. Henry III's naming of popes was not a one-off: Emperor Otto I had deposed the pope in 963 (Wickham 2016, 113), and over the next one hundred years, Ottonians and Salians appointed twelve out of twenty-five popes (Oakley 2010, 218). German emperors further claimed legitimacy as both holy successors to Roman emperors and as military leaders. Not surprisingly, then "in late tenth and early eleventh century, the German emperors seemed destined to overwhelm the rest of Latin Christendom" (Møller 2021, 920).

The empire's territorial ambitions extended to Italy, directly threatening the papal lands. Yet as we will see, the empire never developed strong central authority, clearly defined borders, a bureaucracy, a standing army, or a central executive. Instead, it became a loosely governed network of powerful nobles and bishop-princes in Germany. Much of the emperor's early authority depended on his physical presence and constant travel to different imperial palaces (*Kaiserpfalzen*):[6] when he was absent, nobles, bishops, and city councils asserted their own local authority. Thanks to the conflict with the church, and the frequent absences that it necessitated, power shifted to nobles, bishops, and towns—and no emperor was able to claw it back or establish a strong central administration.

---

6. Emperors had their preferred residences: Charlemagne's was at Aachen, for example. Charles IV (r. 1346–1378) effectively made Prague his permanent imperial capital.

Elsewhere, new polities arose, but few had consolidated by the eleventh century. France remained an archipelago of powerful banal lords, who exercised extensive local control. The kingdom of al-Andalus in what is now Spain broke up into 30 successor states after 1030, and new kingdoms arose in Castile and Hungary (Wickham 2016, 100). Germany itself descended into civil war after 1077. Only England could claim a relatively coherent and centralized government, as William quickly reasserted power after the conquest of 1066.

Church Liberation: 1054–1122

After centuries of control by temporal rulers, the Church asserted its autonomy in the 1050s. The eastern and western churches split in 1054, and the history of Byzantium diverged from that of Rome. The western church underwent a series of centralizing reforms and eventually developed a robust hierarchy with an elected pope at the head. The reformist papacy sought to liberate the church from secular control, consolidate papal power within the church, and reform the church from within. These efforts launched the papacy on a collision course both with secular rulers who were loath to concede control and with its own clergy, skeptical of the power grab of the popes.

A series of reformist popes began to work to free the church from secular domination. Emperor Henry III (r. 1046–1056) decided to transform the papacy into a more reliable partner and to that end appointed his relative, Bruno of Egisheim-Dagsburg, as Pope Leo IX (r. 1049–1054). The zealous Leo IX held at least twelve synods from 1049 to 1053, issuing decrees against simony (the sale of ecclesiastical privileges) and nicolaitism (clerical marriage), and developing new canon law in the process (Harding 2002, 97; Cowdrey 2004, 36; Wilson 2016, 53).[7] Leo was followed by other reformist popes. When Henry III died in 1054, his successor, Henry IV, was only five years old, and would remain a minor for the next sixteen years. The papacy exploited this power vacuum and instability to launch a far more comprehensive reform that would liberate the church from imperial and secular control.[8] The first milestone was in 1059, when Pope Nicholas II decreed that popes be elected by a newly founded College of Cardinals, rather than being appointed by emperors, and that papal authority extended over all the churches.

The arrival of Pope Gregory VII (r. 1073–1085) heralded a new era of intense reform. His reforms sought to instill greater discipline and clarity of purpose among the clergy, to ensure that the church gained autonomy from secular interference—and to make the pope the apex of the church hierarchy. Beyond

7. The four Lateran Councils, held over 1122–1215, reinstated the bans on simony and nicolaitism.

8. Since Henry IV was a minor, there was no effective imperial protection for Rome. Roman nobles tried to regain control over the papacy and force it to ally with the new Normans regime in southern Italy and Sicily (Oakley 2012, 9).

the supremacy of the pope over the clergy, he further asserted the primacy of the clerical order over the lay. In 1075, Gregory drew up the *Dictatus Papae*, a collection of twenty-seven papal privileges and prerogatives, including the exclusive right of the pope to use imperial insignia and the insistence that princes kiss the feet of the pope, and the pope's alone (Jordan 2001, 91). The *Dictatus* declared that there were no limits to papal authority, either within or beyond the church, and that the papacy was the sole universal authority. Critically, the decree included provisions that only popes could depose emperors or release subjects from oaths to wicked princes (Schatz 1996, 88). Gregory also prohibited lay investiture, the naming of bishops by secular rulers. Only the pope could now name bishops, a move Gregory justified on the grounds that such offices were often sold to the highest bidder, generating revenue to the emperor but doing little to ensure proper spiritual care.[9]

Thus began the Investiture Conflict (1075–1122), which first pitted Pope Gregory VII against Henry IV (r. 1054–1105), who by this time had become an ambitious ruler in his own right. When Gregory VII banned lay investiture, he posed a challenge to Henry, who began to establish his power in the empire in the 1060s. Controlling the bishoprics was critical to consolidating Henry's authority. He deposed several bishops that he had no role in naming as part of asserting control. The stakes were fundamental: "much of the emperor's power depended on his investiture right, since it linked high church officials to the crown as a counterweight against German territorial nobles" (Clark 1986, 668). When Henry IV asserted his traditional rights a few months later by naming the Bishop of Milan in September 1075, the Pope excommunicated him and called on his lords to forsake Henry. Nobles and bishops both began to abandon the king, already worried by his centralizing ambitions. Henry found himself increasingly isolated. To regain his position, he had to seek forgiveness from the Pope, which he did by marching through the Alps in the winter of 1076–7 to meet the Pope at the fortress of Canossa. He then famously (if apocryphally) stood barefoot in the snow for three days, as a penitent begging for forgiveness. The Pope, by convention and doctrine, had to forgive Henry and lifted the excommunication. The wayward princes and bishops rallied around Henry again.

A renewed and prolonged struggle followed. Henry IV again began to name his own bishops, and Gregory VII again excommunicated and deposed him in 1080. This time, however, the bishops sided with the king: they were less than enthusiastic about Gregory's monarchical ambitions and refused to pay to defend Rome. Henry's Norman allies besieged Rome from 1081 to 1084 and eventually pillaged it, and Gregory VII himself fled Rome only to die

---

9. That said, these Gregorian reforms were not uniformly accepted within the church, and it was only in 1100 that the clergy widely accepted church autonomy (Wickham 2016, 115).

shortly thereafter. Henry IV again summoned his bishops and named a rival pope (the "Anti-Pope" Clement III), who enthroned Henry as the emperor. His triumph appeared complete. Meanwhile, the struggle over investiture had spread to France and England, as rulers and clergy both debated whether the land holdings of the bishop and his office were a single juridical entity. The conflict and negotiations continued with Henry V (r. 1099–1125). When Pope Calixtus II assumed the papacy in 1119, he made ending lay investiture a priority, and the conflict was formally settled at the Concordat of Worms (1122). The contest gained greater autonomy for the church and delineated more distinct spheres of authority. Emperors would no longer control the church.

Thanks partly to the Investiture Conflict, central power weakened in Germany and in Italy. German dukes deposed Henry IV in 1077, and Germany descended into a civil war that spread into Italy in 1080 and lasted for two decades. Henry IV won in Germany and resumed power—but failed to do so in Italy. That allowed cities and communes to arise as autonomous polities (Wickham 2016, 102).[10] In northern Italian territories nominally under imperial control, city-states arose in the power vacuum created by the absence of central authority in the late eleventh century. By the mid-twelfth century, more than fifty of these collectively governed cities would gain coherence, call themselves communes, and establish power over neighboring rural areas (Wickham 2016, 109). When Frederick I Barbarossa (r. 1152–90), the most successful of the Hohenstaufen emperors, attempted to regain control in Italy in 1158 and again in 1177, these communes banded together and decisively defeated him. Frederick II (r. 1212–1250) tried to reestablish authority in 1235 and was also defeated. Instead, the communes grew more powerful, developing strong trade networks and even colonizing the Mediterranean.[11]

Rulers in England, meanwhile, gained an advantage. The papacy blessed William the Conqueror's invasion of England in 1066, which enabled him to consolidate his authority more easily. William extirpated the existing Anglo-Saxon nobles and bishops, confiscated their lands, redistributed them to his own followers—and the papacy tolerated it all.[12] William retained the tight

10. The communes were initially governed by councils and evolved new institutions to ensure stability. By the end of the twelfth century, salaried leaders such as the *podestá* took over. By the mid-thirteenth century, *capitani del popolo* (captains of the people) were the modal leaders, and after 1300, we see the rise of *signori*, noble autocrats who soon became hereditary (Wickham 2016, 148). The imperial legates or viceroys sent out in the thirteenth century became the hereditary lords of Milan, Savoy, Modena, and others, reducing the emperor to dispensing legitimation in exchange for cash, and "imperial sovereignty thus slowly evaporated in Italy" (Guenée 1985, 13).

11. Genoese sailors became so predatory that a formal Office of Plunder reimbursed foreign victims of Genoese piracy (Rohan 2021, 57).

12. These new nobles held the land in fief from the king, ensuring their loyalty—and their subsequent attendance at Parliament (Boucoyannis 2021, 30–1, 74).

rule of earlier Anglo-Saxon kings, based on large-scale royal land owner-ship and land taxes (Wickham 2016, 104). Even as popes fought to liberate the church from imperial rule, they allowed English kings to have control over the English episcopate and thus the church. As a result, England largely stayed out of the conflict with the papacy—and royal power could rapidly centralize and develop its own endogenous institutions such as common law. By the late twelfth century, English kings centralized the administration, including the treasury, chancery, and the "semi-judicial" exchequer, and created the distinct system of English justice (Mundy 2000, 225).

Church Triumphant: 1198–1302

After throwing off the imperial yoke, papal power grew immensely during the twelfth and thirteenth centuries. The era of the so-called papal monarchy, and the consolidation of papal power within the church, began. The papacy also assumed a new "power of intervention and direction in both spiritual and secular affairs" (Southern 1970, 34). Popes grew far more powerful, both within the church and in the temporal realm, from the election of Pope Innocent III in 1198 to the downfall of Pope Boniface VIII in 1303.

A spectacular example of papal power is Innocent III (r. 1198–1216). A propo-nent of papal supremacy and a determined leader, Innocent III threw himself into temporal politics, crowning and deposing kings, and settling disputes. He reinvigorated the fifth-century concept of the "fullness of power" (*plenitudo potestatis*), which now implied universal papal jurisdiction over all Christian-ity,[13] and asserted secular power as the ruler of the Papal States (Morris 1989, 421; Watt 1999, 117). He convened the Fourth Lateran Council (1215), the most magnificent and most representative of the councils to date, which defined the Catholic doctrine of transubstantiation, condemned heretics, addressed sev-eral disputes among secular rulers, empowered bishops and called on them to better oversee their dioceses, required annual confession, and reiterated bans on the sale of office and clerical marriage.

Claims of papal authority grew ever more ambitious. When Innocent III took over, neither imperial succession nor the temporal powers of the pope had been settled. He argued that the pope was the source of power on earth, as Christ's vicar, and "proclaimed and practiced a papal near theocracy" (Ozment 1980, 143). His successors went further: Innocent IV (r. 1243–1254) argued that popes were above human law, and Boniface VIII (r. 1294–1303) asserted that papal authority directly extended over all beings. In short, during the era from

---

13. *Plenitudo potestatis* extended beyond the papacy: other rulers used it in their strug-gles to claim authority. By the thirteenth century, the canonist Hostiensis noted that both the pope and the emperor had *plenitudo potestatis* in their respective domains (Costa Lopez 2020, 235).

1050 to 1350, we see the rise of a "papal monarchy" that "appropriated to itself the status of sacred kingship" (Oakley 2012, 3).

Conflict with the Holy Roman Empire continued. Not content with their German and central European holdings, successive emperors sought to control the papacy. In the mid-twelfth century, Frederick I Barbarossa sought to unify the empire by conquering Italy. He fought with Pope Alexander III and the Lombard League (*Lega Lombarda*) of northern Italian cities, and was forced to retreat. Emperor Otto IV (r. 1209–1215) and Innocent III quarreled openly, and as a result, the pope backed Barbarossa's grandson, Frederick II, as emperor instead. Innocent's interference backfired: Frederick II then invaded Italy and struggled with three different popes—Honorius III, Gregory IX, and Innocent IV—and was repeatedly excommunicated and deposed. He consolidated control over vast swaths of Italy in the south and Germany in the north, establishing an efficient regime in Sicily[14] and threatening the Pope and the rest of Italy. Gregory IX (r. 1227–1241) excommunicated Frederick in 1227 and again in 1239, allied with the Lombard League, assembled an army, and ordered foreign troops to conquer Sicily (Fried 2015, 277). Innocent IV (r. 1243–54) launched armies against Frederick II, instigated a crusade against the wayward emperor, and called a council at Lyon in 1245 to condemn and depose him.[15] Another civil war followed. Once again, armies fought each other, once again the Lombard League convened, and again the emperor was routed in 1248. Frederick II died in 1250, and his son Conrad IV in 1254, leaving a paralyzing power vacuum in the empire.

After Frederick II's death, imperial ambitions in Italy withered away, and the empire retreated beyond the Alps to central Europe, leaving behind a fractured Italy and an atomized Holy Roman Empire (Canning 1983, 4). A lengthy succession dispute, known as the Great Interregnum (1250–1312), meant there was no accepted ruler until 1273 and no emperor crowned until 1312.[16] In 1266, Charles of Anjou defeated Manfred, the last king of Sicily from the Hohenstaufen line, and then pursued Manfred's nephew, Conradin. The Hohenstaufen line ended with the execution of Conradin in the market place of Naples in 1268, with the support of the papacy.[17]

14. Sicily under Frederick had an efficient bureaucracy, centralized finance, standard currency, a wage-earning economy, a professional judicial system, and a legal code that culminated in the Constitutions of Melfi (1231) (Fried 2015, 277; see also Titone 2013).

15. The Bull deposing Frederick II called the emperor "the special cause of . . . discord and suffering" and accused him of seizing papal territory, perjury, sacrilege, heresy, breaking peace, impiety, and failure to keep his oaths. The papacy also coolly contemplated Frederick's assassination (Abulafia 1999, 505).

16. Kings still ruled Germany: but they could not become emperors without crowning by the pope. The monarchy also suffered from an excess of pretenders: there were at least eighteen anti-kings from 983 to 1410 (Wilson 2016, 303).

17. The image of Pope Clement IV's foot on the neck of the dead emperor, lying on the ground, "was to become one of the most potent antipapal propaganda images of the entire Reformation" (Fried 2015, 248).

The papacy exploited the crisis and "even deliberately made sure the dispute lasted longer than seemed absolutely necessary for the church" (Fried 2015, 242). In the process, the popes secured areas lost to previous emperors, including the Marches, Spoleto, Ravenna, Umbria, and Tuscany. After the collapse of the Hohenstaufen hegemony in 1254, and through the centuries that followed, emperors were unable to centralize their authority. Many imperial estates north of the Alps were dispersed, and the emperor's ability to intervene in northern Italy was greatly reduced (Watts 2009, 65). Subsequent emperors "had no pretension to direct rule over the German lands as a whole, and nor did any successor before 1866" (Wickham 2016, 150). The papacy had abetted the destruction of imperial authority in Italy and its permanent fragmentation in Germany.

Even as the Holy Roman Empire fractured, the twelfth and thirteenth centuries saw the expansion and consolidation of political systems elsewhere in Europe. Monarchs grew stronger, partly as a result of adopting ecclesiastical templates. They expanded their administrations and reduced the prerogatives of nobles and barons who would oppose the concentration of royal power (Ergang 1971, 164; Poggi 1990, 42; Reinhard 1996). Several kings laid the foundation for strong monarchies by building regional administration, the judiciary, and new fiscal regimes. Rulers shifted from relying on income from their own lands, to collecting taxes on the property of others (Ormrod 1999). These state builders include Henry II (r. 1154–89) and Edward I Longshanks (r. 1272–1307) in England, Philip II Augustus (r. 1180–1223) and Louis IX (r. 1226–70) in France, and Alfonso VI (r. 1065–1109) and Ferdinand III (r. 1230–52) in León and Castile. Frederick II may not have been able to centralize authority in the Holy Roman Empire, but he did so in Sicily, where he was also king after 1198. These new powers meant that conflict in domains where church and kings overlapped in jurisdiction, such as taxes or justice, would become increasingly likely.

In England, a series of powerful monarchs built the English state. They centralized justice (the system of royal writs and new courts gave rise to common law in the twelfth century), representative institutions (parliament increasingly assented to taxation and policy, with representatives of both cities and shires attending), and administrative advances. Henry I (r. 1100–35) laid the foundations of the administrative state, including the Exchequer, and strengthened the earlier system of territorial administration.[18] Henry II (r. 1154–89) consolidated the fiscal administration and asserted greater control over regional administration; he expanded the reach of royal justice with circuit royal judges, the formalization of grand juries and inquests with the Assize

18. The main unit of administration was the shire, with a shire reeve from the tenth century onwards as the royal official in charge of both justice and taxation. Shire assemblies also met regularly in shire courts. Shires were subdivided into hundreds, whose officials (hundredmen) answered to the king as well (Stasavage 2020, 198).

of Clarendon in 1166, and new jurisdiction over civil and land cases in addition to criminal trials. John (r. 1199–1216) had a tumultuous relationship with both his barons and the papacy: Innocent III placed the country under interdict and John under a sentence of deposition for not accepting Stephen Langton as Archbishop of Canterbury.[19] Langton led the struggle against John, along with numerous barons, and the crisis led to the signing of the Magna Carta in 1215 (and its almost immediate annulment by the same Pope Innocent III). Edward I Longshanks (r. 1272–1307) reformed the royal administration and law, and was the first to summon representatives of shires and towns to the Parliament, making it a more representative assembly (Ergang 1971, 47).

The French kings also grew far more powerful, extended royal lands, and sent out paid officials of the king to administer these new territories (Wickham 2015, 143). Given the violence of the local nobles against both lay people and clergy, and the constant insecurity this engendered in the eleventh century, this centralization of power was fully supported by the church. Clergy enthusiastically anointed Capetian kings and legitimated their rule (Downing 1989). If Louis VII (r. 1137–80) directly controlled only the area around Paris, Philip II Augustus (r. 1180–1223) quadrupled royal holdings by declaring English holdings in England forfeit, leaving only Aquitaine in English control. Philip Augustus also reformed his royal council, replacing nobles with legally trained experts, and expanded the system of territorial administration with *prévôts* (much like sheriffs) and *bailis* and *sénéchals* (two kinds of royal officials) to oversee them. France became a power on par with the Holy Roman Empire only in the 1220s (Wickham 2016, 102–3). Louis IX (r. 1226–70) did not extend territory, but he reformed justice and drew up a division of labor in the royal court.

In Spain, Castile and Aragon emerged as the two strongest unifying powers (Ergang 1971, 119). The kingdoms of Léon and Castile were joined in 1037–8 under Ferdinand I (r. 1035–65), Portugal spun off in 1109–40, and Aragon joined Catalonia in 1150 (Wickham 2016, 160). Roger II of Sicily (r. 1105–54) unified the Norman principalities in southern Italy over the course of 1127–44, attracting artistic and scientific luminaries to his court and expanding and consolidating a powerful bureaucratic administration. Further afield, the church played a direct role in the consolidation of royal power. In Scandinavia in the twelfth and thirteenth centuries, Christianity had a centralizing impact, as kings replaced pagan chieftains with their own Christian loyalists and bishoprics served as outposts of royal administration (Bagge 2014, 66, 82). Poland converted to Christianity in 966 and then joined Pope Gregory VII in his conflict against Germany (Ertman 1997, 279). The kingdom fragmented after

19. The conflict with the pope was resolved when John placed England under papal fief in 1213 and promised the papacy an annual payment of 1000 pounds sterling, which was not abolished until 1366 (Jedin 1993, 85).

1138 in a succession struggle, but Władysław Łokietek (r. 1306–33) reunified Poland, and Casimir III the Great (r. 1333–70) further consolidated territorial authority with church support.[20]

Broadcasting Church Power

Even as kings gained power, the church remained the single most powerful geopolitical player of it time. Its human capital and its spiritual authority were unmatched, as was its geographic reach. Bishops, monasteries, and cathedrals were omnipresent in the lives of medieval peoples, critical to both transmitting the church's teachings and institutional innovations and reaching people where they lived.

BISHOPS

Bishops were indispensable secular administrators and religious leaders. As such, they were an important conduit of church influence. They were the chief pastors of the dioceses, which were the basic administrative units of the church and among the few infrastructural legacies left behind after the collapse of Rome in the fifth century. [21] In Charlemagne's day, bishops served as administrators and governors, both local lords and imperial representatives: "an imperial official and an important instrument of political unity," a key link in the far-flung net of local administrators (Zacour 1976, 71). When local authority collapsed, they stepped in to keep order and deliver justice.[22] The church was often the only source of stability and guarantee of order, and bishops assumed governing responsibility in many territories. Bishops were judges, offered asylum and settled disputes, and gave shelter to refugees and counsel to warring parties (Dębiński 2010, 47). They were vital to the temporal

20. Poland remained a single bishopric during the time of fragmentation, and several bishops ardently supported reunification. Pope Gregory VII raised Duke Bolesław to the rank of king in 1076, and Poland allied with the papacy against the German empire. The church also benefited and gained land (Ertman 1997, 280). Bolesław joined the Gregorian reform party and championed ecclesiastical reform (Wyrozumski 2004, 281).

21. The diocese is the district administered by a bishop, while a bishopric is the office belonging to a bishop, whose authority does not always coincide with the diocese. The two terms are used interchangeably when discussing the jurisdiction of a bishop.

22. In the eleventh century, bishops responded to the failure of central authority to maintain order, and to the violence against clergy and churches (Morris 1989, 144; see also Bisson 1994). Many ecclesiastic buildings were fortified, so that churches and monasteries took the form of castles and forts (Mitterauer 2010, 119). Bishops launched the Peace of God movement in the last quarter of the tenth century in southern France (Kaeuper 1988, 145). The Truce of God prohibited violence from Wednesday evening to dawn the following Monday in early eleventh-century Languedoc (Jordan 2001, 27). Similar church efforts took place in Norway (see Helle 2003, 348).

power of both popes and emperors, since they served as both feudal vassals of the secular monarchs and spiritual envoys of the pope.[23] They simultaneously held both high secular and ecclesiastical office, ruling vast lands, and exercising extensive judicial, administrative, and spiritual authority. These were merely their natural powers: "the processions organized by bishops could hold off the plague, cause rain to fall, put out fires and confound enemy armies, if we believe the saints' lives" (Wickham 2009, 183).

Bishops served as papal deputies, as local governors, and as central administrators. First, bishops were delegates of the pope, strengthening his reach, collecting taxes, and keeping records: "just as the king shared his authority with the great barons of the realm, the pope governed the church with his bishops" (Pennington 1984, 4). Figure 1.1 shows their presence in Europe. Spread out over 800 dioceses in Europe by the thirteenth century (Jedin 1993, 134; Hay 1995, 289), bishops oversaw a body of lower clergy that was anywhere from 1 to 3 percent of the population (Cipolla 1993, 67). They were responsible for the well-being of the diocese and sworn to obey papal will.[24] Bishops collected taxes on behalf of the church, adjudicated ecclesiastical disputes, and administered local benefices on behalf of the pope. They were the main intermediaries of papal authority—which also meant that bishops interpreted canon law and wrote their own statutes, simplifying, ignoring, and altering papal decretals and conciliar decrees (Dorin 2021, 37).

Second, bishops served as regional administrators for kings and emperors, adjudicating disputes, settling contracts, and protecting local peace (Robinson 1990, 423). Bishops were especially important in the empire: the Carolingians and Ottonians relied on bishops to govern, a practice continued by the Salians, who took over the throne in 1024. In the absence of a well-developed regional government, bishops played the role of imperial representatives in their territory for German emperors, who "relied heavily on bishops as chief administrative agents in the royal government" (Angelov and Herrin 2012, 170). Bishops were so important that under the Hohenstaufens, bishops obtained the rights to govern counties and ducal powers after 1168. This led

23. The bishops were *not* vassals of the pope: they swore an oath of obedience, rather than feudal fealty, and he owed them no protection. Monarchs and secular lords could become feudal vassals of the pope by the mid-eleventh century. Monarchs entered this relationship by surrendering land, receiving it back as a usufruct, and paying an annual tribute. They received papal protection and legitimation in return (Ullmann [1955] 1965, 332–7).

24. Despite these vows, bishops had enjoyed considerable autonomy. Some were so powerful (and predatory) that monasteries and mendicant priests sought exemptions from their rule, so that they would be answerable to the pope alone (Blumenthal 2004, 12). Gregory VII absolved parishioners from obedience to recalcitrant bishops (Ott 2015, 14).

FIGURE 1.1. Bishoprics in Europe by 1250.

to the rise of ecclesiastical princes, or "prince bishops," who were *ex officio* regional governors and secular officials with formal political powers, capable of electing emperors and claiming a seat in royal councils. Their status was formalized in 1220 (Wilson 2016, 93). By the fourteenth century, sixty out of the ninety bishops in the Holy Roman Empire held the rank of prince (Eldevik 2001, 777). Prince bishops were essential to the administration of the Holy Roman Empire, where they played a critical role in the balance of internal power, and where their role as electors of the emperors was enshrined in the Golden Bull of 1356 (Wilson 2016, 305–6). They were so involved in politics that many of these prince-prelates hired subsidiary bishops to carry out their religious functions (Hughes 1992, 31). Thus, even after their liberation from secular princes, bishops served as judges, advisors, and royal representatives.

Bishops were also local magnates, wealthy lords with authority over those living in their lands. As ecclesiastical princes, bishops taxed, defended, and exploited their own territory. They held between 31 percent of European land in the eleventh century and around 20 percent in the thirteenth (Morris 1989, 393).[25] Around 1000, bishoprics "were small states, with almost everything which corresponds to our conception of a state: rulers, governments, central places, citizenship, legislation, taxation" (Reuter 2011, 23). Bishops kept order, delivered justice, and protected their own wealth. They were the rulers of their own dioceses, serving as judges and overseeing an auditory or consistory staffed by legal advisers (Morris 1989, 532).[26] In the earlier Middle Ages, they even commanded military forces to defend their territories (Arnold 1989, 169; Houghton 2018, 275; Kotecki, Maciejewski, and Ott 2018, 2), contributing as much as three-quarters of the armed forces in Germany (Mitterauer 2010, 111).

Bishops reified the territorial division of authority in their roles as papal emissaries and local rulers. Dioceses were territorial designations, reinforcing the notion that administration extended over a contiguous land and its people, rather than a list of estates or tribes. After 1100, a bishop's spiritual authority was defined geographically, and it coincided with their secular control of the land, resources, and trade in that region. In Scandinavia, the borders of bishoprics corresponded almost exactly to national borders, favoring geopolitical stability (Bagge 2014, 83). Bishoprics also inevitably centered around a city, a legacy of Rome: in the later years of the Roman empire, all administrative units (*civitas*) had a bishop.[27] The church thus administered territorial units, at a time when many kingdoms did not have territorially based administrations or even stationary capitals (Morris 1989, 220; Tabacco 2004, 76).

Finally, and perhaps most importantly for the development of state institutions, bishops and other clergy staffed royal administrations. They held central positions in royal administrations across Europe, from England and France to Poland and Norway (Hamre 2003, 664). Depending on where they served, and under what monarch, their specific roles differed—but nearly everywhere they dominated the high administrative, financial, and judicial offices well into the fourteenth century, and in some cases beyond. For example, English medieval bishops served as judges and councilors, and they were "especially active in institutions such as parliament, chancery, and the council, which offered justice to the king's subjects on a discretionary basis" (Dodd 2014, 213). They

25. The decline reflects the consolidation of noble and knightly families: it made more sense to hold wealth within the family than to hand it over to the church (Morris 1989, 393).

26. Bishops also had courts of their own, with chaplains, chancellors, officials and servants (Obertyński and Kumor 1974, 325).

27. Roman cities retained their bishoprics, but new medieval cities did not necessarily have their own bishop: as populations expanded and new cities arose, existing bishops incorporated these.

served eagerly and saw judgment as part of their spiritual vocation, not simply career advancement or lordly obligation (Dodd 2014, 225).

Kings appointed bishops as senior judges and administrators, and conversely, they chose bishops from a pool of legally trained clerks. High clergy, including abbots and bishops, attended first the royal councils and then the national assemblies. In their role in the parliaments, they served to administer justice, legitimate the monarchs, and eventually to agree to new legislation. Bishops even served as substitutes for kings, thanks both to their expertise and to their inability to inherit the throne. For example, French churchmen frequently served as regents during the Second, Third, Seventh and Eighth Crusades (Jordan 1979, 117, Jordan 2009, 131). High clergy filled the high councils that advised the king even in the early modern era, with archbishops serving as chancellors in Tudor England and cardinals directing foreign policy in seventeenth-century France. Bishops were thus integrated into royal and princely governance.

MONASTERIES

Thousands of monasteries dotted the landscape, as figure 1.2 shows. After the collapse of the Roman empire, monasteries were a source of theological advances, a literate culture, and reformist zeal (Blum and Dudley 2003; see also Doucette and Møller 2021). During their heyday from 1050 to 1150, monks often served as local leaders and advanced both economic opportunity and social order: they cleared forests and marshes, served in the military orders as soldiers, and formed quasi-monastic foundations that housed the age, sick, destitute and fallen (Morris 1989, 35; Mundy 2000, 14). Donations to the monasteries and the restoration of their lands by reforming popes made many monasteries wealthy (Morris 1989, 61; see also Lawrence 2015, 28–30).[28] Noble lords also founded monastic houses across Europe, including the reformist centers of Cluny, Brogne, and Trier; endowing monasteries, cathedrals, and churches; and bolstering their own status (Howe 1988, 334).

CATHEDRALS

Cathedrals exemplified the daily presence of the church and its wealth. They served multiple roles: solemn houses of worship, town halls, marketplaces, warehouses, and even fortresses (Reynolds 1997, 91).[29] As figure 1.3 shows,

28. The monasteries' tax-exempt status also led to considerable controversy: local churches resented monastic wealth (see Morris 1989, 536). When monasteries gained exemptions from episcopal rule in the twelfth century, bishops also looked askance. The result was a slew of lawsuits, pursued both locally and at the papal courts (Lawrence 2015, 136), and the gradual decline of monasteries in the fourteenth century.

29. Reynolds argues that these multiple temporal roles mean that cathedral building does not simply reflect popular devotion (Reynolds 1997, 80).

FIGURE 1.2. Monasteries in Europe, 1000–1300. Darker crosses indicate
earlier establishment.

they were initially concentrated in the Italian peninsula and later spread across
Europe. These soaring buildings were a source of local pride and prestige, sought
after by townsmen even when bishops opposed them (Kraus 1979, xiv). Cathedrals were funded by enthusiastic lay and religious donations, bequests, indulgences, and direct appeals (Morris 1989, 292).

   Cathedrals and monasteries were also an early source of human capital (see
chapter 4). Charlemagne founded a system of schools connected to monasteries and cathedrals (Herzog 208, 79). Many trained clergy to prepare them
for their roles as statesmen and administrators, with some dozen schools
emerging at the turn of the tenth century (Jaeger 1987, 574). Education in cathedral schools was a prerequisite for advancing to higher office in the imperial church, and so demand for cathedral schools expanded (Wieruszowski
1966, 17; Morris 1989, 45). Between 960 and 1100, twelve new major cathedral

FIGURE 1.3. Cathedrals in Europe, 1000–1300. Darker squares indicate
earlier establishment.

schools emerged in Germany (Jaeger 1987, 574). The 1078 Council of Rome
and the 1079 Third Lateran Council required all bishops to provide schooling at all their churches, emphasizing the link between education and liturgy
(Witt 2012, 269), and the schools expanded in the eleventh and twelfth centuries to teach the sons of local nobles (Wieruszowski 1966, 19).

Church Overreach and Political Losses: 1302–1417

As rulers grew stronger, especially in England and France, they increasingly
chafed at papal intervention and sought to contain it. An important episode
was the conflict between Pope Boniface VIII and King Philip IV of France; the
consequences are explored in chapter 2. The clash, the "first medieval conflict of church and state which can properly be described as a dispute over

national sovereignty" (Tierney 1964, 172) began in earnest in 1294, when Philip IV sought to subdue Aquitaine. To do so, he imposed taxes on the church within the territories he controlled. Edward I also declared the clergy would be taxed in England. The pope refused to pay, arguing that this was neither a war to defend the faith nor a case of legitimate self-defense. He forbade the clergy from paying the levies. In 1296, Boniface issued an unprecedented bull, *Clericis Laicos*, commanding clergy to contravene established practices and refuse to pay taxes to both the French and English rulers.[30] The pope found especially galling the idea that the French and English kings would use ecclesiastical revenue to fight each other, instead of the "enemies of Rome and Christ" (Watts 2009, 265). Boniface declared that clergy could not pay temporal taxes without his permission and that rulers who insisted on extracting taxes would be excommunicated.

Clericis Laicos would have been momentuous: "the Pope intervened as legislator in important areas of the life of the state, which was becoming ever more keenly conscious of its autonomy. In practice kings in their wars would have become dependent on the good will of the Pope, who could permit the paying of taxes" (Jedin 1993, 158).[31] Philip responded by forbidding the export of gold, silver, and coins from France, a critical source of papal revenue. From Philip's perspective, "his sovereignty within his kingdom was damaged if he could not tax his clerical subjects, a pre-eminent economic group, without the approval of another ruler" (Canning 2011, 15). As he told the papal legates in 1297, "in governmental affairs the French crown is subject to nobody, and nobody means nobody" (Wilks 1963, 427). The Pope relented in 1297, once the funding from France dried up.[32]

Meanwhile, in England, Edward I prohibited clerical loyalty to the pope (Hay 1995, 83). Edward I's Statue of Mortmain in 1279 already made gifts to

---

30. Despite the Fourth Lateran Council's declaration, in practice, popes acquiesced to secular taxation and conceded tax rights over the church (Watts 2009, 54).

31. *Clericis Laicos* declared that "likewise emperors, kings, or princes, dukes, counts or barons, podestas, captains or officials or rectors—by whatever name they are called, whether of cities, castles, or any places whatever, wherever situated; and any other persons, of whatever pre-eminence, condition or standing who shall impose, exact or receive such payments, or shall anywhere arrest, seize or presume to take possession of the belongings of churches or ecclesiastical persons which are deposited in the sacred buildings, oi shall order them to be arrested, seized or taken possession of, or shall receive them when taken possession of, seized or arrested-also all who shall knowingly give aid, counsel or favour in the aforesaid things, whether publicly or secretly: shall incur, by the act itself the sentence of excommunication. Corporations, moreover, which shall be guilty in these matters, we place under the ecclesiastical interdict." *https://sourcebooks.fordham.edu/source/b8 -clericos.asp*, accessed 11 May 2021.

32. Boniface was also under enormous pressure from both the Franciscans (who resented his wealth) and the Roman Colonni (prominent Roman nobles who resented that his nepotism favored the pope's own family, the Gaetani).

the church conditional on royal permission. He then asked clergy for a subsidy and flew into a rage when they refused. The king threatened the ecclesiastics with confiscation and the withdrawal of security. They relented, and Edward I set the precedent of royal taxation of clergy. Subsequently, when Edward invaded Scotland, and Pope Boniface VIII objected, Parliament sent the Pope a letter in 1299 with 100 signatures declaring that Scotland was not part of the papal remit, and the pope had no right to interfere in English internal affairs (Ergang 1971, 77–9).

The French conflict then focused on sovereignty. In 1301 Philip arrested Bishop Bernard Saisset, who was suspected of treason. Boniface lashed back that only popes can try bishops and called a council of French bishops. Philip forbade them from attending: they complied, largely because they feared losing their benefices (Spruyt 1994, 97). In response, an incensed Boniface VIII then excommunicated Philip and issued the famous *Unam Sanctam* bull in 1302, which insisted that the pontiff was supreme above all men, and all "temporal authority subjected to spiritual power." Further, Boniface insisted, "it is absolutely necessary to salvation for every human creature to be subject to the Roman Pontiff."[33] The bull was an "unqualified extreme statement of papal monarchy, fashioned to overawe the disobedient by sheer weight of sacerdotal authority" (Watt 1999, 161).

The bull badly backfired. It infuriated the French rather than inducing them to obedience. Denunciations of Boniface as a heretic, usurper, and simoniac followed. Philip made common cause with the traditional enemies of the papacy, the Roman aristocratic Colonna faction. Philip's deputy (and skilled administrator), Guillame Nogaret, marched to Italy with armed troops and took the Pope prisoner. Boniface VIII himself died of shock on October 11, 1303. The papacy was moved to Avignon, an area firmly under Philip's control. Philip's furious response was prompted not by his desire to control the flow of resources, but by his avowed need to autonomously govern his country free from outside interference. In effect, Philip asserted sovereignty: he was the undisputed lord of his own domain, not subject to an external lord. *Unam Sanctam* turned out to be a "magnificent swan song of papal supremacy" (Ullmann [1955] 1965, 456).

Boniface's defeat meant the beginning of the Avignon residency (or the "Babylonian captivity," as it was also known), which lasted from 1305 to 1376. Boniface's successor would be French—and for the next seventy years, the papal seat was in Avignon, France, rather than in Rome.[34] The papacy

33. *Unam Sanctam, https://www.papalencyclicals.net/bon08/b8unam.htm,* accessed 11 May 2021.

34. The first Avignon pope was Clement V (r. 1305–14), who spent most of his time dealing with heavy pressure from Philip IV to suppress the Templars (and thus gain their wealth for Philip) and to call the Council of Vienne (1311–2), which absolved Nogaret and denounced Boniface VIII.

flourished here, even if it was dependent on French generosity.[35] Papal administration and financial efficiency reached their peak at Avignon (see chapter 3). In some analyses, the move also "demonstrated that the papacy had snapped the links that had bound it to a definite place and a specific local church. More than anything else it denoted that the papacy had become a truly universal monarchy" (Wilks 1963, 407).

The Avignon papacy also led indirectly to the Great Schism—and the steep decline of the papacy's secular powers. In 1376, Pope Gregory XI decided to move the papal court back to Rome, only to die two years later. This simple decision would have momentous effects on the power of the papacy relative to the European monarchs. Gregory's newly elected successor, Urban VI (r. 1378–89), quickly showed himself to be erratic and despotic. In attacking simony and clerical wealth, he went after the very cardinals who had just elected him. Without a procedure to oust Urban, these cardinals declared his election invalid and began to lobby rulers abroad. The cardinals then elected Clement VII. In response, Urban VI appointed a new college of cardinals and Clement fled to Avignon in 1379.

The Great Schism thus began, deeply unsettling society and politics.[36] The next forty years saw multiple competing popes, two centers of papal power, and papal rivals urgently building coalitions with secular rulers (Hay 1995, 302). Clergy were anxious—not even canon law experts could decide which pope was legitimate. Lay rulers were more serene—and took advantage of the opportunity to form coalitions and eventually weaken the papacy. All of Europe took sides: Urban and other Roman popes could count on England, the empire, Hungary, Poland, Scandinavia, and the city-states of Italy. Clement and the Avignon popes had the Spanish kingdoms, Scotland, Burgundy, Savoy, Naples, and France as allies. Each pope negotiated and conceded his way to gain backing from secular rulers, who themselves saw their alliances coalesce or disintegrate depending on which pope they chose to support (Fried 2015, 181). These monarchs, not clergy or canon lawyers, eventually resolved the schism at the councils of Constance (1414–8) and Basel (1431–9). A notable leader was Emperor Sigismund (r. 1410–1437), who hoped to revive imperial control over the church in the name of protection and reform (Scott 1998, 352).

During and after the Great Schism, the church relied on the good graces of kings and emperors for protection. With the Protestant Reformation, this

35. Nearly half the funding for the Avignon papacy came from French church dues, and popes conceded that the French kings could now tax the church for wars with the English (Wickham 2016, 213).

36. Beyond the schism and the decline of papal power to interfere in secular politics, the fourteenth and fifteenth centuries also saw the Black Death, which raged across Europe from 1347 to 1353, decimating (and in some cases halving) the population, and the Hundred Years' War (1337–1453), which began with territorial disputes over the autonomy of English Gascony and led to the loss of nearly all English conquests in the continent.

dependence was solidified, in *both* Catholic and Protestant countries, as secular rulers now protected their clergy and churches, exacting clerical loyalty and wealth. As a result, "the church changed its political role over time. For centuries, it had been the teacher of the state, not only in ideology, but especially where institutions were concerned . . . after the Reformation it changed into an obedient instrument of control and resource extraction" (Reinhard 1996, 18).

Conclusion

The church first liberated itself from imperial control in the late eleventh century; grew in power, ambition, and administrative capacity in the twelfth and thirteenth; and then overreached, fractured, and lost most of its political influence in the late fourteenth. This arc sets the stage for the story of rivalry and emulation, the two processes that drove early state formation in Europe. Some secular rulers clashed with the papacy and lost power, while others benefited from these conflicts, amassing authority, asserting their independence, and gaining new capabilities.

CHAPTER TWO

Rivalry and Fragmentation

MEDIEVAL POPES AND rulers clashed constantly over authority and territory. The papacy wanted to ensure autonomy for the church. Popes targeted their main perceived threat, the Holy Roman Empire, even as they supported the Norman Conquest of England or the reconquest of Spanish territories. Using coalitions, balancing strategies, awarding of titles and privileges, and joint efforts such as the Crusades, they assiduously worked to deepen the fragmentation of the Empire. Monarchs eager to consolidate their rule resisted these papal assertions of worldly power. A ruler who sought control over the provision of justice, taxation, and order faced "conflict, first, with representative institutions, which were his rivals for the control of government and were usually dominated by the nobility, and secondly, with the Church, which was the only Western institution to have survived the barbarian invasions and had been the focal point of European unity during the High Middle Ages" (Bireley 1999, 9).

These struggles between the papacy and temporal rulers gave rise to some of the defining features of the European state system: the differentiation of the secular and the temporal, the fragmentation of territorial authority, and the equal standing of monarchs. The church's efforts to fragment territorial authority also enabled communes to grow. These developments emerged between 1100 and 1300, during the heyday of papal power. Without them, the European state system would look very different, and their roots lie in the church's efforts to ensure greater autonomy for itself and to throttle imperial hegemony.

The popes were especially anxious about the Hohenstaufens, the dynasty that first arose in 1079 and ruled the Holy Roman Empire until 1254. Denounced by the popes as "a brood of vipers" (Abulafia 1999, 506), the Hohenstaufens sought to rebuild the Carolingian empire and reunify Italy and Germany by controlling both northern Italy and Sicily. They were even more interested in imperial Italy than in Germany itself (Toch 1999). Control over these territories would surround the papal domains and expose them to enormous political and military pressure. Frederick II's was the most ambitious effort, and had he succeeded, the papal states would be encircled by a powerful adversary. Popes sought to contain these aspirations, and to ensure that Germany would remain fragmented and Italy under papal control. The papacy was so successful that it took until the mid-nineteenth century for Germany and Italy to unify as states (see Ziblatt 2006).

The conflict was ongoing because the rivalry between the papacy and the monarchs could not be decisively settled. Both sides were as ambitious as they were relatively weak: neither could fully enforce laws or agreements, nor could they claim full control of territory. As a result, "no lasting power sharing between popes and emperors could be established . . . each claimed to be universalist, enjoying supremacy over the other" (Angelov and Herrin 2012, 168). Spiritual and secular authorities were intermingled, as were morality and the law—and this meant these conflicts were not the familiar interstate rivalries, but rather personalized struggles over authority. Both popes and kings also faced internal defiance, whether from clergy skeptical of the reform program or nobles eager to preserve their privileges.

Below, I examine how the papacy wielded both spiritual and temporal weapons, and sought to ensure its interests in several episodes of medieval rivalry between popes and rulers: the Investiture Conflict in the late eleventh and early twelfth centuries; the fragmentation of Europe that began in the twelfth century; early assertions of sovereignty at the beginning of the thirteenth century; and the consequences for the Great Schism of 1378–1417.

Weapons of the Meek: Spiritual and Temporal Warfare

The church could rely on an arsenal of weapons in its conflicts with secular rulers. First, there were spiritual weapons: curses and maledictions, the excommunication of rulers and placing whole countries under interdict,[1] cutting them off from the community of the faithful. Popes could reward as much as they punished, with gifts of indulgences, dispensations, papal appointments, and absolution. The papacy also waged wars by proxy and formed alliances with secular rulers who bore the military burdens and shared geopolitical goals (and the material profits). Popes even endowed some of these expeditions with crusade privileges, turning conflict with kings into a holy war.

---

1. The interdict applied to the entire community, who could no longer celebrate mass or receive sacraments. Hundreds if not thousands of interdicts were imposed across medieval Europe. The most common causes including supporting a person condemned by the church, the misappropriation of ecclesiastical property, political opposition to papal interests, and destroying church property (Clarke 2007, 114–5). The heyday of the interdict was the early thirteenth century, when Pope Innocent III put France, Norway, Germany, and England under interdict at various times (Mundy 2000, 203).

EXCOMMUNICATION

The most serious sanction available to the church was excommunication (Helmholz 2015, 402; see also Helmholz 1994 and 2004). Excommunications punish by excluding individuals from the sacraments and religious communion. Excommunication released vassals and lords from their oaths of fealty to the monarch and could thus lead to a loss of allies: for example, after his first excommunication in 1076, Henry IV found himself deserted by his princes. Excommunicated rulers could even be deposed from office. To regain good standing, some kings would even become papal vassals, as John I of England did in 1213 and Valdemar I of Sweden did in 1274 (Jordan 2001, 248).

Popes excommunicated rulers, monarchs, princes, and emperors for political reasons more than one hundred times from the third to the twentieth century.[2] Boniface VIII, the last of the powerful popes, issued no fewer than seven royal excommunications. Not surprisingly, given the papal obsession with its biggest rival, fully 44 percent (twenty-two) of the fifty medieval political excommunications between 1000 and 1400 targeted Holy Roman emperors and princes for defying the papacy.[3] The record holder was Emperor Henry IV (r. 1054–1105), who was excommunicated five times by three different popes. Perhaps the starkest comparison is to England, whose aid the popes sought. From the eleventh century to the Reformation, only two English kings were excommunicated: Harold I in 1066 to pave the way for the Norman Conquest and John I in 1209 for allying with Holy Roman Emperor Otto IV, who threatened Rome. Even the murder of Thomas Becket did not lead Pope Alexander III to excommunicate Henry II: English support (or at least detachment) was too important.

Excommunications for political reasons peaked in the medieval era, as figure 2.1 shows. They drop off rapidly after the fourteenth century, as a papacy greatly weakened by the Great Schism stopped sanctioning leaders.

Yet excommunications were not decisive weapons. They destabilized monarchical rule, but did not end tenure in office. Excommunicated kings and princes vary enormously in the duration of their rule. Their office holding is unstable and does not increase over time, as figure 2.2 shows. Here, Blaydes and

2. "Political reasons" consist of disobedience to papal orders, refusal to go on crusade, failure to pay taxes, the appointment or removal of bishops contrary to papal wishes, and so on. Papal excommunications were coded as such only if the pope deliberately pronounced sentence on the ruler, as opposed to automatic excommunication for certain sins, the *latae sententiae*. The data come from the *Catholic Encyclopedia* and the *New Cambridge Medieval History*.

3. The pattern is robust to other periodizations: forty-two political excommunications took place during the heyday of papal power, from 1050 to 1302, and eighteen, or 43 percent, targeted Holy Roman rulers. In the entire data span, 46 percent of excommunications were imposed on Holy Roman rulers.

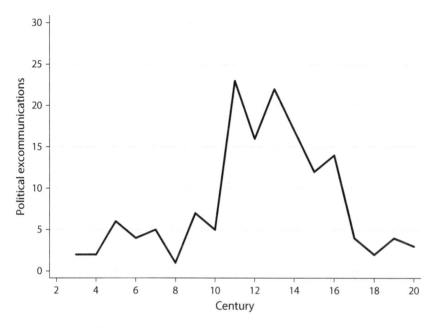

FIGURE 2.1. Papal excommunications of rulers for political reasons by century.

Chaney (2013) identified a steady increase in the duration of western European rulers in office from 700 to 1500. I augment the same data set (taken from Bosworth 1996 and Morby 1989) with new data on dynasties in Eastern Europe and papal excommunications, and calculate the duration of rule for both excommunicated and non-excommunicated rulers. Rulers who avoided excommunication exemplify the pattern identified by Blaydes and Chaney. In contrast, for excommunicated rulers, tenure in office is unstable and does not increase over time. It is only with the Great Schism, and the loss of papal authority, that their rule becomes secure.[4]

Instead, excommunication only affected more vulnerable, younger rulers. Figure 2.3 reports results from Kaplan-Meier survival analyses, using the same data. It shows that rulers in their first fifteen years of rule are more threatened by excommunication. If they survived beyond the first fifteen years, excommunicated rulers were actually *more* likely to survive in office than non-excommunicated ones. Henry IV regained his allies and did not lose them when he was excommunicated subsequently. Despite his five excommunications, he was king and then emperor for fifty-one years, from 1054 to 1105. Frederick II

4. Blaydes and Chaney (2013) argue that the longer duration of officeholding is attributable to feudal institutions and the power-sharing and executive constraint they induced in rulers. But a major medieval transformation is the church's introduction of stricter rules on marriage and primogeniture, which lengthened tenure in office (Kokkonen and Sundell 2014).

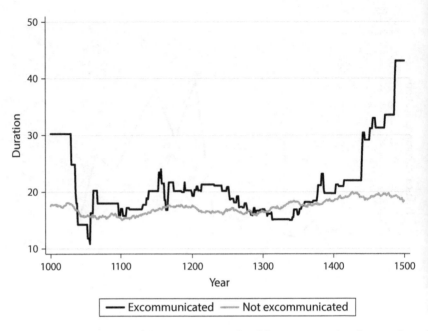

FIGURE 2.2. Duration of rule for excommunicated and non-excommunicated monarchs, 800–1500.

was similarly undeterred after his excommunication. He insisted that God was on his side and continued the seizures of papal territory in Italy that got him excommunicated in the first place (Watt 1999, 136). He may have had a point: he, too, lasted in office for more than fifty years, as king and emperor from 1198 to 1250. Popes targeted rulers whose power posed a threat: and that same power allowed these rulers to survive.

Spiritual weapons lost their edge when used too often, as Innocent III himself warned (Obertyński and Kumor 1974, 166).[5] Already in 1245 at the Council of Lyon, "Innocent IV both anathematized Frederick II as a heretic and launched a Crusade against him. After this fulmination, one that harked back to Europe's civil wars of the Gregorian age, no new weapons were found in the papal arsenal" (Mundy 2000, 203). By the fourteenth century, excommunications and interdicts were used more sparingly, and this "ultimate papal weapon had ceased to be a sanction on a different level from any other" (Southern 1970, 135). The penalties were frequently ignored (Herde 2000, 543), both because they were overused, and because they were "discredited by virtue of being used as an instrument of political pressure" (de Sousa 1998, 632). Not even clergy complied: when Poland-Lithuania defeated the Teutonic Order

5. Innocent tried to bolster the power of excommunication by making annual confession mandatory once a year, and enforcing it "by a real executive officer, the confessor" (Smith 1964, 52).

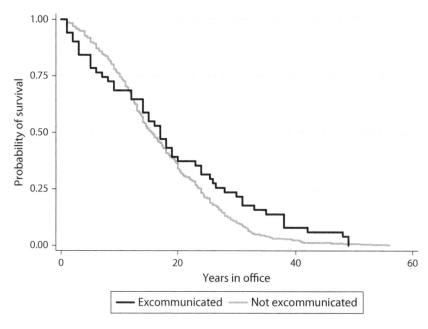

FIGURE 2.3. Probability of survival in office over time for medieval monarchs only, 1000–1350.

in 1410, Popes Calixtus III and then Pius II placed Poland under an interdict "which the people and clergy promptly ignored" (Gieysztor 1998, 737).

THE CHURCH MILITANT?
COALITIONS AND PROXY WARS

Fundamentally, the papacy had to rely on *temporal* strategies to defend its interests. Popes sought to protect the papal territories from encroachment from both north and south, and they waged war to prevent the empire from completing a pincer movement and gaining both northern Italy and Sicily and Naples. Spiritual weapons were not effective, and the few direct military campaigns led by medieval popes ended in disaster: when Pope Leo IX (r. 1049–54) fought the Normans in southern Italy in 1053, the Normans easily defeated his army and took him prisoner (Jordan 2001, 87). When Innocent II (r. 1130–43) took the field himself against Roger II of Sicily in 1139, he, too, was taken prisoner and had to accede to Roger's demand for control of Sicily and Apulia (Brooke 1938, 276). History repeated in 1156 (Robinson 1990, 367). Medieval popes may have been savvy diplomats and reformers, but they made poor military commanders.[6]

6. The Council of Constance (1414–18) freed popes to declare war (Chambers 2006, 37). The largest papal expenditure in the fifteenth century was the upkeep of the armies and its garrisons. Even in peacetime, military expenditures ate up over one-quarter of papal

Instead, the papacy allied with secular rulers, offered protection, and sub-sidized joint ventures. The popes' goals were to protect their temporal holdings in the papal territories, and to ensure that no hegemon could arise to threaten their interests. The results of the balancing strategies and interventions were the fragmentation of Europe and the survival of smaller states.

Popes and rulers entered into strategic coalitions, which shifted as the balance of power changed. Already in 800, Leo III crowned Charlemagne emperor in exchange for the monarch's help with both personal enemies in Rome and the Lombard invasion of papal lands. Urban II (r. 1088–99) and Pascal II (r. 1099–1118), threatened with schisms, found it expedient to favor the Normans: when Roger I conquered Sicily, Urban recognized him and named him the legitimate papal legate on the island (Fried 2015, 195). The papacy also pitted rulers against each other to preclude the consolidation of bigger claims on territory or authority. Popes recognized the territorial grabs of their allies, but not the conquests of their foes, and urged "powerful vassals to aban-don the emperor's cause" (Hoffman 2015, 132). Shifting and unreliable alli-ances meant that popes had to deploy their own resources and closely monitor their allies (Robinson 1990, 29).

In building these alliances, the papacy was opportunistic. The Lombard League of city-states was traditionally an enemy, but Pope Alexander III allied with the League to prevent Frederick I from taking over Italy in the mid-twelfth century, and Pope Gregory IX did so again to battle Frederick II nearly a century later (Gregory also helpfully excommunicated Frederick II on multiple occasions). The papacy could even ally with the German emperors. After the Concordat of Worms, hostilities ceased from 1125 to 1156, allowing the pope to break the costly alliance with the Normans and instead align with the empire (Brooke 1938, 264). Similarly, popes subsequently sought German help to contain Angevin ambitions in Sicily. Even the fourteenth-century Avi-gnon popes, residing in Angevin lands, tried to prevent Angevin kings from controlling the whole of Italy. For example, Clement V (r. 1305–14) gingerly encouraged Emperor Henry VII to balance Robert the Wise of Anjou (r. 1309–43), only to switch sides and support Robert when Henry of Luxembourg tried to invade Italy (Abulafia 2000, 489).

Popes invested heavily in their defense and subsidized their allies. Popes readily funded potential counterweights to the German emperor and the Normans in Sicily, such as Henry I in twelfth-century England or the anti-king Henry Raspe in thirteenth-century Germany (Whalen 2019, 185). In the

income (Hay 1995, 316). Sixteenth-century cardinal-princes raised, funded, and led armies, and popes declared war on hostile secular rulers and defended their territory. The Papal States became the "most formidably defended zones of Europe" (Chambers 2006, 101), with well-stocked armories to defend against insurrection and looting during papal elections, and to fight against baronial armies. Pope Julius II (r. 1503–13) even led the siege of Miran-dola in 1511 in person and formed a Holy League against the French with Venice and Spain.

mid-thirteenth century, both Gregory IX and Innocent IV raised armies to fight the emperor, desperate to prevent the union of Sicily with the empire that would have consolidated imperial power on the Italian peninsula. Innocent IV even sold the rights to invade Sicily to the English king Henry III for the ungodly sum of 90,000 pounds.[7] When Henry III failed to come up with the money, the papacy negated the sale and let Charles of Anjou take Sicily instead.[8]

Just as papal alliances shifted, rulers similarly switched coalitions and even religions depending on their strategic needs. Secular allies fought for the papacy, but expected to benefit (Weiß 2016, 234). Alliances could thus shift quickly: Innocent III crowned Otto IV emperor in 1209, only to have him renege on his promises, turn on the papacy, and try to take over Sicily. Even conversions could be instrumental: Poland converted in the mid-tenth century to strengthen its position against Germany and Bohemia (Gieysztor 1979, 58–9). The Lithuanian king Gediminas converted to Christianity in 1324, only to declare once peace had been secured and confirmed by the Pope that "he had never wished to be baptised and that 'the devil can christen me!'" (Rowell 2000, 709).

Rulers allied with the papacy when they sought legitimation: an expensive proposition, but a mutually beneficial one. Monarchs entered into a feudal relationship by surrendering land to a pope and receiving it back as a fief. The benefit was that a vassal kingdom could not be legitimately offered to another ruler, and any injury to king or country was an injury to the church (Ullmann [1955] 1965, 336). In return, kings had to pay annual tribute or perform military duties. Religious legitimation was thus anything but cheap, contrary to some analyses (Rubin 2017). Becoming a papal vassal was attractive to monarchs whose rule needed bolstering, where succession struggles had weakened the monarchy, for example. Thus, "on Europe's frontiers, kings were papal vassals. Scandinavia, Hungary, Poland, Bohemia and Bulgaria and the British Isles were all at one time or other under papal lordship" (Mundy 2000, 200).

THE CRUSADES

With Pope Urban II's rallying cry of "Deus Vult!" (God wills it!) at the Council of Clermont in 1095, and the council's enthusiastic acclamation, the first Crusade began in 1096.[9] The Crusades contributed to state formation by facilitating

---

7. The episode prompted huge concern among barons in England and led to the Provisions of Oxford, which set limits on royal authority in favor of baronial governance (see chapter 5).

8. Charles ruled Sicily from 1266, but the Sicilian Vespers rebellion of 1282 overthrew Angevin rule and divided Sicily into two kingdoms: mainland Naples and the island of Sicily. Angevins ruled Naples until 1435, while the crown of Aragon assumed control in Sicily. The two kingdoms reunited in 1816.

9. As early as the ninth century, Leo IV and John VIII gave assurances of forgiveness and eternal life to those killed in battle against heathens. The eleventh-century Gregorian reformers already lauded holy war as essential to the reform of the church (Morris

taxation, sales of feudal land, reintegration into global trade networks, and the elimination of rivals to ruling monarchs (Blaydes and Paik 2016, 563–4).

Yet these joint ventures between popes and monarchs were also an exercise in flexing political power—and the fragmenting of authority. The Crusades quickly took on an explicitly political tone and were summoned against the enemies of the papacy, rather than defending the faith. Papal expeditions against secular states in Europe were increasingly endowed with crusade privileges as an incentive to rally troops. At the 1135 Council of Pisa, Innocent II expanded crusade indulgences to all those who fought against the pope's enemies (Riley-Smith 2004, 545). The Baltic Crusades, designed to convert northern Europe to Christianity and to gain the pope political influence, began in 1147 and lasted through the sixteenth century. The Reconquista of Spain was endowed with crusade privileges. After excommunicating John in 1209, Innocent III threw his support behind Philip II of France and declared his war against England a crusade (Jedin 1993, 85). In 1241, shortly before his death, Gregory IX commissioned a crusade against German Emperor Frederick II (Whalen 2019, 121). Pope Innocent IV also launched a crusade against Frederick II in 1245 and then against Frederick's son, Conrad IV, excommunicating and deposing both. He summoned Germany, Lombardy, and Sicily, and offered indulgences to the crusaders as if they had been on a crusade to the Holy Land, "creating an equivalency between the two theatres of holy war" (Whalen 2019, 186). Subsequently, Popes Alexander IV and Urban IV called for a crusade against Manfred, son of Frederick II, who invaded papal territories in 1258. This crusade was launched in 1255 and lasted until 1266, with boundless privileges granted to Charles of Anjou, who defeated Manfred (Jedin 1993, 166). Boniface VIII subsequently launched a crusade against his political enemies in the papal states, including the Colonna family in Rome, in 1297 (Mundy 2000, 43). Urban V gave crusade privileges to his attempts to overthrow the Visconti in Milan in 1362, and his successor Urban VI launched a crusade against Flanders in 1383 (Jedin 1993, 180–1).

Popes thus used crusades as political weapons against their secular enemies.[10] Holy war was "debased by being used by popes for purely political

---

1989, 145). Leo IX (r. 1049–54) justified wars on the basis of religion, and Gregory VII (r. 1073–85) declared wars against heretics and wayward kings. After 1096, six other main crusades followed, in almost two centuries of constant crusading, ending in 1270. Crusades of various magnitude took place into the seventeenth century.

10. Heretics were another target. Innocent III made crusades into weapons against religious dissent, whether against schismatic Greeks (the Fourth Crusade of 1204), Muslim Spain, the Waldensians, or the vicious Albigensian Crusade against the Cathars in 1209, in concert with the French king (who stood to gain control over Languedoc as a result). The Cathars were virtually extirpated, but other heresies remained. Gregory IX, unlike Innocent III, quickly realized crusading against heretics was ineffective—and turned to the Inquisition instead (Rist 2016, 321).

purposes" (Hay 1995, 279). The aim of these military ventures, especially after the thirteenth century, became "less religious than hierarchical; it implied the domination of Church over State, and of clergy over laity, the demonstration of the civil power's derivation from ecclesiastical" (Smith 1964, 54).

Popes could thus use both spiritual and temporal weapons to achieve their aims. Excommunications were largely ineffectual, but alliances with secular rulers and crusades were far more potent weapons. The church wielded them to achieve both its own autonomy, and the fragmentation of Europe.

Liberta ecclesiae: *the Investiture Conflict and Liberation of the Church*

The Investiture Conflict was a major episode in the rivalry between the papacy and secular rulers. The papacy used both excommunications and alliances to ensure its autonomy. The conflict differentiated sacred authority from secular rule, even as the rivalry continued without decisive settlement. The eventual separation of church and state, in turn, was a critical prerequisite for European constitutional state development (Fukuyama 2011, 267, 273; see also Ertman 1997, 54).[11]

The Conflict, nominally a series of disputes over the naming of bishops, lasted from 1075 to 1122 and had at its core the mutually constituted powers of popes and German emperors.[12] Prior to the Gregorian reforms, popes delegated their worldly rule to emperors, and the papacy relied on imperial protection. In practice, this meant the popes' authority over their own clergy was limited. Lay investiture, or the right of secular kings and princes to name bishops,[13] was a key prerogative for rulers, precisely because the bishops were such important agents for both monarchs and popes. These offices were also

---

11. Boucoyannis (2021) argues that the separation of church and state is neither necessary nor sufficient for constitutionalism, citing the cases of the United Kingdom, Denmark, Sweden, and Norway. Yet in all these cases, while the state *subordinated* the church during the Reformation, the two remained distinct.

12. The debate over the character and consequences of the controversy is considerable. Maureen Miller (2009) identifies three main interpretations: a) reform as an attempt to rectify the abuses plaguing the church, and the rise of papal monarchy as the most significant result of the reform conflict; b) lay influence in the church as the key occupation of the reformers, and the investiture crisis as a struggle for the right order; and c) the church's institutional practices fostering the development of bureaucratic techniques and the rule of law. Historians also disagree about the longer-run effects of the controversy (see also Oakley 2012, 17).

13. As part of the ceremony, the king would present a bishop with the symbols of religious office: the staff and the ring, and rights and privileges (the regalia). The clergy swore fealty to the ruler who named them and promised services to the king including counsel, military support, and the payment of taxes and fees.

enormously lucrative and a major means of patronage, so both secular and ecclesiastical authorities vied to nominate bishops (and profit from vacant sees). In short, the naming of bishops was essential to both medieval government and ecclesiastical authority.

The Investiture Conflict began after Gregory VII prohibited lay investiture in 1075 as part of his broader reform program. The German king Henry IV (r. 1054–1105) rejected Gregory's authority and insisted on naming his own bishops, as we saw in chapter 1. Nearly five decades of excommunications, denunciations, and mutual depositions followed, spanning the reign of two emperors and six popes. Both sides argued that doctrine and law supported their claims.[14]

After lengthy negotiations, the Concordat of Worms formally settled the controversy in 1122. The biggest bone of contention, lay investiture with ring and staff by the emperor, had been resolved in favor of the pope. The emperor could no longer formally invest bishops with their *spiritual* authority. In return, the monarch could confer regalia with scepter and receive homage from the elect bishops (Robinson 1990, 437).

The Concordat is sometimes seen as *the* decisive point in church-state relations in Europe, "a monumental contract that would change the world" by driving a permanent wedge between kings and popes, incentivizing the former to promote economic development and the latter to hamper growth as they named bishops (de Mesquita 2022, 8). In some accounts the "Concordat of Worms ensured autonomy for the church as an institution" (Fukuyama 2011, 289; see also Strayer [1970] 1998). The church did gain greater autonomy from secular rulers, and the conflict did distinguish ecclesiastical and secular authority (Clark 1986, 669). The agreements drew clearer lines between the two spheres and wielders of authority, desacralizing the monarchy (Mitterauer 2010, 152–3; Oakley 2012, 39).

Yet the Concordat did not end the struggle between secular and ecclesiastical authority: it was a compromise, not a resolution. The naming of bishops and filling episcopal vacancies was only one of many disputes: bitter conflicts also raged over the authority to tax, the extent of jurisdiction over legal disputes, and sovereignty. Rulers in England, France, and Spain repeatedly asserted control over churches in their lands, not only naming clergy (as in England or Poland), but extracting resources and asserting legal control. Kings "continued to use the language of divine authority. The monarchy . . . laid even more emphasis upon its religious doctrine" (Morris 1989, 227).

14. The fifth-century Gelasian doctrine of the two swords distinguished between the earthly power of secular kings and the sacred authority of the pope. Gregory VII and his successors insisted this implied the primacy of the sacred, while Henry IV and his followers argued it meant distinct spheres of authority. The reference to the two swords comes from Luke 22:38.

The Concordat did not even settle the status of investiture itself. Secular rulers continued to informally influence the naming of bishops everywhere, and lay investiture continued where the papacy needed the support of rulers. Popes tactically tolerated lay investiture, despite agreements with the English king as early as 1107 and the French in 1108. Even Gregory accepted it to preserve alliances outside of Germany, France, and Italy (Cowdrey 1998, 550).[15] For example, the papacy let William the Conqueror assert primacy over the English church in 1066. William replaced the Anglo-Saxon bishops with Norman royalists and required royal consent for papal bulls to enter England, for councils to enact canon law, for the recognition of the pope, and for the excommunication of lords. Subsequently, even Paschal II (r. 1099–1118), a fanatical reformist, conceded homage of ecclesiastics to William's son, Henry I (r. 1100–1135), which allowed him, and generations of English kings, to retain control over investiture (Cantor 1958, 287–8). The papacy acquiesced because it could ill afford conflict with both the Holy Roman Emperor and the King of England. Similarly, in France, the formal abandonment of lay investiture did not change the close blood relations, shared elite networks, or the bishops' services to the Capetian monarchy (Leyser 1994, 105; Baldwin 2004, 515–6). Some French kings, such as Louis VII in 1149 and Philip II Augustus in 1203, even voluntarily withdrew their rights to name bishops, yet canon chapters continued to elect bishops favorable to the king (Baldwin 2004, 518 and 524). By refusing to accept homage, even the emperor could effectively exercise a veto. A decisive settlement of investiture would wait until the Great Schism (Millet and Moraw 1996, 75).

Nor was it the case that secular rulers gained the upper hand. By the end of the twelfth century, Pope Innocent III achieved the position of supreme judge of western Europe, compelling kings of France, Portugal, and Léon to take back wives they had discarded, stopping the incipient conflict between Castile and Aragon, nullifying the Magna Carta, and insisting that the barons who broke the oath of fealty to John go to court—specifically, the papal court in Rome (Ergang 1971, 19). Even in the Holy Roman Empire, despite the assertion of the electoral principle in the Golden Bull of 1356, popes would continue to crown emperors as late as 1530.[16] This form of religious legitimation did not come cheap—but it held the empire together, given the weakness of its central institutions.

15. Kings retained control over church affairs all over Europe. In Scandinavia, Gregorian ideals spread slowly in the twelfth and thirteenth centuries, and kings retained control over investiture (Bagge 2014, 79, Cantor 1958, 12). Hungarian kings continued to preside over ecclesiastical synods, appoint bishops and move them to different sees, despite formally giving up investiture in 1106 (Berend 2004, 312). In Poland, despite an alliance between King Bolesław the Bold and Gregory VII, kings continued to invest bishops, give monasteries to nobles, and benefit from vacant benefices (*ius spolii*). As late as the fifteenth century, Polish kings named the bishops (Obertyński and Kumor 1974, 60, 360; Kotecki 2018, 308).

16. The last Holy Roman Emperor to be crowned in Rome was Frederick III in 1452.

The Investiture Conflict and the Concordat of Worms had three ancillary effects. First, the controversy led to the growth of the law as a political weapon, in lieu of appeals to the divine. Gregory VII fought not only with excommunications and appeals but also with legal arguments, using the papal archives to buttress his arguments. Henry IV could not do so at first. With the rediscovery of Roman law at the height of the conflict, both popes and emperors invested heavily in legal expertise, and in the law schools and universities that began with the founding at Bologna in 1088 (see chapter 4). As a result, popes and Hohenstaufens first clashed over investiture, but eventually shifted to jurisdiction: which legal cases and appeals could be tried by the pope, what limits there were on his legislative activity, and what legal sanctions he could use (Tierney 1964, 97). These debates redefined religious and lay domains of authority.

Second, the Investiture Conflict empowered nobles against monarchs by affirming that elections, rather than divinely sanctioned ascension, were a legitimate mechanism of leader selection. Gregory VII and subsequent popes advocated royal elections: inherited rule could not guarantee a religiously suitable leader (worse yet, dynastic rulers did not need the church's blessing). Naturally, elections and papal vetting were a more reliable mechanism (Fried 2015, 199). With little else in common, German lords joined the church in pressing for royal elections, gaining a powerful weapon against the crown (Zacour 1976, 105). Innocent III's *Venerabilem* decree (1202) formally endorsed royal elections. The Holy Roman Emperor became an electoral office after 1254, during the 1250–1312 interregnum when no pope anointed an emperor (Watts 2009, 64). Eventually, the contested royal election in 1314 led one of its protagonists, the future emperor Ludwig IV of Bavaria (r. 1328–47), to realize that election meant that the papacy could be excluded from the selection of the emperor (Wilks 1963, 239–40).[17] With the Golden Bull of 1356, popes and German king-emperors finally reached a lasting rapprochement: the emperor would be elected, but the pope would have no role in these elections (Black 1993, 56). Popes would continue to anoint the emperor: in fact, the value of papal recognition was highest where kings emerged from elections rather than dynasties (Kern [1948] 1985, 33). The conflict thus indirectly shifted the domestic balance of power where royal elections were held.

Third, as we will see below, the Investiture Conflict contributed to the fragmentation of the Holy Roman Empire. Having gained relative autonomy, the church sought to ensure it by reducing the threat of a resurgent empire. While Henry IV and his successors focused on the conflict with Rome, they neglected to broadcast power within their territories. With each conflict and

17. Pope John XII (r. 1316–34) insisted on inspecting both candidates, Ludwig and Frederick the Fair, at Avignon, and invalidated the election because he played no role in choosing the emperor.

excommunication, independent towns, princes, lords, and bishops gained power relative to the emperor, who had neither time nor resources to stem these leaks.

The Gregorian reforms and the Investiture Conflict led to greater autonomy of the church from secular authorities. Law, rather than charisma, would increasingly become the organizing principle of European governance. Election, rather than anointment, could legitimate rulers. And the focus on high politics meant an opportunity for cities and magnates alike to gain politically and carve out their own sphere of autonomy.

The Fragmentation of Europe

The fragmentation of territorial authority after the collapse of the Carolingian empire in Europe is often the starting point for analyses of the rise and consolidation of modern territorial nation-states. A wide consensus casts this "multifarious polycentric fragmentation" as the foundation for subsequent political and economic modernity (Scheidel 2019, 348).[18] It is the point of departure for both Hintze and Tilly, who emphasize the fragmentation that occurred after the Carolingian center disintegrated.[19] Proposed causes of this initial fragmentation vary. Scholars have pointed to the uneven emergence of urban life (Abramson 2017), the rise of local warlords (Bisson 1994), and low levels of religious legitimation (Rubin 2017; see also Fischer 1992). Frustratingly, this fragmentation remains largely unexplained (Boucoyannis 2021, 39).

Once we incorporate the church into the analysis, however, the fragmentation of territorial authority in Europe becomes more legible. Fragmentation was a deliberate policy of the medieval papacy. The papacy first sought to free the church from imperial influence—and then to preclude an imperial resurgence. As a result, fragmentation is not evenly distributed across Europe, and it is closely associated with papal conflict.

First, not all territorial authority was equally fragmented. Figure 2.4 shows the number of states over time within the borders of European states as they existed in 1900.[20] Where the church and rulers had fought the hardest, in the

18. See Jones (1981) 2003; Ertman 1997; Landes 1998; Van Zanden 2009; Rosenthal and Wong 2011; Stasavage 2011; Voigtländer and Voth 2013; Hoffman 2015; Dincecco and Onorato 2016; Cox and Weingast 2017; Mokyr 2017; and Dincecco and Wang 2018.

19. Early Germanic rulers could not tax effectively and instead exchanged land for services, which fragmented the imperial landholdings (Stasavage 2020, 105).

20. "States" here are defined using Abramson's (2017) criteria: principalities, lay and ecclesiastical, duchies, baronies, and cities that are not occupied by a foreign power can tax and have a common executive (Abramson 2017, 103). The shape files for state borders are from Abramson (2017), augmented by European country borders in 1900 from the Mosaic historical maps project: *https://censusmosaic.demog.berkeley.edu/data/historical-gis-files*, accessed August 2021.

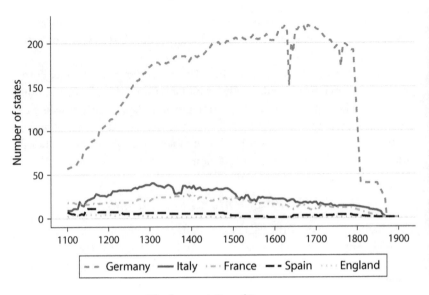

FIGURE 2.4. The fragmentation of Europe, 1000–1900.

German and Italian lands, territorial political fragmentation persisted and no central authority arose for centuries. The fragmentation of the empire was both extraordinary, and extraordinarily durable, dipping only briefly with the temporary Swedish conquest in the Thirty Years' War (1618–48). Italy is a distant second, but here, too, cities and principalities benefited from the zealous focus of the popes on Holy Roman emperors. The rulers and territories most involved in conflict with the pope over political authority and territorial rule remained decentralized, disorganized, and disunified until the 1870s. In contrast, the church supported the early Capetian consolidation of power in France and efforts in the Spanish territories.

Second, the fragmentation of territorial authority *increases* during the heyday of papal rule, in the twelfth and thirteenth centuries. This is most visible in the case of the Holy Roman Empire, the church's chief enemy. Here, territorial fragmentation rises sharply in 1100, continues until 1300, and then tapers off after 1400. It is therefore not the case that the collapse of the Carolingian empire left behind a fragmented but stable landscape—instead, the fragmentation of territorial authority was dynamic. Italian fragmentation also increases during this period, although at a more moderate rate.

Third, the fragmentation was persistent. Contrary to the bellicist narrative, fragmentation did not end in the early modern era. Tilly observes that the number of states decreased from five hundred in 1500 to thirty in 1900 (Tilly 1992, 45–6), but fragmentation persisted through the early modern era, and only ended in the nineteenth century. The vast majority of these states were in the Holy Roman Empire, and these tiny principalities, city states, and *kleinsta-aterei* survived (Abramson 2017; Bagge 2019, 24). Of the fifteen kingdoms of the twelfth century, seven still existed as independent units with their own rulers in 1648: England, France, Castile, Portugal, Denmark, Sweden, and Poland (Bagge 2019, 23). City-states were also remarkably durable (Abramson 2017, 116–7).

The papacy deepened and maintained these patterns of fragmentation and consolidation. Popes worked assiduously to keep any one ruler from getting too strong and reassembling Charlemagne's empire (Hoffman 2015, 132).[21] They deliberately played rulers against each other and used doctrine, intimidation, and wars by proxy to ensure that no powerful rival could arise that might threaten the papacy's political interests. Popes made successive efforts to move states out of the emperor's sphere and into their own. Markus Fischer argues that the church failed to maintain European unity (Fischer 1992, 438), and Jared Rubin (2017) agrees that Europe was fragmented because relatively weak religious "propagating agents" poorly legitimated monarchs. But this has the historical record backwards. It is not that the church failed to legitimate monarchs—it is that the church deliberately sought to balance them against each other and preclude any from gaining too much authority.

Conversely, popes did not hamper royal centralization of power where they needed support (or at least non-interference). In countries farther removed from territorial conflicts with the popes, monarchs could centralize their rule and consolidate into powerful administrators and tax collectors in the late twelfth and thirteenth centuries. In England, a relatively strong state existed before the Norman Conquest. English kings already issued coins, collected taxes, and put forth royal legislation. After 1066, the pope needed English support in his conflict with the empire and limited his interference in England. The centralization of English royal power could proceed unhindered.[22] Latin Europe was also centralizing over the course of the twelfth and thirteenth centuries with papal blessing (Mundy 2000, 218). The French king Philip Augustus (r. 1180–1223) began the arduous process of wresting authority from regional strongmen, and the royal city of Paris became the core of a centralizing project that took off in the thirteenth and fourteenth centuries (Ergang 1971, 56; Genet 1990, 261; see also Fried 2015, 197). For its part, a series of dynastic unions and the Reconquest transformed the kingdoms on the Spanish peninsula into an increasingly powerful and consolidated monarchy.

21. After Charlemagne's death in 814, the magnates pursued their own interests in the absence of royal protection. These lords obtained control over royal estates, and the king's power declined in tandem. The church would benefit if a landholder would donate land to the church and continue to use it, and then the land would revert back to the church (Zacour 1976, 73, 79).

22. Some recent work has questioned this historical consensus, suggesting that the court system was not as centralized as previously thought (Herzog 2018, 113).

The patterns of fragmentation persisted, even after papal power waned in the fourteenth century, because it had created powerful vested interests that stymied centralization in the empire. The emperor lost power to princes, bishops, and towns. The constant expeditions over the Alps to conquer Italy meant the diversion of imperial attention and resources. After expending so much effort on waging war with the papacy, emperors had few resources to consolidate central authority within the empire. Frederick II spent so little time in Germany that his rule has been characterized as "government by remote control" (Angelov and Herrin 2012, 154). Local princes, bishops, and lords gained in territorial and economic power at the expense of the emperor, the number of towns grew tenfold, and the territory of the Holy Roman Empire remained politically riven and decentralized.

The conflict between popes and the German emperors entrenched cities and nobles at the expense of the emperor's central authority. First, the power vacuum after Henry III's death in 1056 meant twenty years without a ruler in Italy, giving the initial impetus to the "communal revolution" and the rise of increasingly autonomous cities in Italy, such as Pisa, Milan, or Lucca (Hyde 1973, 49). These cities then began to control neighboring territory, and in effect, became regional powers. Italy then entered a protracted period of internecine warfare in the twelfth and thirteenth centuries that further precluded the consolidation of central authority. In Germany, after Frederick II's death in 1250, towns were much more likely to become self-governing (Møller and Doucette 2021, 209).

Second, local princes and bishops gained durable power at the expense of the emperor. Princes first assumed *de facto* and then *de iure* control over serfs, taxation, and justice (Clark 1986, 668; Mitterauer 2010, chapter 5). To legitimate themselves, emperors gave bishops further secular jurisdiction and ducal powers. These ecclesiastical lords became powerful secular princes: the archbishops of Mainz, Trier, and Cologne served as *Kurfürsten*, electors who chose the king and gained enormous autonomy. The interregnum entrenched the electors as a small and powerful group, disintegrated the Hohenstaufen royal estates, and made future emperors more dependent on their private estates (Watts 2009, 169).

Cities and princes maintained the fragmentation long after the church's power declined. They "grew in strength as a result of the conflict between kings and popes . . . [and] could defeat any imperial plans to centralize administration or tax collection" (Hay 1995, 317). Italian cities turned into republics that governed their surrounding areas and competed for power and wealth. The German electors began to rule independently of the monarch, raising armies, summoning diets and even ruling collectively as a committee of regency (*Kurverein*) in 1394, 1399, 1424, and 1438 (Watts 2009, 301). The empire survived, but as a loose confederation of principalities, towns, and fiefdoms (Oakley 2012, 10).

FIGURE 2.5A. Europe in 1000, showing the territories of the Holy Roman Empire.

As a result, until its dissolution in 1806, the Holy Roman Empire never became a centralized territorial state (Stollberg-Rilinger 2018, 20).

The maps in figure 2.5 show how Germany and Italy became fragmented. If the German empire was relatively cohesive in 1000, it fragmented over the next two hundred years and remained fractionalized, even after the Thirty Years' War. In contrast, authority in other kingdoms of Europe consolidated, and these states grew larger and more centralized.

FIGURE 2.5B. Europe in 1300, showing the territories of the Holy Roman Empire.

The emperor's loss was the church's gain. Thanks to the Investiture Conflict and deliberate papal fragmentation, "the Church had a political importance in Germany only equaled in the papal states. Its landholdings were huge and many of its prelates, archbishops, bishops, abbots, abbesses, deans, and the heads of the Teutonic Order and the Order of St. John were political rulers of states as well as senior clergymen" (Hughes 1992, 31). Bishops and abbeys strengthened their lordship rights within territories, so that "next to the Papal States, the Empire became the only European polity in which ecclesiastical dignitaries like archbishops, bishops, abbots, and abbesses could also be temporal rulers and, as such, sometimes Imperial members as well" (Stollberg-Rilinger 2018, 22).

FIGURE 2.5C. Europe in 1648, after the Thirty Years' War, showing the territories of the Holy Roman Empire.

PAPAL CONFLICT AND TERRITORIAL
FRAGMENTATION

To see more systematically how the papacy helped to fragment Europe, I turn to the analysis of the historical data on fragmentation, papal and secular conflict, and other potential explanations. I first examine the patterns of papal and secular conflict, and then show how they are associated with the fragmentation of territorial authority and the rise of self-governing city-states.

The takeoff in fragmentation coincides with the rise in papal conflict in the twelfth and thirteenth centuries, as the papacy reached the acme of its

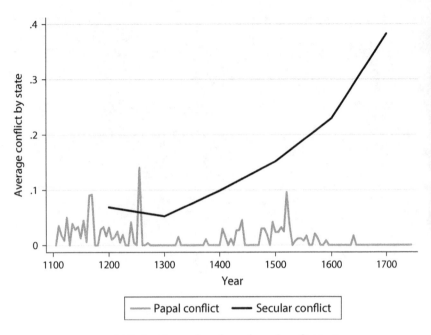

FIGURE 2.6. The incidence of secular and papal conflict in Europe.

ambitions. Figure 2.6 shows the average number of papal conflicts experienced by a state over centuries. Papal conflict here consists of clearly identifiable wars by proxy against papal enemies by allied rulers (including crusades against rulers), papal depositions of secular rulers, and attacks either led or financed by the popes directly (compiled from *The New Cambridge Medieval History* 1998–2009, and Dupuy and Dupuy 1993). The secular conflict variable relies on data from Dincecco and Onorato (2016) and codes the share of cities that experienced a siege, battle, or other conflict. The conflict drops in the fourteenth century: during the Avignon papacy and then the Great Schism that lasted until 1417, the weakened papacy did not launch conflicts at anywhere near the same rates. Papal conflicts spike again in the sixteenth century, thanks both to proxy wars of the Reformation and to the ventures of militant popes such as Julius II (r. 1503–13), who personally led armies to defend papal territories. Secular conflict, in contrast, takes off later, consistent with the bellicist account of more intense early modern warfare.

If the church deepened the fragmentation of territorial authority in Europe, we would expect conflict with the popes to be strongly associated with the fragmentation of medieval authority. To see whether this is the case, I divide the territory of Europe into 100km × 100km cells and proxy territorial fragmentation with the number of state boundaries in a given cell. I use ordinary least squares (OLS) regressions with two-way fixed state and year effects, which control for time- or space-invariant factors, such as climate,

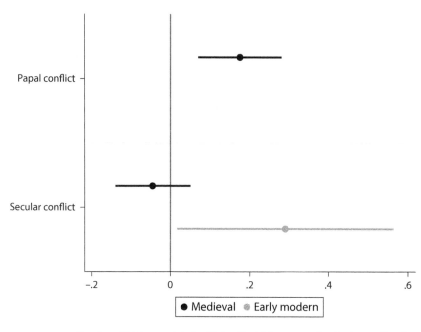

FIGURE 2.7. Papal conflict is associated with territorial fragmentation in the medieval era (1000–1350). 100 km × 100km grid cell data (OLS regressions with city and year 2FE). Horizontal lines indicate 95% confidence intervals.

elevation, agricultural suitability, and proximity to ports and coasts. To capture the theorized difference between the medieval and early modern periods in papal strength, I split the sample into medieval (1000–1350) and early modern (1500–1800) periods (see the appendix, section C). All subsequent analyses in this book rely on the same periodization.

Figure 2.7 shows that papal conflict is clearly and positively linked to territorial fragmentation. The figure summarizes the results for papal and secular conflict. The lines represent the likely range of the actual relationship between the type of conflict and fragmentation (95% confidence interval). If they cross 0, we cannot conclude that a variable has an impact. Papal conflict in the medieval era is represented by the top horizontal line: it shows a strong positive association with territorial fragmentation. This finding is consistent with the proposition that medieval popes actively fragmented territorial authority.[23] Its impact disappears in the early modern period, swamped out by the impact

23. An alternative interpretation may be that popes were more likely to enter into conflict with rulers in fragmented areas. Yet popes deliberately and consistently targeted those rulers they considered to be their biggest threat at the time. Moreover, the empire fragmented *after* papal efforts began in earnest in the twelfth century, not before. Smaller and weaker rulers did not pose a threat to church autonomy and were not the target of papal efforts.

of the Protestant Reformation. In contrast, secular conflict has no impact in the medieval period, but is associated with early modern fragmentation.

To examine the positive association between papal conflict and fragmentation more closely, and to subject it to more stringent tests, I include several potential confounders and alternative explanations. *Parliaments* may help to consolidate authority, since they constrain monarchs and lead to power sharing, thus stabilizing rule (Ertman 1997; Stasavage 2010; Blaydes and Chaney 2013). I use the indicators of parliamentary presence from Van Zanden, Buringh, and Bosker (2012), which measure the number of years per century that parliaments met in a given state. *Cities* may also contribute to fragmentation, since the rise of cities drove the survival of smaller units in Europe (Abramson 2017), and dense urban populations drove both economic growth and institutional development (Abramson and Boix 2019). Urbanization also serves as a standard proxy used in the literature for economic development. I therefore use the average city population within a grid cell, using data from Bairoch, Batou, and Pierre (1988). I include whether or not a given cell belonged to the Holy Roman Empire, to ensure that the results are not simply driven by papal hostility to the emperor. I also include coding for Protestant status in the early modern period, in case the results are driven by the Reformation.

Two alternative explanations for fragmentation are also tested. First, the rise of *communes* in the late eleventh to the twelfth century could preclude the easy consolidation of territorial authority. In the "city belt" that stretched from central Italy to northern Germany, numerous and relatively strong cities prevented rulers from establishing and centralizing authority (Rokkan 1975; Tilly 1992; Blockmans and Tilly 1994; Wickham 2015; Wilson 2016; Abramson 2017). Thus, it is no accident that the "city-studded center" (Rokkan 1975) arose precisely where rulers were preoccupied with papal conflict.

Second, inheritance regimes may also explain fragmentation. Specifically, *primogeniture* (the inheritance of all land and office by the oldest son) prevents territorial fragmentation, while partible inheritance divides the land under a ruler's control among several heirs.[24] Primogeniture emerged around 1000, adopted by the Capetians in twelfth-century France and in many families within the Holy Roman Empire by the thirteenth and fourteenth centuries (Goody 1983, 118; Wilson 2016, 425). A response to changes in the church's family law,[25] primogeniture greatly lengthened tenure in office for kings (Kokkonen

24. The church offered a highly lucrative career path for younger sons excluded from inheritance, ensuring families would support the regime (Sharma 2015, 166). Henrich (2020) argues that the consequence of primogeniture was to break up kinship ties, and Goody (1983) argues that the church's aim was to enrich itself. But another consequence of the church's family law could be to further fragment territory, by making dynastic unions and legitimate inheritance more difficult. I am grateful to Jared Rubin for this point.

25. By the tenth century, the church laid down a regime of family law, including monogamy, consanguinity restrictions, prohibitions on adoption and divorce, legitimacy of

and Sundell 2014) and thus stabilized monarchical rule (Goody 1983; Brund-age 2009; Sharma 2015; Acharya and Lee 2019). The combination of female inheritance and primogeniture resulted in dynastic politics that consolidated and expanded territorial rule (Teschke 2003, 225; Sharma 2015, 169).[26] I therefore include both communes (Van Zanden, Buringh, and Bosker 2012) and primogeniture (Kokkonen and Sundell 2014) in the analyses.

Table 2.1 reports the full regression results.[27] Over the entire time period (1000–1800), papal conflict powerfully correlates with territorial fragmentation. (Model 1. See also figure A.1 in the appendix.) Once we split the sample, three important patterns appear. First, in the medieval period, papal conflict remains consistently and positively associated with fragmentation (models 2–4). This strong positive relationship survives the inclusion of all control variables save primogeniture (model 5). Primogeniture swamps out papal conflict, but it has no independent impact on fragmentation. Instead, primogeniture is itself a consequence of earlier changes in the church's family law regime: papal policy through a different channel.[28] Being part of the Holy Roman Empire does not contribute to fragmentation independently of papal conflict in the Middle Ages. Second, parliaments, urbanization, and communes are all associated with fragmentation, and the signs run in the expected direction: parliaments decrease fragmentation, while urbanization and communes increase it.

Third, in the early modern period, secular conflict becomes more important. The association is *positive*, however, suggesting that war breaks up states rather than consolidating them, contrary to the bellicist literature. Papal conflict is collinear with Protestant status in the early modern era. It is positively associated with fragmentation in model 6, but once we include status as Protestant for a given cell of territory, papal conflict disappears in this and all specifications that include Protestant status as a variable (models 7–10). Parliaments, urbanization, and communes no longer show as statistically significant

---

children, and female inheritance (Moody 1983; Ekelund et al. 1989 and 1996; Sharma 2015; and Henrich 2020). Fewer marriages could take place as a result (and could be dissolved more readily on the basis of consanguinity), and fewer heirs could potentially inherit. Both would benefit the church, which was the natural alternative beneficiary (Goody 1983).

26. Others argue that despite prominent examples, such as the union of Aragon and Castile through the marriage of Ferdinand and Isabella, or the expansion of early modern Austria, the main reasons for contracting such marriages were alliances rather than uniting territory. Territorial acquisition through dynastic unions only emerged after the fifteenth century and is not responsible for medieval territorial fragmentation or consolidation. Even in Habsburg Austria, the rapid accumulation of dynastic possessions in 1477–1536 did not expand the empire. Finally, dynastic gains in the other most likely case, England, were temporary (See Fichtner 1976; Sharp 2001; Bonner 2003; Joseph 2015; and Wilson 2016, 436).

27. Figure 2.7 reports the results for secular and papal conflict from models 3 and 8.

28. Mediation analysis suggests that 33 percent of the impact of papal conflict was mediated by primogeniture. See appendix table A.5.

Table 2.1. Papal conflict is associated with fragmentation, cell grid 100km × 100km (OLS 2FE)

	1000–1800		Medieval				Early modern			
	(1)	(2)	(3)	(4)	(5)	(6)	(7)	(8)	(9)	(10)
papal conflict	**0.285****	**0.146****	**0.175****	**0.137****	-0.110	**0.487*****	0.000	0.000	0.000	0.000
	(0.087)	(0.046)	(0.054)	(0.046)	(0.080)	(0.077)	(.)	(.)	(.)	(.)
secular conflict	0.060	-0.004	-0.045	-0.066	0.043	0.032	**0.290***	**0.288***	**0.328***	**0.560*****
	(0.033)	(0.048)	(0.048)	(0.045)	(0.036)	(0.022)	(0.138)	(0.141)	(0.149)	(0.162)
parliaments	**-0.245****		**-0.153*****	**-0.283*****	**-0.130****			-0.539	-0.637	**-1.277***
	(0.080)		(0.042)	(0.065)	(0.044)			(1.025)	(1.036)	(0.605)
urbanization	0.066		**0.718*****	**0.358****	0.042			0.154	0.192	0.118
	(0.040)		(0.133)	(0.121)	(0.079)			(0.151)	(0.151)	(0.151)
communes	**0.504*****			**0.654*****	**0.303****				-1.241	**-1.596***
	(0.142)			(0.132)	(0.111)				(0.629)	(0.665)
primogeniture	**0.500*****				-0.063					0.418
	(0.088)				(0.078)					(0.303)
HRE	**-0.298****	-0.258	-0.244	**-0.365***	-0.057	**0.412*****	**0.938*****	**1.052*****	**1.055*****	**0.653****
	(0.107)	(0.160)	(0.147)	(0.170)	(0.188)	(0.106)	(0.250)	(0.241)	(0.247)	(0.217)
Protestant							-0.816	-0.879	-0.920	-0.219
							(0.701)	(0.728)	(0.765)	(0.729)
constant	1.594***	2.018***	1.874***	1.913***	1.953***	1.511***	4.488***	4.482***	5.210***	4.522***
	(0.103)	(0.038)	(0.049)	(0.052)	(0.057)	(0.039)	(0.544)	(0.643)	(0.764)	(0.760)
$\partial=0=\beta$ for papal conflict[a]	-2.69	-1.05	-1.34	-1.21	3.89	18.78	.	.	.	.
N	3656	1650	1650	1650	1081	3665	548	548	548	486
adj. R^2	0.816	0.754	0.778	0.795	0.824	0.968	0.971	0.971	0.971	0.980

* $p<0.05$, ** $p<0.01$, *** $p<0.001$

[a] The rule of thumb for the sensitivity tests ($\partial=0=\beta$) developed by Oster (2019) is that if the beta is 1 or above, the likely effect of the observables is as high, or higher, than the unobserved

RIVALRY AND FRAGMENTATION [67]

a relationship as in the medieval era. Fragmentation is also strongly associated with status in the Holy Roman Empire in the early modern period. (Please see appendix tables A.1 through A.4 and figure A.1 for other specifications and robustness tests.)

In short, medieval conflict with the papacy is strongly associated with territorial fragmentation, independent of parliaments, urbanization, and communes. In the early modern period, secular conflict becomes more closely associated with territorial fragmentation, once we control for the Protestant Reformation. Early modern secular conflict *increases* fragmentation, however, rather than consolidating states. Many states either consolidated before the early modern period (England, Spain, Portugal) or long after (Germany, Italy, Poland). Further, devastating early modern wars, such as the Thirty Years' War, were fought mostly on the already fragmented territory of the Holy Roman Empire, and did little to consolidate it.

THE RISE OF COMMUNES

The close association between communes and fragmentation exists also because papal conflict and fragmentation made it possible for towns to escape imperial rule and govern themselves. As Max Weber and Otto Hintze have already noted, towns seized autonomy and control during the conflict between popes and emperors in the late eleventh century and the subsequent imperial power vacuum (Weber 1958; Clark 1986, 662; Ertman 2017, 61; Ringer 2004, 206).

Both popes and kings enabled self-governing cities to arise and flourish in the Middle Ages. To curry local support, popes and emperors granted new charters with substantial privileges to lay officials and new political rights, which "only strengthened the sense of agency that the urban population felt," giving new agency, urgency, and responsibilities to communal self-government (Witt 2012, 206). The church itself diffused norms of local self-governance through bishops and monastic reform (Møller and Doucette 2021), and further afield, through its restrictive family law (Schulz 2022). Bishops often cooperated with the creation of communes, and communal institutions then mirrored religious ones (Coleman 1999, 394–5; Schwartzberg 2014, 51; see especially Møller and Doucette 2021). Of course, bishops and urban self-government could be at odds, erupting in violence and murder, as in the famous case of Laon in 1112.[29] Communes could thus serve as "an instrument of liberation from the captivity of worldly and abusive bishops" (Malegam 2013, 231).

29. The people of Laon murdered Gaudry, their bishop, after he disbanded their commune; rose up against their rulers; and proceeded to riot violently until Thomas de Marle invaded and subjugated the city. The Roman commune also arose in the 1140s to rebel against papal authority, also eventually resorting to violence.

As a result, local self-governance started to take off in the late eleventh century and then grew further in the shadow of imperial-papal conflict (see Jones 1997; Watts 2009, 99; Wickham 2015, 9; Wickham 2016, 148ff; Møller and Doucette 2021, 84). In the twelfth century, self-governing cities affiliated in "communes of communes," such as the Lombard League, which banded against Frederick I Barbarossa and his efforts to reestablish imperial power in Italy in the mid-twelfth century. In Germany, the protracted succession struggles and Frederick II's conflict with the papacy also meant that more and more cities gained their freedoms, including the withdrawal of the royal reeves and the rise of municipal councils (Fried 2015, 243). Cities expanded greatly in the thirteenth and fourteenth centuries, *after* the fragmentation of the eleventh and twelfth centuries.

Communes thus appear to emerge thanks to fragmentation. To test whether communes are associated with papal conflict and the fragmentation it engenders, I use the same data and two-way fixed effects OLS regressions as above, but now the presence of communes (from Van Zander, Buringh, and Bosker 2012) is the dependent variable. I also include the presence of bishoprics in a given cell, to proxy for the influence of bishops. (Please see appendix tables A.6 and A.7 for full regression results, including the impact of urbanization and parliaments, and robustness tests.)

Figure 2.7 shows that medieval conflict with popes is strongly and positively associated with communes. Secular conflict is not, in either the medieval or early modern eras. Fragmentation, measured by the number of state borders in a grid cell, is also strongly and positively associated with the rise of communes, as is the presence of bishops. This is consistent with the argument that the power vacuum associated with papal conflict and territorial fragmentation allowed medieval communes to flourish. In the early modern period, in contrast, these variables no longer predict the rise of communes. Communes were typically founded in the eleventh and twelfth centuries, rather than the early modern period. Moreover, aristocratic oligarchies and dictators replaced local self-governance in the fourteenth century.

These empirical regularities are all consistent with the core argument of this chapter: conflict between the papacy and secular monarchs, and especially the Holy Roman Empire, fragmented territorial authority. This medieval rivalry also allowed other forms of autonomous governance to arise and escape imperial control.

Sovereignty

In their desire to quash the imperial threat, popes relied on concepts as well as conflicts. They articulated the first notions of sovereignty, even if there was no widespread *practice* of sovereignty. The medieval struggles between church and empire led to new concepts of sovereignty as supreme authority over territory (Latham 2012, 29), although these ideas did not yet possess "the secular character of modern sovereignty" (Costa Lopez 2020, 224; see also Ullmann 1977;

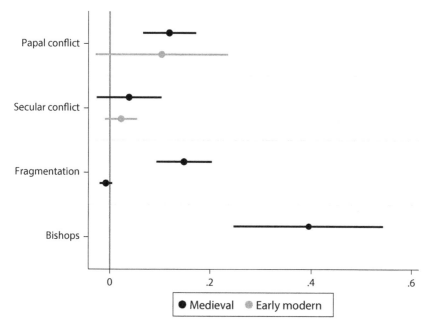

FIGURE 2.8. Papal conflict and fragmentation are associated with the rise of medieval communes, grid cell data (OLS regressions with city and year 2FE). Horizontal lines indicate 95% confidence intervals.

Friedrichs 2001). Conflicts between popes and kings in the fourteenth century would reflect these notions and pave the way for the eventual triumph of lay authority over the religious.

Sovereignty, or a ruler's exclusive right to control his territory and to defend it from external demands,[30] implies "supreme authority within a territory" (Morgenthau 1985) and the mutual recognition of this status by other states (Wendt 1999, 280). This conception of sovereignty is associated with the sixteenth- and seventeenth-century theories of Jean Bodin and Thomas Hobbes, who viewed sovereignty as supreme power over citizens and subjects, unconstrained by rival powers or legal constraints (Skinner 2009, Poggi 1990, 44). The concept is also often, if incorrectly, identified with the 1648 Peace of Westphalia (Philpott 2001, but see Osiander 2001; Teschke 2003; de Carvalho, Leira, and Hobson 2011).[31]

Yet concepts of sovereignty are a medieval innovation. In the conflict between empire and the church, popes and canonists formulated many of the ideas later articulated by Bodin (Costa Lopez et al. 2018, 496). The medieval

30. Sovereignty invokes supremacy as a necessary but not sufficient condition: a sovereign actor brooks no higher power, such as an emperor, pope, or an international organization. For a genealogy of the concept, see Costa Lopez et al. (2018).

31. At Westphalia, "the Holy Roman Empire and its members still eluded this sovereignty principle." For his part, the Pope refused to sign because it codified the equal status of Protestant heretics (Stollberg-Rilinger 2018, 104).

papacy first promoted concepts of sovereignty to stifle imperial claims, asserting that monarchs were not beholden to other secular authorities. These arguments culminated in the doctrine of *rex in regno suo imperator est*: a king is an emperor in his kingdom, or the king does not recognize a superior in temporal matters, articulated by Innocent III in his famous 1202 *Per Venerabilem* decretal.[32] The *rex in regno suo* formula was a dig against imperial ambitions and a rejection of imperial hierarchy, and the canonists' arguments emphasize the equality of secular rulers (Black 1992, 113). These concepts may have been honored more in theory than in the actual, messy (and often bloody) practice, but they represent an early articulation of sovereignty nonetheless.

The doctrine meant the rejection of imperial hierarchy but also, eventually, of papal supremacy (Spruyt 2017, 85). Legal experts soon realized that if rulers did not have to recognize a secular superior, they could also reject *papal* claims. Monarchs eagerly took up this analogy. They had grown weary of the constant papal demands for military and monetary assistance, and worse yet, the papacy's insistence on intervention in royal governance even as it jealously guarded its own privilege: the papacy increasingly grew more "preoccupied with fiscal gain and political advantages, and pretentious in its claims to universal power" (Gottfried 1983, 83). They wanted autonomy from the pope and the *plenitudo potestatis* that allowed him to intervene in governance (Rigaudiere 1995, 23). This, in turn, led to wider acceptance (and practice) of the principle that rulers do not recognize superior powers, including that of the papacy, in England, France, Spain, much of Italy, and even some German territories. Over the thirteenth century, "everywhere, civil and canon lawyers made a case for the rediscovered sovereignty of their own country and made the famous formula . . . victorious from Sicily to England" (Rigaudiere 1995, 21; see also Guenée 1985, 7). Subsequent political thought would emphasize the autonomy and authority of rulers over people and territory (Jedin 1993, 205).

These new understandings of sovereignty had momentuous consequences for the papacy itself, as shown by the episode between Philip IV the Fair of France (r. 1285–1314) and Pope Boniface VIII (r. 1294–1303). The critical issues were royal autonomy from the papacy—and the king's rule over both clerical and lay subjects. The conflict centered around taxation in its first stage (1296–7) and the autonomy of the clergy in its second (1301–2), as we saw in chapter 1. Boniface VIII claimed clergy required papal permission to pay taxes, and that clergy were exempt from lay jurisdiction. He was badly defeated on both points, when Philip first withdrew funding for the papacy and then sent his henchmen to imprison Boniface, who collapsed and died.

---

32. Twelfth-century interpretations of Roman law also recognized the king as the supreme legislator with two other principles: *quod principi placuit legis habet vigorem* (what the king decides has the force of law) and *princeps legibus solutus est* (the king is above the law).

The conflict was a turning point. The papacy moved to Avignon, a territory it did not control. Within a few years, Pope Clement V reaffirmed with his 1311 bull *Rex Gloriae* that the King of France was sovereign in his kingdom—a papal concession that simply recognized the new reality. Kings replaced popes as guardians of the national churches in both England and in France (Harding 2002, 239). Boniface's ignominious defeat constrained subsequent papal intervention in secular affairs and shifted the papacy's attention to internal control. New notions of autonomy and independence subsumed the earlier differentiation of temporal and ecclesiastical authority: "from the early fourteenth century onwards, a widening circle of the governing and educated elites expressed a consciousness of secular power as separate in origin, purpose, scope, and legitimacy from the church" (Black 1992, 188). Not surprisingly, Boniface's papacy has been judged as "particularly disastrous," ruining church supremacy within one hundred years of papal triumphs (Rabb 2006, 23).

Missa Finita Est? *The Great Schism and the State Triumphant*

Ironically, these outcomes of rivalry—differentiation, fragmentation, and concepts of sovereignty—made the church more vulnerable to secular rulers. Wars by proxy and political crusades undercut the church's spiritual authority, and the papacy demanded ever more resources. Fragmentation meant no one power could protect the church, and concepts of sovereignty fueled a new skepticism of papal claims. The faithful grew weary, and the rulers wary, of the political activities of the papacy and its continual involvement in European politics.

After Boniface's defeat, Philip IV relocated the papacy to Avignon, where it remained until 1376. Seven decades of relative calm followed, to be broken by Gregory IX's return to Rome in 1376 and the contested succession of Urban VI. The result was the Great Schism, which divided the church from 1378 to 1417 among two (and sometimes three) rival popes, each sponsored by his own ecclesiastical factions and royal supporters (see chapter 1). It was not the first split within the church: competing popes and internal factions had emerged earlier in the church, especially during the eleventh century.[33] But it was the longest division, and the most consequential.

The schism itself was a politically motivated rupture, sustained by rulers backing rival papal factions. It was not motivated by theological disputes or

---

33. There were several papal schisms earlier, notably from 1061 to 1177–80. The clergy itself was initially very skeptical of the Gregorian reform program, especially the bishops. It was not until 1100 that the church coalesced around reform. The Holy Roman Empire also saw two rival kings five times between the eleventh and thirteenth centuries (Fried 2015, 399). These earlier schisms brought the French and English churches more closely under the leadership of the king.

competing doctrinal interpretations. Earlier, popes such as Innocent III and Boniface VIII could put forth a full theory of papal world government and universal papal monarchy and authority (Tierney 1964, 152–3). Now, rival claimants would depend on the French king and the German emperor to settle their dispute. Rulers were fully aware of the political benefits: as Lorenzo de Medici noted in 1477, "the division of power is advantageous, and, if it were possible without scandal, three or four Popes would be better than a single one" (Hay 1995, 304).

The fragmentation of Europe meant that there was no one powerful actor who could resolve the impasse. Nor was the church itself able to heal the rift: at Pisa in 1409, prelates from both camps convened a council that deposed both popes, but one refused to step down. The result was the simultaneous claim to the papacy of *three* claimants: Alexander V, Gregory XII, and Benedict XIII. Secular rulers eventually became involved. With their consensus, the Councils of Constance (1414–8) and Basel (1431–9) eventually reconciled the church. The protracted length of the councils reflected the complexity of the rift—and bought more time for secular monarchs to extract concessions from the papacy.

The Great Schism and its resolution further empowered secular rulers (Kaminsky 2000, 680). Kings negotiated with popes and councils, sent representatives, and concluded treaties. They also gained more control over the hierarchy and property of the church in their realms (Watts 2009, 411). The English Parliament restricted appeals or payments to Rome and required approval before a papal document could be published. The clergy became a "separate and distinct order or estate," and the church's role was much diminished (Hay 1995, 62). In France, the Pragmatic Sanction of Bourges of 1438 asserted "gallican liberties" for French clergy and deprived the popes of their power to appoint, judge, and tax clergy in France. In Hungary, Sigismund announced the *placetum regium* in 1404, which asserted "the king's supreme right of patronage in the Hungarian church and prohibit[ed] appeals to Rome" (Hay 1995, 243). Even staunch Catholic monarchs such as Ferdinand and Isabella in Spain asserted their prerogatives, brooking no appeals to Rome for Inquisition cases, and allowing the publication of papal bulls only with royal consent (Ergang 1971, 141).[34]

The papacy had lost its standing vis-à-vis kings and princes and had to negotiate individual, bilateral agreements with them, which meant "the parceling out of the pope's sovereign authority over the universal church" (Oakley 2015, 137). Such individual agreements had been signed in the early twelfth century to help resolve the Investiture Conflict, but they now became widespread. Pope Martin V (r. 1417–31) and then Eugenius IV (r. 1431–47) had to obtain separate concordats with the crowns of Germany, England, France, Castile, Aragon,

---

34. By the end of the fifteenth century, Pope Innocent VIII, desperate for Spanish military aid, conceded patronage to all major appointments in the Spanish (and subsequently, colonial) church (Ozment 1980, 189).

and others, before these monarchs would recognize them. These concordats diminished papal authority over the churches in these lands.

The schism weakened the pope's reach within the church. Cardinals and bishops now had the upper hand, both at Rome and in the national churches across Europe (Obertyński and Kumor 1974, 305). The Council of Constance (1414–8) affirmed conciliarism, or the primacy of councils over popes, even if at the Council of Basel (1431–49), the papacy defeated it (see chapter 5). The bilateral concordats and the rise of national churches meant that even as the pope continued as the spiritual leader of the church, "his effective reach into the management of the Church would be limited" in individual countries (Whalen 2019, 176).

As a result of the schism, the church was impoverished, and its attempts to regain revenue streams further decreased its moral authority. Papal revenues were only one-third of pre-schism amounts. Papal rights to taxes and office nominations were limited. Popes could no longer count on secular subsidies: in some cases, such as France and Castile, kings began to wield powers previously exercised by popes, with Charles VII going as far as imposing a three-tenths tax on the French church during the Council of Basel itself (Watts 2009, 296). To pay its ever-increasing bills, the church turned to selling offices and benefices.[35] Centuries earlier, simony was the target of Gregorian reforms: now it became an overt papal practice. The sale of offices proved so profitable that popes formalized the practice, and secular rulers in the fifteenth century adopted it (see chapter 3). This avarice, even if necessary, cost the church moral authority. What followed was a lurching spiral of newly empowered states contributing fewer funds and, in turn, a more grasping church with lower revenues and less moral authority to ask for more.

The papacy would reassert its *spiritual* role, "unquestionably strengthened in the later 15th century . . . as a spiritual authority over the European laity" (Watts 2009, 357). The pope also reconsolidated his authority within the Papal States.[36] Cardinal-legates took charge of the provinces, and papal governors were installed in cities and towns, reducing municipal self-governance. By 1600, the Papal States were as consolidated, if not more so, than other European states (Bireley 1999, 72). The discovery of alum at Tolfa, the taxation of the cities, and the sale of offices, meant that by the 1480s, papal finances recovered, but with two-thirds of the money now coming from central Italy (Watts 2009, 356).

Yet the schism marked "the end of the medieval papacy" and its claims of unquestioned moral and political authority (Kaminsky 2000, 696; Greengrass

---

35. The church administration became too lucrative for reform to be feasible, with something like 2,000 marketable posts with capital values of 2.5 million gold florins and interest of 300,000 (Jedin 1993, 305).

36. The two critical moments were the reconquest of Bologna in 1506 by Julius II and recovery of Ferrara by Clement VIII in 1598 (Bireley 1999, 72).

2014, xxvii). The Great Schism showed popes to be petty politicians vying for power, rather than men of God. The intense secular partisanship and competing factions belied the notion of a true and universal church.

The papacy no longer claimed universal power or the dominance of the spiritual over the temporal. Most church hierarchies were now organized along regnal lines, subject to the temporal legal order, and heavily influenced by the prevailing politics of a given land. Secular rulers forced papal nominees to withdraw, insisted on nominating their own bishops, and generally ignored the pleas and requests of the papacy. The church's considerable achievements—the differentiation of secular and religious authority, the fragmentation of Europe, and new notions of sovereignty—backfired.

Conclusion

The medieval rivalry between rulers and popes led to the differentiation of ecclesiastical and temporal authority, the survival of smaller states in a fragmented Europe, and the concept (if not the practice) of sovereignty. This was not simply a linear and inexorable progression towards a full separation of church and state or the modern state system, but a series of protracted negotiations, alliances, persuasions, and setbacks.

Contrary to dominant accounts, which claim that early modern secular wars winnowed out large, consolidated states, medieval religious conflict enabled smaller states to survive and self-governing communes to arise. If anything, early modern warfare exacerbated fragmentation, rather than consolidating states. As a result, the Holy Roman Empire and Italy remained fragmented for centuries, even as rulers in Spain, England, France, and Scandinavia consolidated their territorial authority.

The irony is that by liberating itself, working to fragment its rivals, and asserting the sovereignty of rulers, the church made itself vulnerable. Rulers grew to resent papal demands, and when the opportunity of the Great Schism presented itself, the crown subordinated the episcopal mitre. By the fifteenth century, the state was ascendant—yet its supremacy would not be possible without the clashing ambitions of medieval popes and rulers, and the political differentiation, territorial fragmentation, and concepts of sovereignty they conceived.

CHAPTER THREE

Governing Institutions

EMULATION IS THE SECOND MECHANISM by which the medieval church influenced state formation, as royal courts adapted church templates for ruling institutions. The bustling judiciary, efficient chancery, and fiscal innovations of the papal court meant that as late as "the 14th century [the church administration] remained a unique object lesson in bureaucracy" (Hay 1995, 288). These governing institutions of the church, and how they shaped royal courts, are the focus of this chapter.

Royal administrations were rudimentary well into the eleventh century. Merovingian (sixth to eighth century CE) and Carolingian (ninth to tenth century CE) rulers of what is now France and Germany relied on revenues from the *fisc:* lands that had been the private preserves of Roman emperors. Taxation was ineffective: Charlemagne declared a tithe for the church in 779, but collected as little as one-thirtieth (Stasavage 2020, 110). Provincial governors and the *missi,* or pairs of emissaries (one temporal, one ecclesiastic), served as regional administrators, but they were too few (and often too hereditary) to serve the emperor's administrative interests effectively. Central state administrations were equally inchoate. Ecclesiastical archives housed property titles and other records, and priests kept track of births, marriages, dowries, wills and burials (Bossy 1985, 66). Private royal households and public administration were indistinguishable, run by the same small coterie of servants. Even the names of the most important tenth- and eleventh-century royal officials suggest the lack of differentiation: cup-bearers, butlers, stewards, and chamberlains. Together, they had no corporate identity as a court or government and did not distinguish between their roles as household members and government officials, traveling with the king when he did.

Yet by the thirteenth century, we see division of labor at royal courts, with different offices for the administration of justice, the adjudication of petitions and sending of writs, and revenue collection and auditing. A bureaucracy of sorts emerges, with skilled royal officials (Eire 2016, 14). Offices are increasingly distinct from the officeholders, specialized, and hierarchical (Bagge 2019, 77). Literacy and record-keeping spread, new schools of higher education emerged, both canon and civil law were systematized, tax collection began in earnest, and the very notion of office, as separate from the person, developed after the ecclesiastical reforms of the eleventh century (Fried 2015, 219).[1] These new technologies "increased the oppressiveness of lordship and strengthened the ambitions of government" (Watts 2009, 73).

What had changed, and why? An earlier literature argued that governing institutions arose as functional solutions to the exigencies of warfare (Tilly 1992), the need for more revenue (Schumpeter [1918] 1991), or as the result of the balance of power between kings and nobles (Hintze [1905] 1975; Levi 1988; North and Weingast 1989; Ertman 1997). Yet many of these institutions rose *before* costly warfare emerged in the sixteenth-century Military Revolution, and before institutionalized bargaining took place in the early modern era. Nor can these accounts explain why particular *forms* of institutions were taken up: why, for example, would petitions become a way to appeal judicial decisions?

This chapter shows that many of the new technologies of governance emerged from the institutional and administrative innovations of the church. The papacy reformed its court in the eleventh century and developed a separate clerical state under papal control (Watts 2009, 52). The Gregorian reformers "came to see that they could only effect their programme by constructing effective, centralized institutions" (Kaeuper 1988, 270–1). Papal chanceries answered petitions and letters, recorded contracts, and sent out instructions and letters. The Camera (financial office) raised revenues, collected taxes, and carefully recorded first gifts and then obligations to the church. The Rota was the papal judiciary, a court for both secular and clerical appeals, and the Penitentiary its counterpart for matters of conscience. These innovations served as precedents for kings and emperors eager to rule more effectively: a similar division of labor (and often the same titles for officials and agencies) spread across Europe in the thirteenth and fourteenth centuries.

These advances flowed from the papal curia at Rome to royal courts largely through the clergy. Rulers needed specialists and experts, who had the literacy, legal training, and experience in formal writing, the *ars dictandi*. They turned to clergy, who served at court administrations to such an extent that "clerk" came to mean both an ecclesiastic and a literate official. Papal legates brought with them papal innovations, instructions, and advice. Canon lawyers gained expertise at Bologna and other universities and then traveled home armed

---

1. In the twelfth century, "crown" was already sometimes used as an abstract for prerogatives of the king, and the use of "our state and our kingdom" followed by the early thirteenth century (Harding 2002, 140).

with the latest legal innovations. Bishops serving at royal courts as judges and councilors also traveled to Rome,[2] exchanged letters and ideas, and came together in church councils.

This was not simply a wholesale transfer of religious administrative formulas and solutions, as an earlier literature sometimes suggested (Hintze [1905] 1975; Strayer [1970] 1998). Not all institutional models were adopted: common law prevailed in English royal courts, rather than the civil law dominant elsewhere. Prohibitions against usury were widely skirted, and the sanctioning of chastity was equally ignored.[3] Nor were these particular solutions inevitable: outside of the church's sphere of influence, as in Byzantium or China, other divisions of labor prevailed.[4] Instead, the process was more of an institutional isomorphism, an imperfect mimicry and borrowing driven by uncertainty, networks of similarly trained personnel, and concerns with legitimation (DiMaggio and Powell 1983).[5] Monarchs and princes made use of the church's extensive human capital, even as they sought to develop their own literate bureaucrats, legal experts, and savvy ambassadors.

Moreover, "state institutions" did not mean what they do today (see Johnson and Koyama 2017). Medieval rulers defended their (rather fuzzy) borders, raised some revenue, and adjudicated disputes. They did not supply clean water, deliver education or health care, relieve poverty, or build regulatory

2. Bishops could only assume office after receiving a pallium (ceremonial stole) from the pope, and by the twelfth century, they traveled to Rome to collect it in person and then to pay regular visits (Blumenthal 2004, 11).

3. The church not only formally accepted commercial transactions under Urban II, but also limited the definition of usury to pawnbrokers and moneylenders who "manifestly exploited the unfortunate" (Morris 1989, 334–5). Limitations on usury thus had little practical import, as the twelfth-century commercial revolution would suggest. See also Dorin (2015).

4. For example, imperial China had a highly developed bureaucracy, with the first written civil service exams in 595 (see Wang 2021). Since the Han dynasty (25–220 CE), it divided administrative labor very differently, however: by stage in the policy process rather than by domain. The Chancellery formulated *all* policies, whether on regional policy, finances, religious rites or military affairs; the Secretary (a vice-chancellor) advised and disciplined; and the Department of State, the most powerful organ, executed the policies (Wang 2022). Moral principles, rather than policy expertise, tended to shape decision making. Nine ranking ministers were in charge of Ceremonies, the Attendants, the Guards, Justice, Agriculture, the Small Treasury, as well as the Grand Herald, the Grand Servant and the Director of the Imperial Clan (Wang 1949, 150–1). A general trend in Chinese history was that the three ministries were weakened over time, and the emperor gained direct control. In the mid-Tang period (around 723 CE), the Chancellery and Secretariate were merged, and by 1380 the Ming dynasty (1368–1644) abolished the offices as the emperor centralized power (Wang 2022).

5. In their explanation of seventeenth- and eighteenth-century state development, Gorski and Sharma also note that actors do not choose "from an infinite set of potential solutions" but instead borrow from readily available institutional domains, in this case, the church (Gorski and Sharma 2017, 122).

agencies. Rather than cohesive states and bureaucracies, medieval rule consisted of rulers and a host of offices, staffed by clerks, bishops, and laymen. Medieval governance was characterized by weak capacity, lack of specificity, and contested sovereignty. Royal administrations were far smaller, less centralized, and less bureaucratic than modern states (Reynolds 1997, 117). Neither the church nor the monarchs were as powerful as modern states are today, and they could not control society or regulate economic relations as effectively. Kings struggled to control recalcitrant nobles and clergy, and to collect revenue. Medieval or early modern European taxation, for example, was never as lucrative or as efficient as its Roman, Byzantine, or Ottoman counterparts (Wickham 2015, 11; see also Stasavage 2020, 12).

Popes, too, were limited in their ability to broadcast power. The papacy in the eyes of some observers established a "near complete dominion" over the church by the early thirteenth century (Watts 2009, 52). Even so, "Rome did not possess the machinery to direct in detail the affairs of the western churches, nor the revenue to finance its enterprises, which often had to depend on self-interested allies and out-of-date information" (Morris 1989, 451). And although "churches took the lead in literate and record-keeping administration . . . the authority of the pope over the whole Church was not statelike. It depended on moral authority and influence, not on coercive control" (Reynolds 1997a, 119). Both kings and popes cajoled, convinced, and threatened rather than demanded or extracted by force.

Despite these limitations, the church vitally influenced both the *timing* and the *form* of secular administrations. First, *rivalry* with the church influenced *when* centralized state institutions arose. Where the church fragmented political authority and sustained its fracturing, as in the Holy Roman Empire, a centralized state administration struggled to arise—in the case of the empire, the first real push to centralize the administration only took place at the end of the fifteenth century. By the end of the Middle Ages, the cities and the territorial principalities of the empire had developed jurisdictional capacity and a bureaucracy—the kingdom itself did not (Reynolds 1997a, 128). In contrast, where the rulers' support was necessary for papal aims, monarchs had more autonomy to develop central state institutions. Secular rivalry with the papacy also spurred administrative growth. The competition between royal and ecclesiastical courts, for example, led kings to limit secular appeals to papal and ecclesiastical courts, in effect subsidizing the growth of royal justice.

Second, secular *emulation* of the church shaped the *form* of the offices. The papal administration "became the model for the beginnings of state bureaucracies" (Mitterauer 2010, 150). Papal templates allowed royal courts to transform from informal and ramshackle households into more formal and specialized state administrations. The centralization and specialization of the papal administration that began in the mid-eleventh century became a pattern for the division of labor and the agencies of royal administrations.

The Papal Chancery governed by answering petitions and issuing rulings, and royal courts followed suit. The church developed new techniques of taxation. Church officials were expected to act on behalf of the organization, rather than themselves, and superiors expected obedience from their inferiors. Limits to this specialization also followed church precedent: given the demand for justice and the flood of petitions, several offices took on judicial roles.

Below, I examine papal administrative reforms and their transmission to royal courts. Thanks to these models, royal courts developed, differentiated, and specialized—and eventually subordinated the very church from which they had earlier adopted these institutional innovations.

Patterns of Papal Innovations and Secular State Institutions

Church administrative reforms were the forerunners of secular state institutions. As Jørgen Møller has noted, "there is a broad consensus in the literature that a series of elements of the modern state were invented by the Catholic Church and then imported by secular rulers as they attempted to augment their own administration" (Møller 2018, 302; see also Ullmann [1955] 1965; Tierney 1982; Berman 1983; Genet 1992, 126). Many administrative prototypes are found in the church, centuries before secular courts adopted them. Some of these, like the *capella* (chapel), were part of Frankish court practice, then refined, formalized, and made into a distinct chancery by the papal administration (Jedin 1993, 19). The Ottonian dynasty (919–1024) explicitly integrated the church into the imperial administrative system, and the church subsequently refined these administrative models to gain capacity and assert itself against secular rulers.

The church initiated techniques of recordkeeping and accounting, with the chancery and the treasury as distinct offices in charge of correspondence, executive orders, and petitions, and fiscal accounts, respectively. The church's near-obsession with archives, written records, and legal exegeses was both an advantage in conflicts with secular rulers and a template worthy of emulation: "the unparalleled advantage which the papacy had over any other institution was its own storehouse of ideological memory, the papal archives" (Ullmann [1955] 1965, 262). Taxes, as rudimentary and ineffectually collected as they were (papal petitions are full of lamentations and grievances from both the collectors and the donors), were instituted by 1100. The original papal court of justice, the Rota, began to receive, adjudicate, and send back petitions from across Christendom.

Figure 3.1 summarizes the pattern of institutional development across several European political entities. The bands summarize when several major state institutions first arose: chanceries, cameras, taxation, legal courts, national assemblies, and the census. Figure 3.2 disaggregates these patterns into

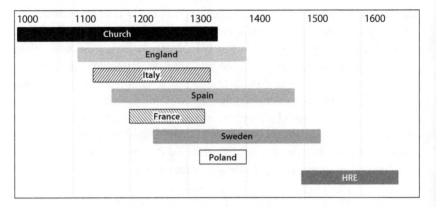

FIGURE 3.1. Summary of the emergence of early state institutions.

individual institutions. Needless to say, these were not Weberian bureaucracies, with impersonal rules and strict division of labor, but far more rudimentary offices.

Three patterns appear: first, the church was an institutional pioneer, developing many institutions before kings and emperors did. After the late eleventh- to early twelfth-century administrative centralization of the papacy, the tripartite division of royal courts into councils, exchequers, and judicial tribunals diffused across Europe, in a strikingly similar process of differentiation (Hintze [1905] 1975, 220). In England and then in France, a chancery, parliament, and a system of royal justice were functioning by the thirteenth century, one hundred years after the popes had established theirs. In general, the development of specific institutions in France lagged behind England by roughly a century. In Spain, some of these institutions functioned regionally, such as the famous parliament of Léon in 1188, or the Castilian chancery, which began in 1168. In Scandinavia and East Central Europe, where Christianity arrived relatively late—in the tenth to twelfth centuries—these institutions took off in the mid-thirteenth to mid-fourteenth centuries. Here, the church introduced the idea of kingship as office and directly led kings to found institutions (Gieysztor 1979, 128–9; Bagge 2014, 57, 78). That said, powerful lords and barons in these lands resisted and delayed the centralization of government (Watts 2009, 128).

Second, central state institutions barely took root in the inhospitable soil of the Holy Roman Empire. While other rulers increasingly concentrated on strengthening their administrations, the Holy Roman Emperor was distracted by both conflict with the papacy and the increasingly powerful princes (both temporal and ecclesiastical), who repeatedly seized both political authority and territorial control. Partly as a result, Italian institutions arose relatively early on, but only on the level of communes. Within the empire, no central taxation, parliament, courts, or chancery emerged until 1500, and many remained weak

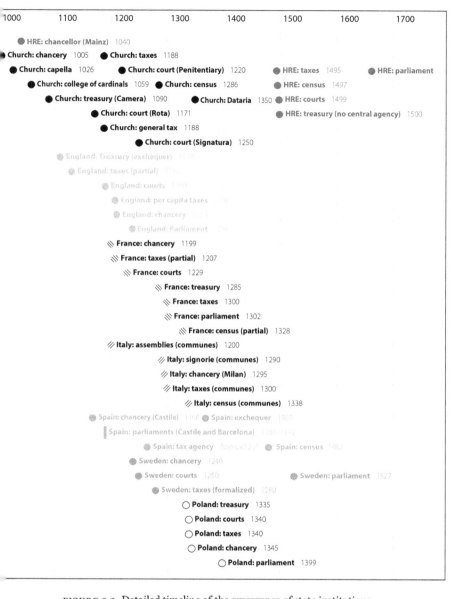

FIGURE 3.2. Detailed timeline of the emergence of state institutions.

and brittle. The Archbishop of Mainz served as the nominal chancellor for Germany since 1040, but no central chancery arose until the early modern period. The emperor himself was itinerant, with no established capital from which to rule, until the 1350s.

Third, where the pope needed rulers as allies, monarchs were free to centralize and consolidate their rule and administrations. For example, successive popes relied on English kings to stay out of European politics and not aid papal enemies. The papacy largely stayed out of English domestic politics (Cantor 1958, 146). The English administration could thus centralize spectacularly in the second half of the twelfth century, partly because "England's church rarely led the magnate opposition successfully, a reason being Rome's need for English friendship while battling the Empire" (Mundy 2000, 233). English kings had freer rein to consolidate power and to develop unique institutional solutions such as the Exchequer and the royal system of courts. Elsewhere, however, the church provided prototypes, precedents, and solutions.

Papal Administrative Reforms

What were these papal innovations, and how did they influence medieval governance? Below, I examine the administrative advances of the papacy, their transmission by bishops, and how they shaped three pillars of royal administration: chanceries, taxes, and the judiciary.

THE GREGORIAN REFORMS AND CENTRALIZATION

With the reforms of the 1050s, the papacy began to transform church institutions. Pope Leo IX (r. 1049–54) laid the foundations for reform, expanding the papal administrative machinery, formalizing governance through legates and councils, and choosing capable clerical officials to run the administration (Southern 1970, 100). Gregory VII (r. 1073–85) pioneered the notion (though not yet the full practice) of a centralized hierarchy at whose top sat an unquestioned ruler. Administrative reforms took off under his successors, who reorganized and centralized the papal curia. The church developed new technologies of governance, such as legates, missives, and charters; new methods of record keeping, contract enforcement, and adjudication of disputes; and novel extraction techniques. The papal court was among the first formalized central administrations to arise in Europe.

The reformers had their work cut out for them. Until the eleventh century, the pope was more or less a provincial official, and the papal court was a regional office, more of a household than a governing institution (Brooke 1978, 7; Morris 1989, 33). Notaries and scribes still used papyrus, and their "distinctive script, littera Romana, could not even be read north of the Alps" (Morris 1989, 165). Seven *iudices de clerii* (judges) served as the chief officials, responsible for finance, almsgiving, and the secretariat. A *vestararius* ran the papal treasury, and a *vicedominus* supervised the Lateran palace (Blumenthal 1988, 72).[6]

6. Other papal offices included *arcarius* (treasurer), *saccellarius* (paymaster), *nomenculator* (poverty relief), *protoscrinarius* (archivist), *bibiliothecarius* (chancery), *schola notarium* (correspondence) and *schola defensorum* (legal matters) (Jedin 1993, 19) Domestic officials rounded out the pope's household.

By 1005, a chancery existed, and by 1026, a pool of clerks toiled in the capella (Ullmann [1955] 1965, 330; Blumenthal 1988, 78).

Gregory's successor, Urban II (r. 1088–1099), transformed the papal court. Urban ignored both tradition and the old bureaucracy as he created new institutions.[7] He revived and expanded the Chancery, assumed new judicial responsibilities, and brought in a slew of new officials with distinct roles.[8] A former prior at Cluny, he applied the model of the monastic institution of the camera to the papal court (Blumenthal 2004, 21; see also Doucette and Møller 2021 on the influence of Cluny). By 1087, the church had documentary proofs of possessions of the church and its claims against the empire, revised in 1187 and 1192 compilations (Bisson 2009, 417).

The Curia Romana[9] emerged as the central set of offices, "an agency with the authority of central leadership furnished with armies of professional notaries and other functionaries" (Fried 2015, 146). Over the period from 1090 to 1130, it began to assume its characteristic specialized appearance (Schwarz 2016, 171). The Camera, along with the Chancery and the Judiciary (the Sacra Romana Rota), formed the three key institutions. These were the linchpins of papal governance and influence: "the Chancery developed not just as a key institution within the Vatican, but also provided an example to numerous princely and royal courts on how to draft and archive official documents," while the reinvigorated Camera ensured that "all sources of papal revenue were scrupulously recorded once more" (Fried 2015, 216). The Curia "was infinitely better organized and had more ramifications than its royal counterparts" (Ullmann [1955] 1965, 319).

These administrative reforms and institutional developments gave the church a considerable, if relative, advantage over the monarchs and emperors of Europe. From the eleventh to the fourteenth century, the church was the largest and most organized public institution in Europe, endowed with the wealthiest intellectual resources and most efficient legal system (Deanesly 1969, 121–130). The papal administration hardly met the modern ideal of impartial and salaried officials, as the sale of offices and the practice of paying the clergy at court with benefices shows—but in relative terms, it was a bureaucratic powerhouse (D'Avray 2010, 136.)

By 1200, the Curia was doing a roaring business in judicial appeals and petitions, and grew further in response to demand for its judgments and decisions. The burgeoning of papal government in the twelfth and thirteenth centuries

---

7. Gregory's chief papal administrators deserted him in 1084 for the antipope Clement III and his imperial patron, Henry IV. These bishops revolted against Gregory's repeated insistence that he would decide all ecclesiastical appointments and matters (Ullmann [1955] 1965, 349). Their departure left enormous discretion to Urban II.

8. Gregory VII and Pascal II also belonged to Cluny. The templates for Urban's reforms remain unclear, but under his papacy the Roman Curia began to assume its characteristic format (Robinson 1990, 17).

9. The term "Curia Romana" itself was first used to denote papal government and household in Urban's letters.

was in part a response to the demands of "clergy and laity across Europe who wanted the papacy to legitimate their own claims to power" (Wiedemann 2018, 503), and the relative ease and convenience of sending appeals to the papacy (Watts 2009, 52). By the end of the thirteenth century, the Curia had grown to more than 1,000 administrative staff and had the most elaborate administrative apparatus in Europe (Watts 2009, 240).

The thirteenth century marked a "golden age" for the institutional papacy. Pope Innocent III (r. 1198–1216) became known as the creator of the papal state, taking Urban II's innovations to a new level of administrative efficiency (Morris 1989, 421). Records of conciliar and other decrees were systematized, synods were held regularly, and legates ensured that papal power would reach the periphery. The papacy could turn to a well-organized college of cardinals and central administration; clear procedures for legal appeals to the Curia; a developed canon law; and other institutions that could be pressed into papal service, such as the international religious orders, crusades, and universities. This thirteenth-century drive to order and efficiency produced "a vastly improved machinery of bureaucratic control" (Morris 1989, 415). A newly powerful "papal lordship reached into distant localities through judges-delegate imposing and enforcing rules of Christian conduct of unprecedented scope" (Bisson 2009, 291). The church shifted from its earlier aim of converting Europe and suffusing Christianity, to a goal that "was less religious than hierarchical; it implied the domination of Church over State, and of clergy over laity, the demonstration of the civil power's derivation from ecclesiastical" (Smith 1964, 54).

The structure endured when the papacy moved to Avignon. Indeed, Urban V (r. 1362–70) further centralized the Curia and gave it additional powers in 1363, such as the filling of all patriarchal and episcopal sees and of all monasteries at a specified income level (Jedin 1993, 193). The fourteenth-century papacy produced enormous quantities of documents, conveyed by petitioners and networks of banking firms, with Clement VI (r. 1342–52) topping out at 90,000 papal documents and Gregory XI (r. 1370–8) at 35,000 (Jedin 1993, 195). Until the mid-fourteenth century, the church enjoyed an increasingly specialized and efficient administration that gave the papacy an administrative advantage over the increasingly ambitious and truculent monarchs with whom it had to contend.

CARDINALS, LEGATES, AND BISHOPS AS OFFICIALS AND CONDUITS

To govern the church and fill these offices, popes relied on cardinals, legates, and bishops. They had wide-ranging responsibilities and powers, and they advised kings and popes alike, transmitting ideas and innovations.

The first step in the Gregorian reforms, then, was to replace the cardinals. After the cardinals gained the monopoly on papal elections in 1059, the College of Cardinals transformed from a group of Roman aristocrats to an institution of the universal church (Robinson 1990, 40).[10] The papacy recruited cardinals outside of Rome and added other officials while reducing the original offices, such as *iudices*, to ceremonial functions (Morris 1989, 168). Under Urban II, the role of these important advisors and officials further shifted from liturgical to increasingly administrative, including attesting bulls, serving as legates, and advising the Pope (Morris 1989, 168). The *Consistorium* (consistory, or council) began under Victor III (r. 1086–7), who was in poor health and relied on the cardinals to guide the church. It served as an advisory council, settling disputed episcopal elections and jurisdictional disputes, but also guiding the pope on specific policy points: for example, Henry IV was excommunicated on the advice of cardinals (Robinson 1990, 100). By the mid-twelfth century (and as a result of a schism in 1130), cardinals participated extensively in papal government, with the pope consulting with the college extensively and relying on the cardinals for strategic advice (Robinson 2004a, 425).

Legates served as papal deputies across Christendom, ensuring uniformity and correctness of the reform implementation. Their charge was to carry out the reforms in distant territories, bind the broader church more closely, and enforce papal claims and decrees (Blumenthal 2004, 25; see also Rennie 2007, 167). These emissaries were direct deputies of the pope, accountable only to the pope, a responsibility enforced by Gregory VII with "characteristic rigour" (Robinson 1990, 151).[11] Traveling across Christendom accompanied by extensive retinues, legates presided over provincial synods, judged bishops, prepared crusades, recognized royal elections, and negotiated peace (Mitterauer 2010, 150). Legates also assumed judicial roles, commissioned to adjudicate specific cases on site and make binding decisions. They issued absolutions and dispensations and systematically recorded these decisions, reporting to the papacy on a regular basis (Müller 2016, 207). Under Gregory, "the effectiveness and strength of the legatine office reached a high point" (Rennie 2007, 179), as these trusted and knowledgeable officials carried out the reform program. Subsequent popes continued to send legates, some permanently, throughout Christendom to represent their policies, serve as judges and emissaries, and ensure the pope's reach into the bishoprics.[12] Notable examples include Guala

10. There were fifty-three formal places in the College of Cardinals, but the usual number was forty or fewer (Robinson 1990, 43). In the Avignon period, there were no more than twenty cardinals total (Hay 1995, 299).

11. *Dictatus Papae* explicitly took up legates and emphasized that they superseded all other bishops at synods (Müller 2016, 203).

12. The legates became especially important between the schisms of 1130–8 and 1159–78, with over 109 legations, undertaken by fifty-one cardinals, or one-third of the total membership of the college of cardinals (Robinson 2004a, 418). By the thirteenth century, their duties were more specific, and their discretion limited, in keeping with the prevalent formalization and specialization (Rennie 2007, 180). The *Audientia literarum*

and Pandulf, papal legates involved in English royal politics in 1216–21, who even lent material support to the regime.

Bishops were an essential part of church administration. Gregorian reforms made them into more reliable agents of the pope: popes alone could issue dispensations and exemptions, establish new dioceses, and approve bishops. Bishops were also were a vital path through which church innovations would travel to royal courts and administration. Not only were they in frequent contact with the papal court in Rome, but they were educated, spoke the same Latin, learned the same canon law, and imbibed the same spirit of hierarchy and fiduciary duty (along with a healthy dose of spoils of office). From the kings' point of view, "bishops and prelates were desirable officers as they had administrative skills and legal learning, as well as the advantage that their offices were not hereditary" (Bagge 2014, 85). They could also be paid in church benefices, making them extraordinarily cost-effective.

At both papal and royal courts, these clergy managed three distinct government roles and institutions: the Chancery, the administrative center; the Camera, the treasury; and the Judiciary, the administration of justice.

The Chancery

Chanceries were the nerve centers of governance for both popes and secular rulers. They responded to petitions and issued letters of justice, so that the chancery and the judiciary coevolved (Strayer [1970] 1998, 39; Zutshi 2000, 663). The huge rise in petitions expanded the offices and the capacity of the papal and secular administrations (Southern 1970, 106; Jedin 1993, 154).[13] Chanceries made it possible to deliver justice and govern through appeals and decrees, as well as to broadcast power through decrees and letters, and to keep track of the letters and documents flowing in and out of the curia.

The Papal Chancery processed requests and appeals to the pope and issued the responses. Urban II introduced a reinvigorated secretariat responsible for papal correspondence, the *Cancellaria* (Robinson 1990, 93). The chancellor was a chief advisor to the pope. The office existed earlier,[14] but the position

---

contradictarum was the chancery office responsible for appointing the judges-delegate. It decayed in the fifteenth century, with the rise of the new offices of *Signatura Gratiae* and *Signatura Iustitae*. Pius X abolished both and created a new Signatura that had little to do with the former two offices. It now functioned as an appeals court and auditing body for Rota decisions.

13. See Zutshi (2007) for scholarly debates over the role of petitions in the development of the papal government.

14. An informal chancery existed as early as the seventh century. In 1044, Peter, deacon of the Roman church, combined the offices of librarian and chancellor and assumed a key role in the papal secretariat that he fulfilled until 1050 (Cowdrey 2004, 261). The chancery registers were revived around 1070 (Blumenthal 2004, 18).

had waxed and waned in importance and was sometimes left vacant (Norr 1982, 329; Blumenthal 2004, 18). The office of papal chancellor was already filled by important advisors in the 1050s, but reformist innovations had not yet led to its overhaul (Morris 1989, 166). In 1082–4, the office was thoroughly reorganized, as part of a reform of the papal household (Schwarz 2016, 177). Under Urban II, the chancellor gained in strength, and his office had undergone a renewal, maintaining official registers and newly responsible for papal documents.

The Papal Chancery became ever more efficient and powerful over the course of the late eleventh to early twelfth century. It replaced Roman scribes with non-Roman ones, in keeping with the more universal outlook of the papacy, adopted the Carolingian miniscule that was legible outside of Rome, and gained autonomy from the city of Rome, whose documentary procedures it had earlier had to follow (Norr 1982, 329). The chancellor was the head of his own department and, along with several notaries, formed the personal secretariat of the pope, writing, dispatching, and recording important letters. He was a powerful figure, with constant access to the pope and a life-time appointment to office (Robinson 2004a, 423). The chancery itself "employed a small army of abbreviators, glossators, correctors, computators, and bullators to prepare, certify, and send out apostolic letters" (Hsia 2005, 104). It coped with (and created) the rapid growth of written records and registers, and this new efficiency spread through the church. For example, if no episcopal registers of parish institutions existed before 1200, by 1250 they were standard, at least in France and England (Morris 1989, 415).

The Papal Chancery became Europe's busiest and the best documented by the late twelfth century (Mundy 2000, 274). Tens of thousands of petitions began to flood the papal curia in the twelfth century, and they were first systematically recorded by the fourteenth (Millet 2003, 1; Zutshi 2009, 92).[15] In response to this deluge, the Chancery expanded under Innocent III, and papal registers begin their continuous history in 1198 (Morris 1989, 534).[16] Papal decretal letters were codified into formulas. Innocent III further reformed the Chancery, tightening rules against forgery, hiring officials charged with fact-checking and proofreading, using watermarks, and ordering the removal of porters from the chancery chambers, to make access to the Chancery easier (and cheaper) (Zutshi 2003, 85). He also fixed the fees paid by papal petitioners (Wiedemann 2018, 517). By the end of the thirteenth century, papal administration was now sending out more than 50,000 papal letters a year to manage complex issues

15. Petitions to the papal curia included requests for graces from the Chancery, letters of justice, benefices, appointments of an auditor to hear a case, and matters approved by cardinal penitentiary: absolution, dispensation, etc. For example, the "illegitimately" born petitioned for dispensations to become priests (Zutshi 2009, 84).

16. These records may have existed before, but many were lost in the papal travels and schisms (Mundy 2000, 274).

such as military orders, exhortations to secular rulers, guidance to monasteries, and exchange of information with bishops and archbishops (Jordan 2001, 189). During the fourteenth century, these numbers grew exponentially (Jedin 1993, 195).

Secular counterparts followed suit. Princely chanceries started to be organized by the late twelfth century, a century after the papal office, with bishops nearly always at their helm. Earlier, Carolingian royal courts had been divided into the *Aula* (hall), the Camera, and the Chapel, but it was not until the late twelfth century that administrative matters became a specialized concern at European royal courts, and the Chancery became distinct from the Chapel (Tullberg 2020, 125).

The church shaped royal chanceries in two ways: administrative templates and staffing. Royal chanceries adopted several papal innovations, from the style of writing used to the legal formulas to templates for documents. Chanceries across Europe used the papal *ars dictaminis*, the style of letter writing. The *cursus Romae curiae*, the rhythmic prose used in the Papal Chancery was also adopted by royal chanceries, including the English from the reign of Edward I (r. 1272–1307) onwards (Brooke 1938, 393; Zutshi 1999, 205; Bombi 2009, 68). Phrasings first used by Gregory IX were adopted in English writs in the mid-thirteenth century, and the royal assignment of livings was modeled on papal provisions (Barraclough 1954, 375). The very rules for petitions for grants of land or office, specifying value, previous grants, and so on, copied the rules of the Papal Chancery (Zutshi 1999, 207). None of there were somehow imposed by the papacy: rather, they were freely borrowed from papal sources (Zutshi 1999, 201). For example, in the 1140s, English bishops were already copying the handwriting, titles, and invocations of papal documents (Sayers 1999, 173)—and using these in the royal chancery.

The English Chancery served the same role as the papal one: to answer royal correspondence and the petitions that flowed to the royal court. It was staffed by clerks and run by bishops: the head was "always a high ranking cleric, by the thirteenth century a bishop" (Strayer [1970] 1998, 33). Clergy wrote the king's letters and orders, preserved laws, and recorded land transactions for the crown. The Chancery also became a court of first instance. It was a source of cheap and swift justice, and a potent jurisdiction since it issued common law writs and dealt with "breaches of trust and contract which the common law courts had not yet learned how to handle" (Harding 2002, 182; see also Haskett 1996, 252). Chancellors themselves "ascended to the first rank of household officials in terms of pay and perquisites and outclassed the others in the rewards of office" (Warren 1992, 79). Under their leadership, the business of the Chancery boomed: from 5,000 letters under Henry III (r. 1216–72) to 30 to 40,000 less than a century later (Bagge 2019, 77). The thirteenth century also saw the decisive separation between the central administration, including the Chancery, which was permanently stationed in Westminster, and the royal court, which continued to move with the king. By the fourteenth century, the English Chancery was so sophisticated that it no longer needed to adopt papal templates (Zutshi 1999, 202ff).

English clergy and its expertise were so much a part of state administration and personnel that the church became "an integral part of the State" (Sayles [1961] 1988, 192). The Lord Chancellor remained a churchman until the time of Henry VIII. "Early in the 1090s perhaps half the bishops and more important abbots had formerly been royal chaplains, and . . . from 1089 to 1109 only two bishops among sixteen appointed had not served in the royal administration in some capacity" (Cantor 1958, 33).[17] Personnel flowed in both directions: clerks in the English royal administration were rewarded with appointment as bishops. Many English bishops were ambitious and well-educated clerks of humble origins who made their way up the ladder and were rewarded with ecclesiastical appointments for their years of service. In the early twelfth century (1100–36), eight out of the eighteen English bishops came from the royal administration (Cantor 1958, 291). Clerics were paid with benefices that had no direct impact on crown finances (Swanson 1989), and in turn the bishops owed military and financial obligations to the King and his Exchequer, further fortifying the ties between clerical and secular governance. They also secured positions for their candidates at court, an "old boy network on an impressive scale" (Morris 1989, 22–3). Angevin administration has been characterized as "an amalgam of royal and ecclesiastical governance," with bishops running the king's administration and courts during the twelfth and thirteenth centuries (Harding 2002, 137).

In the late twelfth century, chanceries also arose in other kingdoms, modeled on the papal chancery. They were inevitably staffed by bishops and clergy and followed the papal model of an independent office, with record keeping, letter writing, and petition administration. They, too, adopted the *ars dictaminis*, the *cursus*, and patterned both letter writing and record keeping after the Papal Chancery. The relationship between the French royal court, the papacy, and the domestic bishops was more fraught than in England, not least because of Philip IV the Fair's conflict with the papacy, and the greater proximity to Rome. Nonetheless, the French chancellor was too a cleric, and all chancery officials and clerks of royal council charged with financial accounts were clergymen.[18] The chancery grew from a relatively obscure office in the eleventh century,

---

17. These fused positions were the core of the fatal conflict between Henry II and Thomas Becket. Henry wanted Becket to serve as both Archbishop of Canterbury and Royal Chancellor—but Becket resigned the chancellorship on becoming archbishop in 1162 (Robinson 2004, 330).

18. The number of personnel serving them also multiplied. Councilors handling the judicial petitions to the king doubled, from fourteen to twenty-nine, over the course of the nearly three decades between 1314 and 1343, as did the number of notaries in the chancery and councilors in the Parlement (Rigaudiere 2000, 35).

was abolished by Philip Augustus in 1185, and then re-emerged as a powerful center when the conflicts between popes and French kings erupted (Hintze [1905] 1975, 227; Brooke 1938, 208). The number of letters grew from 15,000 under Philip IV to 35,000 within two decades, by the 1330s (Bagge 2019, 77).

Elsewhere, Castile had a chancery by 1168, and by 1204, had developed rules and conventions for writing in the vernacular, as well as ties to the university (Linehan 2004, 503). Once again, clergy served as chancellors and judges, and played an active role in record-keeping, including the compilation of *Liber feudorum maior*, the 'Great Book of Fiefs', in 1194 (Linehan 2004, 503). The chanceries of Léon, Castile, and Aragon were closely tied to the church as well (Ertman 1997, 79). In Hungary, King Béla III (r. 1172–96) detached the chancery from the royal chapel, made it an independent body, and staffed it with high-ranking clerics, many trained at Paris (Berend 2004, 315). In the early to mid-thirteenth-century Kingdom of Sicily under Frederick II, the office of chancellor was reserved for a bishop or archbishop holding a degree in law—and the vice chancellor was explicitly a doctor of laws who was not in the holy orders (Ryder 1976, 19). In Poland, clergy dominated the administration throughout the medieval period: chancellors and vice chancellors were bishops, and they, too, reproduced papal formulas and institutions (Obertyński and Kumor 1974, 31).[19]

Thanks to the bishops' common educational and religious background, "procedures and ideas of these chancelleries passed from country to country, from court to court, and that in this way a certain uniformity of thinking about politics and administration was established" (Hintze [1905] 1975, 318). Partly as a result of ecclesiastical influence, the chancery also preserved a certain ambiguity between its judicial, administrative, and governing roles: as the oldest office of the medieval state, it maintained a peculiar multifunctionalism (Ribalta 1996, 29).

Medieval royal courts thus adopted and developed chanceries as centers of administrative correspondence and record-keeping. They relied on both the administrative models from the Papal Chancery—and the clergy who diffused these across Europe.

The Camera

Taxation is a state function *par excellence*. It structures the relationship between state and society, it requires organized collection and accounting, and it necessitates some form of societal acquiescence. Here, the church developed administrative record-keeping, direct taxation, and compliance techniques.

---

19. In Poland, a 1507 law stipulated that one of the chancellors had to be lay and the other a cleric, and the rule operated until 1795 and the dissolution of Poland (Millet and Moraw 1996, 177).

Even specific forms of accounting have connections to the church: "the Carolingian practice of surveying estates was preserved by the Church in the ninth century, and transmitted to England in the tenth via the monastic reform movement" (Oldroyd 1997, 24).[20] Secular rulers copied these templates, with varying degrees of success.

Urban II established a new office to administer taxes and papal finances, the *Camera Apostolica*. The office of the chamberlain, or Camerlengo, first established under his papacy, rapidly grew in importance. Thirty years later, under Calixtus II (r. 1119–24), envoys from the archbishop of York were already reporting on its considerable influence (Weiß 2016, 221). By the early twelfth century, the church both expected secular rulers to contribute to church coffers and began to tax the clergy and the faithful. The various taxes collected included per-capita tithes, feudal dues, the census (paid by princes who were not vassals but had papal protection), and Peter's pence (paid by England, Denmark, Norway, Sweden, and Poland).[21] A century later, the Camera ensured that "in contrast to all other European rulers, who were still financing themselves in kind from their domains, St. Peter's deputy was able to tax the whole of Europe, to transfer monies from the whole of Europe to the papal court" (Weiß 2016, 238).[22] Bishops collected these papal taxes, along with royal ones (Loyn 1963, 255–60).

The Camera kept careful track of the various properties of the church: in 1192 Celestine III's Camerlengo, Cardinal Cencio Savelli (later Pope Honorius III, r. 1216–27), drew up a comprehensive property register, the *Liber Censuum*. It included 528 out of 682 dependencies (Jedin 1993, 46). Organized by diocese, it was the "the most comprehensive geographical survey of Europe in the era in question" (Fried 2015, 216; see also Bisson 2009, 418). The *Liber* listed churches, abbeys, bishoprics, and kingdoms that were *censuales*: census-payers of the church.[23] It was thus a list of the legal claims to revenues, rather

20. The survey techniques in the Domesday Book (listing first treasures, then incomes) were no longer used in post-Carolingian states but were preserved in the church. This suggests that "Carolingian techniques which are seen at their apogee in the Domesday Book were transmitted to England by the church" (Campbell 1986, 165). The church also preserved accounting practices after the collapse of the Roman Empire in the West (Oldroyd 1997, 13, 20).

21. The per-capita Peter's pence was collected on behalf of the church before the Crusades by Anglo-Saxon rulers in England. The earliest documentation of such taxes is a letter to King Canute, dating back to 1031.

22. Other sources of income included fees paid by monasteries to be put under papal protection; taxes on Patrimonium holdings; fees collected for penances, absolutions and penalties; taxes paid by bishops on their nomination, confirmation, and first year of tenure; shares of oblations; profits of curial law courts, feudal dues; and taxes paid by minor clerical benefices (Hay 1995, 296). See also note 6.

23. Census books were both financial and legal records: paying the census strengthened claims of ownership. Payments were voluntary, but they were the majority of papal income in the late twelfth century (Wiedemann 2018, 509–10).

than the revenues obtained, but popes began to exact taxes to which the *Liber Censuum* entitled them.[24] By the 1270s, the papacy developed the *rationes decimarum*: estimates of diocesal wealth all over Europe, and their expected contributions to crusade taxes.

As the papacy found new sources of revenue, the Camera administered these. Innocent III established the legal right of a pope to bestow clerical offices (benefices), which other popes enthusiastically took up.[25] The system of papal provisions began in earnest in 1265 (Watts 2009, 52) and greatly expanded in the fourteenth. Under this system, popes reserved clerical offices for themselves and appointed their preferred candidates. Provisions benefited the papacy through rewards and taxes, and they centralized papal power even further, even as they earned the enmity of bishop by forcing candidates on them (Zutshi 2000, 671). In the late thirteenth century, popes also turned to Italian banks and letters of credit to collect dues, since secular rulers were liable to seize tithes, as Edward I did in 1283 and 1294 (Boase 1933, 109).

The Camera derived its power not simply through the collection of taxes and fees, but from their *exemptions* (Hay 1995, 297). Church finances were a tangle of tithes, income from land, various fees paid by ecclesiastical office holders, and payments for appeals to papal courts—and the church could provide relief from these obligations. These discretionary exceptions, and the lengths to which their would-be beneficiaries went to procure them, helps to explain the growing power of—and exasperation with—the Camera.

Finally, the Camera also pioneered techniques of direct taxation and compliance. Here, the big innovation was crusade taxes, first imposed in 1188 on all clergy (Cazel 1989, 140).

DIRECT TAXATION

Medieval taxation in Europe was not consistent, lucrative, or efficient. The tax burden was thus relatively light, especially when compared to the Roman empire, Byzantium, China, or the Abbasids (Wickham 2016, 151; Stasavage 2020, 204–5). Yet taxes steadily increased in importance in the twelfth century, as kings shifted from self-financing their rule with revenues from royal domains, to extracting resources from their subjects. They moved from occasional taxes collected to fund defense and military campaigns, to more systematic and direct taxation. And here, the church played a critical role.

The crusade taxes, as the first per-capita taxes levied on European populations, set the precedent for subsequent secular taxation (Harriss 1975, 16;

---

24. This amounted to around 1.5 percent of English royal revenue at the time (Weiß 2016, 229).

25. In 1363, Urban V confirmed the pope's right to appoint all bishops and archbishops (Pennington 1984, 123).

Blaydes and Paik 2016). The Crusades were not only called by the papacy, but they also provided a model for European rulers: "the scale of the crusading enterprise taught kings how to mobilize the resources of their countries, and the pope's authorization of the taxation even of the clergy for the purposes of the crusade made them aware of their powers" (Harding 2002, 114). As a result, "the collecting of these taxes brought into being real financial organization, which became useful not only to the Curia but also the state administrations" (Jedin 1993, 167). If the First Crusade in 1096–9 was a self-funded and ramshackle affair, subsequent ventures relied on more systematic fund raising. Kings began to collect levies for the Second Crusade in 1147. In 1165, Pope Alexander III had already issued a plea to aid the Holy Land, and both Louis VII and Henry II responded with a per-capita penny tax. This levy "begins the history of general taxation for financing the crusades" (Cazel 1989, 126). In England, priests were responsible for delivering the revenues to the bishops, who then turned them over to the king. Honesty was the main enforcement mechanism (Lunt 1926, 3).

The development of taxation was further catalyzed by the Saladin Tithe of 1188, which introduced new taxation technologies. After the fall of Jerusalem to Saladin in 1187, the pope urged the rulers of England, France, and the Holy Roman Empire to collect a new tithe on all subjects, clerical and lay, to support what would become the Third Crusade. Henry II and Philip II Augustus accepted (Frederick I Barbarossa demurred).[26] The Saladin Tithe, as it was known, was different from previous levies: rates were very high (one-tenth), collection was intensive, and the pope, for the first time, *required* rather than recommended or exhorted that the clergy pay. The levy profoundly shaped subsequent lay taxation systems: "the Saladin tithe, with its strong and orderly administration, was a turning point in the development of non-feudal taxation" (Lunt 1926, 8).

In England, the Saladin Tithe changed how English kings collected taxes. One innovation was the *basis for taxation*: the Saladin Tithe was collected as a flat rate on personal property (movables and revenues), and both clergy and laity had to pay. Earlier taxes on land (tallage) and in lieu of knightly service (scutage) were familiar and widely accepted.[27] The new taxes on personal property were far more controversial. As one historian characterized it, "the Saladin tithe marked both in the machinery of assessment and the basis of the tax the beginning of a new epoch in financial history" (Mitchell 1951, 122).

26. The 66-year-old emperor nonetheless set out on the Crusade, supported by thousands of fellow German crusaders, but drowned while crossing the Saleph River in Turkey in 1190.

27. The tallage was a land tax levied on cities, boroughs, and royal domains, imposed first by the Normans, last levied in England in 1332. Another tax, the carucage, was an infrequent land tax, a replacement for the danegeld (last imposed in 1162). It began in 1194 and was levied for specific purposes, such as Richard's ransom in 1194, and last collected in 1224.

Another innovation was the *technology of collection*, through itinerant teams of local tax collectors. English clergy were deeply invested in the tithe's success, and local boards of assessment and collection involved a parish priest, a dean, sergeant, clerk of the baron, and a clerk of the bishop, as well as a Templar and a Hospitaller.[28] Each taxpayer paid his tax before the board, and self-assessments could be called into question by sworn juries. Self-declarations were no longer enough: those who swore a false valuation or refused to pay could be imprisoned (Mitchell 1951, 88). The commissions traveled in groups and coordinated with each other. This precedent of appointed groups of tax collectors was taken up by the English state, "partly guided in its choice of means by the example of the church" (Mitchell 1951, 64). After the Saladin Tithe, commissioners were sent regularly to each shire and unit to supervise royal taxation, as they did in the two other great English levies: the tax for Richard I's ransom in 1194 and the one-thirteenth tax of 1207, as well as the carucage of 1198 and at least seven levies under Henry III from 1217 to 1235 (Mitchell 1951, 67).

In France, collection was far more decentralized and relied on feudal enforcement: local seigneurs and churchmen collected the tithes of their tenants (Lunt 1926, 8). In contrast to England, there was no royal backing of the tithe, and instead it faced wide opposition (Cazel 1989, 127). As a result, the French "Saladin Tithe went nowhere. Philip Augustus was soon forced to abandon the levy, to renounce its future use, and to fall back on revenues from his expanding domain" (Maddicott 2010, 403). There was no opportunity for the secular machinery of taxation to develop as it did in England, and the Saladin Tithe did not lead immediately to a national tax in France. The French clergy paid several subsequent tithes to the king between 1215 and 1294, but it was not until Philip the Fair in the 1300s that "such taxes began commonly to be imposed upon the clergy and upon laymen by the king" (Lunt 1926, 8).

Heartened by its success in England, the papacy expanded its taxation regime. Innocent III levied a one-fortieth tax on every clerk in Christendom, and in 1199, he made it mandatory (Lunt 1926, 10). With his *Ad liberandam* decree of 1215, he further declared that the pope had the right to tax the clergy without their consent. The Fourth Lateran Council established a one-twentieth clerical tax and a one-tenth tax on cardinals (initially for three years) that became the precedent for subsequent, regular, taxation of the clergy (Canon 71). But the

---

28. The Templars and Hospitallers were both monastic fighting orders based in Jerusalem with a vested interest in the effective collection of the crusade tax. The Templars gained formal recognition by the pope in 1138. They became bankers to the church and royal rulers alike, which eventually led to their destruction by Phillip IV the Fair of France, deeply in debt to the order. The Hospitallers (The Order of the Hospital of St. John of Jerusalem) began as a nursing order but became a military brotherhood, recognized by the pope in 1113. The Teutonic Knights were founded around 1190 as a militant order protecting German pilgrims. They were exempt from the authority of bishops and reported directly to the pope.

clergy could pay far more, as in 1212, when the church in Castile pledged half its income to support Alfonso VIII's mustering of forces against Muslims (Jordan 2001, 166). For the Fifth Crusade of 1217–21, Innocent III and Honorius III developed central control of the fiscal machinery, with papal emissaries rather than local bishops in charge of collection (Padgett and Powell 2012, 129). With Innocent IV (r. 1243–53), we see "regular superintendents with defined areas, elaborate rolls of assessments, and fixed depots for the sums collected. Europe had not seen machinery so complete and well ordered" (Boase 1933, 133).

These taxes meant not only financial resources for the pope but also political authority to decide where and how they would be deployed (Riley-Smith 2005, 186). The church provided the ideological justification for taxation: "the notion that taxation was part of the great business of the realm was sharpened by the development of the doctrine of necessity. By the second decade of the 13th century, the papacy was appealing to this doctrine to demand contributions for a Crusade to defend the Holy Land since this concerned the common good of the Church" (Harriss 1975, 33). From 1247 to 1274, the papacy raised these taxes twenty-one times, and this "regularity made the papal tithe Europe's most advanced tax except for those in the urban republics" (Mundy 2000, 215).

As the need for financing grew, so did the refinements. The crusade taxes, and the associated spending, had to be assigned, levied, and audited. The Camera both collected and distributed these revenues. The Camera shifted from payments in kind to strictly monetary payments. The taxes paid by bishops and abbots were fixed at an annual sum and increasingly regulated. Assessments were more effective and detailed. Papal agents in each diocese could summon and compel answers and financial disclosures from any cleric. The assessors were authorized to excommunicate anyone who gave a fraudulent account, and collectors could depose clergy and reserve the vacant benefices for the pope. The entire collection was overseen and centralized by the Papal Camera (Lunt 1926, 21–2). A 1274 decree by Gregory X, *Zelus fidei*, created twenty-six districts staffed by a hierarchy of collectors and sub-collectors that encompassed Europe (Riley-Smith 2005, 175, 212). Kings and princes were asked to impose a per-capita tax to build up the papal reserves. This sophisticated system of collection in turn spurred more complete financial accounting by the late thirteenth and early fourteenth century in the Papal Camera (Wiedemann 2018, 520).

For secular rulers, the crusade taxes were a critical part of developing their financial systems. Thus, in England, after the tithes of 1166 and 1188, the first systematic lay tax was collected in 1207, when King John I took one-thirteenth on movable goods and revenues (Kaeuper 1988, 36). This tax on property was familiar from the ecclesiastical tithe and used in both the Saladin Tithe of 1188 and the ransom of Richard I in 1194. Building on these precedents, the 1207 tax was another important step to national taxation, "levied against an unspecified

future need, on property not land, and paid by most classes of society, except-
ing some clergy. It was collected nationally by royal justices. It was legitimized
because it had been agreed with a council of barons who represented the community in general who would suffer it" (Hughes and Oats 2007, 94).

Taxation in England changed after the Saladin Tithe. Previously, kings
would occasionally tax land and focus on barons and financial settlements
with communities. These were arbitrary, personal, and determined at the
discretion of the king, who would also sell own lands and debase coinage if
necessary (Harriss 1975, 6). In contrast, the 1207 levy, much like the Saladin
Tithe, was a uniform tax on movable property, with "a national incidence and
a high yield which could be justified by the needs of the realm" (Harriss 1975,
10). As the Saladin Tithe showed, taxes on movables were far more lucrative
than the land taxes, such as the tallage (town) or carucage (estate) taxes, both
of which ended in the thirteenth century. Teams of county commissioners in
England collected the taxes in each county, much as bishops and emissaries
had done so with the Saladin Tithe in the dioceses nearly twenty years earlier
(Mitchell 1951, 64). Most of these assessors were knights who had earlier
served in the royal administration as local officers. The king negotiated and
issued exemptions, much as the church had done (Mitchell 1951, 379).

The secular analogue of the Camera in England, the Exchequer, managed
these revenues and financial obligations.[29] The office was not patterned on
the Papal Camera, but it was strengthened by the Saladin Tithe, which was
collected in the bishoprics, but received, recorded, and transmitted by the
Exchequer (Mitchell 1951, 13). The Exchequer itself was first established
under Henry I (r. 1100–35), perhaps in preparation for Henry's daughter
Matilda's marriage, and it was initially an event rather than an institution, an
annual audit session held at the king's council meeting (Chibnall 2004, 212).
It rapidly grew from temporary expedient to formal institution under Roger,
Bishop of Salisbury, who served as a bishop from 1102 to 1149 (Jones 2009,
269). The Exchequer began to audit the accounts of the king's local agents,
the sheriffs, and to authorize expenditures (Ormrod 1999, 19). The Pipe Roll of
1129–30 represents the first formal and systematic record of royal finance, and
its "near-universal system of assessment" preceded its continental counterparts by more than a century (Campbell 1986, 171). The office relied on extant
techniques: the use of Latin and royal scribes; the abacus; the justices in
the eyre; the representatives of the king sent out to monitor sheriffs, collect
revenue, and administer local justice; and the shire and hundreds system of
administrative sub-units, which dated back to the seventh and eighth centuries (Jones 2009, 272). The Exchequer itself was divided into two bodies: the

29. The Exchequer was named for the checked cloth that served as an abacus for tally-
ing accounts (Chibnall 2004, 212).

lower Exchequer (Treasury), founded around 1124–30, and used for regular payments from the Exchequer, and an auditor.

With the crusade taxes, the Exchequer grew both in responsibility and capacity. Both the Exchequer and the Chancery were administrative departments, but they also developed jurisdiction over their domains, with the Court of Exchequer arising in the 1190s to deal with financial matters and the Court of Chancery gaining formal recognition in the late 1280s.[30] In the thirteenth century, the royal Chancery emerged as a court of equity to meet the growing number of disputes for which common law had no answer (Ormrod 1995, 111).

The French treasury gained neither the experience of the Saladin Tithe nor the fiscal capacity. The first records of royal accounting in France go back to 1202–3 (Jones 2009, 268), but the failure of the Saladin Tithe meant that direct taxation would be delayed by nearly a century. As late as the thirteenth century, French kings were expected to self-fund the royal administration. Here, too, the first steps towards taxation were the crusade tithes, which mostly fell on clerical benefices. Some kings, such as Louis IX (r. 1226–70) and Philip III (r. 1270–85), managed to persuade the clergy to give them tenths for non-crusade purposes. In contrast to the centralized English system, French taxation lacked a clear division of labor. Stewards, bailiffs, and wardens collected the king's revenue while also administering justice, military affairs, and local governance (Wolfe 1972, 13). No formal treasury existed until Philip IV created a new Trésor in 1285 to supervise receipts and expenditures (the Templars held onto most of fiscal powers until 1295). After a failed attempt to impose a national excise tax in the 1290s, Philip finally switched to direct taxation, and specifically the *fouage* (hearth tax, which became the *taille*), alongside *aides* and *gabelles* (salt taxes). Nobles, nonetheless, remained exempt.[31]

There were thus important differences between England and France that are not simply reducible to church influence: English kings were more powerful from the start and pursued deliberate strategies of centralization and overcoming regional loyalties, such as employing nobles in royal justice (Brewer 1989, 4). French royal institutions were superimposed on regional authorities, who retained their various taxation powers and local assemblies. This particularism eventually led the French monarchy to adopt private financiers and tax farming for tax collection, while the English taxes would be

30. At both the Chancery and the Exchequer, legal action began by buying a formal command to the court, known as the original writ. By the late fourteenth century, Chancery also permitted private cases begun by bills, or informal requests. These were generally cheaper and faster (Haskett 1996, 252; Tucker 2000, 791). The Court of Chancery's Victorian successor, ironically, was known for its protracted and sluggish procedures, where cases could take generations (see *Bleak House*).

31. Nobles in the Holy Roman Empire, Poland, and Hungary were also exempt from taxation (Rady 2000, 145).

collected by centrally appointed officials. It is also not clear that the new methods of collection led to a radical rise in revenues.[32] Yet the Saladin Tithe in England is still notable for its legacies of direct taxation of movable property, assessment by itinerant teams and sworn juries, and new enforcement regimes.

Other secular rulers began to collect the first substantial direct levies in the thirteenth century, largely following the papal model of emissaries and local notables sent out to assess and collect. Castile and Sicily developed such taxation in the 1260–70s (prompting the Sicilian Vespers in 1282 as an anti-tax rebellion against Charles of Anjou). In Sicily, the treasury was physically transferred out of the king's residence in 1277 (Ryder 1976, 16). Using ecclesiastical templates, rulers could develop new techniques of resource extraction. By the mid-fourteenth century, "England, France, Castile, Venice, Genoa and Florence and the Papacy all succeeded in establishing workable fiscal regimes, involving high but realistic levels of taxation and a reasonable degree of political consensus" (Watts 2009, 226). Aragon, the city-states of Italy, and German principalities also began to raise taxes, but more modestly and less systematically, while in Scandinavia and East Central Europe, both nobles and peasants objected to taxation too vociferously (Watts 2009, 233).

COMPLIANCE

The crusade taxes also set a precedent for ensuring *compliance*, an important step in making taxation both mandatory and enforced. The papacy relied on three techniques: law, deputies, and profit-sharing. First, the Fourth Lateran Council (1215) declared that tithe payments had priority over all other charges or taxes (Canon 54), and participation was mandatory. Second, papal deputies such as bishops collected the taxes, even if kings could refuse to let bishops transfer the payments. Third, the papacy shared the profits. What monarchs and bishops alike wanted "was not the elimination of the charges, but their own cut. A considerable share of 'papal' exactions actually stayed in local pockets, clerical and lay" (Swanson 2000, 13). By the early thirteenth century, clerical tithing and taxation became subjects of ecclesiastical legislation and litigation, resulting in several schemes that let bishops dispose revenues in favor of particular tithe possessors (Górecki 1993, 4). The papacy also shared the profits of its levies with powerful monarchs such as the kings of France, England, Castile, Aragon, Angevin Sicily, and subsequently with the Scandinavian monarchs. Cooperation with local princes and rulers was a precondition of papal taxation of the clergy, not least because the money had to be

32. The analysis of English exchequer documents (the pipe rolls) shows that English tax revenues took off dramatically after 1194, when Richard returned to England (Barratt 2001; see also Barratt 2007). Royal commissioners were sent out to the shires to collect the ransom levy of 1194, following the Saladin Tithe precedent (Hughes and Oats 2007, 84).

exported—and sharing profits benefited both the papacy and the monarchy (Hamre 2003, 663). This "accustomed these kings to the benefits of taxation and gave them ideas about how to achieve it" (Watts 2009, 225).

Kings then applied the same techniques to their own noble lords and barons. For example, in Castile, the *servicios* were first granted in the 1370s, extensively involving the Castilian nobles and urban elites in the royal tax system. This enabled its expansion and allowed some taxes, like the royal *alcabala* sales tax, to be collected without the consent of the Cortes (Watts 2009, 226–7). Similarly, the French king allowed nobles to raise taxes in tandem with the king, bought off towns with jurisdictional privileges, and developed a system of taxes (*aides* and *gabelles*) for which the nobles were formally responsible—but which they easily delegated to peasants and town dwellers (Watts 2009, 227). More broadly, royal taxation in France succeeded when the king shared the proceeds with the various local powers in France (Mundy 2000, 233).

In England, these kinds of bargaining, exemptions, and profit sharing were critical to the success of the tallage. When Pope Innocent IV imposed taxes on English clergy in 1250–4, Henry III used the interval between the sanction of the tax in 1250 and the assessment in 1254 to negotiate with the clergy and the pope over the share of the revenues (Lunt 1926, 83). Even as tax-sharing expanded, tax farming was reduced: by 1236, sheriffs could no longer farm taxes and fees, and their discretion was greatly reduced (Warren 1992, 222ff).[33] When Edward II put the assessment of the tallage in 1332 into the hands of the council, prelates, lay magnates, knights and towns all united in opposition—largely because they would not bargain over and share the revenues. In short, compliance with taxation could be more easily evoked if notables could share in the revenues, a lesson learned from the papacy.

THE AVIGNON PAPACY AND THE GREAT SCHISM

During the Avignon exile, the Curia, and especially the Camera, actually grew stronger. The move to Avignon in 1309 initially sharply reduced papal income, necessitating new efficiencies and centralization. The Camera became the chief administrative office, and the chamberlain, not the chancellor, now occupied the highest rank at the papal court. The chamberlain himself became the pope's most important adviser: his bedroom in the papal palace at Avignon was located directly beneath the pope's, and the two rooms were connected by a staircase (Weiß 2016). The office transformed from a financial administrator

---

33. In tax sharing, the ruler collecting the taxes gives a kickback to his nobles (or in the case of the papacy, to the secular rulers). Tax collection can still be formal and centralized. In tax farming, local "farmers" collected taxes on the ground, kept a share, and forwarded the rest, a procedure that did not centralize taxation or increase central state capacity.

to the leading agency of the Curia. The responsibility for accounting now devolved to treasurers and their assistants (Weiß 2016, 234).

Centralization and efficiency marked the Avignon administration. Most Avignon popes were thrifty and acute administrators, aided by capable cardinals who served as "princely co-governors" (Kaminsky 2000, 676). Together, they asserted a new degree of control over the church, with Urban V in 1363 reserving for the papacy all patriarchal, episcopal, and high monastic offices (Jedin 1993, 193). Regular clergy and university seats also came under papal control (Hay 1995, 291 and 293). The centralization of appointments made the Chancery "into a large and expensive bureaucracy of legal and financial experts" (Zacour 1976, 186). The scope of papal provisions peaked, enriching the popes and expanding their authority as dues flowed to the Camera (Partner 1999, 360).[34] Fees from litigants at the curia also accrued. Taxes on clergy were fixed at 10 percent, and an exchequer audited the clerics, effectively compelling them to pay taxes (Ormrod 1999, 301). Local collectors, each responsible for a given region, gathered the dues and deposited them at Avignon. The Avignon papacy, moreover, was far more stable than the earlier, itinerant curia. Officials stayed behind, even when Urban V (r. 1362–70) and Gregory XI (r. 1370–78) left for Rome in 1367 and 1376, respectively, allowing the administration to continue and to develop (Zutshi 2000, 662). This machinery was so effective that the first three Avignon popes left a surplus (Zutshi 2000).

The admirably competent governance of the Avignon era could not withstand the effects of the Great Schism of 1378–1417, which weakened both the church's standing and its finances. After the schism ended, lay rulers resisted paying taxes to fund Rome, and spiritual revenues also fell. Over the fifteenth century, popes made further concessions to secular rulers, agreeing to delay taxation and conceding patronage. Total papal income fell to around one-half of what it was before 1368 (Partner 1999, 362). The result was that "when financial and other pressures undermined the curia's administrative practices, and lay princes increased their control over the Church at the expense of the papacy. It was not possible after the end of the Schism for the Renaissance popes to reestablish the old system" (Zutshi 2000, 673). The papacy was weaker and poorer, while national churches reasserted their independence.

As a result, the papacy turned to the Papal States as a source of income and began to heavily tax these areas. The taxation was intensive, with enforcement entrusted to *condottieri* and most papal revenue collected by banking houses. With the Reformation, the financial situation of the church worsened,

34. The scope of the financial requests, and the papacy's association with Avignon, led English kings to try and limit papal influence: new laws abolished appeals to foreign courts (and thus the papal court) in 1353, with an explicit reference to papal courts in 1365. In 1351, the Statute of Provisors made appointments without royal approval null and void. Not all of these laws were equally enforced, but they paved the way for subsequent assertions of royal authority, such as Henry VIII's Act of Supremacy (Ergang 1971, 107–10).

both because ecclesiastical revenue dried up in Protestant areas and because the church had to make concessions to stay on the good side of Catholic monarchs (Hsia 2005, 105). The Papal States went from being least taxed state in 1500 to most heavily taxed state by 1600, quadrupling tax extraction between 1520–1620 (Partner 1999, 368ff). Three-fourths of papal revenue now came from the states (Bireley 1999, 72).

SALE OF OFFICES

Beyond taxing the Papal States, the sale of ecclesiastical offices became a major source of revenue, especially after the Great Schism. Some of these practices reach back to Innocent III, whose administration pioneered the *"resignatio in favorem tertii"*: a benefice holder would resign in favor of a third party, who then transferred it to the intended recipient, with both the first and third party getting paid but avoiding the charge of simony (Gorski 2003, 147). To finance the Crusades, the church had also sold offices—or rather, the profits from offices.

With the expansion of papal administration, and in the aftermath of the Black Plague (1348–53) and the Schism, the papacy energetically turned to the sale of offices and indulgences. Full-fledged venality ensued, and the papacy institutionalized the system of office selling. A special office, the *Dataria*, was founded in the fourteenth century to dispense and record the sale of offices, the awarding of provisions, and indulgences (Hsia 2005, 104).[35] Boniface IX (r. 1389–1404) sold whatever he could, including offices, indulgences, and expectancies (benefices not yet vacant), often to multiple buyers. Not surprisingly, he was seen as "corruption incarnate" (Kaminsky 2000, 684). By the late fifteenth century, most offices in the Chancery, Penitentiary, and Camera were for sale. The 700 benefices were the single most profitable source of papal income, with younger sons of noble families repeatedly appointed to bishoprics, often for a brief time. This churn in office was lucrative: each new appointment brought in another fee to the Camera. Both the papacy and the officeholders profited, with an estimated return on investment of around 9 to 11 percent, considerably higher than the return on bonds at the time (Partner 1999, 374). At the Fifth Lateran Council (1512–17), the income from the sale of offices made up one-sixth of the papal budget (Gilchrist 1969, 95ff). As Barbara Tuchman acidly put it, "every office, every nomination, every appointment or preferment, every dispensation of the rules, every judgment of the Rota or adjudication of a claim, every pardon, indulgence, and absolution, everything the Church had or was, from cardinal's hat to pilgrim's relic, was for

---

35. In the mid-sixteenth century, the office took on marital dispensations (previously under the purview of the *Apostolica Penitentaria*), benefices, and various indults (favors, dispensations, and privileges).

sale" (Tuchman 1978, 26). The Camera's new reputation for avarice and corruption was not helped by its role in the subsequent collecting and accounting
for these profits.

The sale of offices intensified with new papal expenditures: the servicing of debt, military expenses, subsidies to princes, and the administrative
costs of the Papal States (Partner 1999, 374). By the mid-fifteenth century, the
papacy developed a lucrative innovation: "the curial office created specifically
for sale; whose holders were in effect purchasing a life annuity" (Ryder 1998,
580). Thus, if 2,232 offices were sold by the papacy in 1520, forty years later,
in 1565, the number increased to 3,635 (Hsia 2005, 105). Under the "reforms"
of Sixtus V (r. 1585–90), several offices of the Chancery became *vacabili*, or
offices for sale, including the regent, the twenty-five solicitors, the auditors, and
the twelve notaries. Prices for offices reflected the potential profitability of the
office. High clerical office became a family investment, with families pooling
their money and borrowing to get a son into a high enough position, so that he
could resign and obtain benefices for his relatives.[36]

Secular rulers adopted these unsavory practices. They treated the pope
more as a fellow monarch than as a spiritual authority, and this cynical
attitude allowed them to tolerate sale of offices as well as nepotism.[37] It even
led them to invest in papal elections, further hastening both the corruption of
the papacy and the ruin of its reputation (Greengrass 2014, 276). By the mid-
fifteenth century, French and Spanish monarchs also sold offices. The papal
template was an easy and obvious one to follow: "the terms of sale and even
the language of the contracts employed were virtually identical to those used
by the Papal Curia" (Gorski and Sharma 2017, 113). The very definition of
offices, formalized in the French ordinance of 1467, "had obvious parallels with
ecclesiastical benefice" (Doyle 1997, 136). The same rules applied: if holders of
church benefices conditionally resigned and died within twenty days of doing
so, then the benefice would revert back to the provisor. In the 1530s, the same
rule was introduced in France. Offices conditionally resigned reverted back
to the crown if the officeholder died within forty days: "the laws governing

36. The story of the Borghese family is emblematic: the family purchased the office of
the chamber-auditory in 1588, only to see it revert back to the pope when the officeholder,
Orazio Borghese, died young. The pope re-sold the office to Orazio's brother Camilo, who
recouped the investment in six years, was elevated to cardinal in 1596, and handed out multiple episcopal offices to his relatives. Ascending ever higher in the papal administration,
Camilo advanced brothers and nephews throughout the papal administration. As a result,
the family became a great aristocratic clan (Hsia 2005, 101). And Camilo? He became Pope
Paul V in 1605.

37. Papal nepotism was a costly and prevalent practice that bloomed from the late
fifteenth century to the eighteenth (Partner 1999, 368). As Alexander III put it, "God
deprived bishops of sons, the devil gave them nephews" (Smith 1964, 19).

French venality were therefore deeply marked by the ways of the Church" (Doyle 1997, 136).[38]

In short, the church provided innovations, both lucrative and unsavory, in the collection and compliance of taxes, accounting practices, and sources of new revenue. Whether the Saladin Tithe or the sale of office, these precedents were closely followed by princes and kings.

The Judiciary

The third pillar of the medieval administration was the judiciary. As the next chapter shows, the systematization of law provided new concepts of justice and led to a flourishing new culture of learning and human capital. Here, I focus on the institutional apparatus of justice: the petitions, judges, courts, and jurisdictions that the church developed and the kings adopted.

The system of papal justice expanded greatly in the Middle Ages. In its eleventh-century incarnation, the papal curia was the first to issue documents and to make the written word the central medium for conducting business at a time when "the usual mode of formal expression was symbolic action," such as public ceremonies (Morris 1989, 11). Popes themselves had long answered petitions, but with the reform era, the papacy settled an ever-growing number of legal disputes and increasingly adjudicated appeals (Connolly 2009, 61; see also Pitz 1971). The papacy issued privileges, annulments, and dispensations, and adjudicated other cases as well.

Over the course of the twelfth century, legal cases, requests for exemptions, and appeals poured into the papal court. The Investiture Conflict unleashed a flood of cases into the church courts, as claimants sought to distinguish rights of the church from rights of lay rulers (Doucette and Møller 2021, 242). Petitions and the appeals system first proliferated under Innocent II (r. 1130–43) and then boomed as canon law standardized across Europe (Wickham 2015, 148). With the development of new legal procedures to facilitate legal appeals to Rome, a surge of legal petitions and cases followed. Both secular and ecclesiastic petitions and appeals inundated the Curia: "starting in the middle decades of the thirteenth century, law came to play an unprecedented role in the day-to-day workings of the medieval church. The papacy lay at the heart of this development, even if it did not consciously direct it. Bishops seeking advice, petitioners begging for redress, litigants pursuing appeals—all turned to Rome for relief, resulting in a flood of papal mandates and judgments being sent back out to every corner of Christendom" (Dorin 2021, 4).

Papal justice was all-encompassing, and often more efficient than the nascent secular courts. Innocent III allowed any person who felt they had

38. The seventeenth century French statesman, Cardinal Richelieu, and others vigorously denounced the practice—but also saw it as necessary and lucrative (Doyle 1997, 137).

been failed by the secular court system to appeal directly to the pope. The lawyer-popes of the twelfth and thirteenth centuries legislated for the whole of Europe on a wide range of topics, including property rights, and the "efficiency of the papal courts went some way towards realizing the ideal of western Christendom as a juridical unit" (Black 1992, 43). Popes conferred (and cancelled) privileges on ecclesiastical institutions, chartered universities, and developed canon law with hundreds of decretals (Robinson 1990, 186).

This huge new demand led the papal administration to expand (and to profit from the inevitable fees that accompanied the requests). The expansion of justice transformed both local and high church offices. Over the course of the twelfth century, as papal offices specialized, the Curia shifted from an executive to a judicial role, and from being a court of appeal to being a court of first instance (Robinson 1990, 186). To cope with the new demand for papal justice, Alexander III (r. 1159–1181) and successor popes appointed local judges-delegate (*iudices delegati*), prelates appointed to hear and investigate individual cases (Robinson 1990, 192; Jedin 1993, 132). With the formation of territorial parishes in the twelfth century "came the development of church courts which were themselves a hierarchy with what was now called the papal curia as its apex" (Cowdrey 2004, 266). The growing importance of the papacy's judicial role is reflected in the Curia's clear preference for graduates in the law, rather than theology: Pope Alexander III scoured France looking for clerics with the legal and canonical schooling to appoint them in the Curia as cardinals. He appointed six eminent lawyers to the college (Robinson 1990, 55).

New papal offices proliferated to meet the demand for papal justice. Three main specialized tribunals arose out of the Curia. These courts handled cases of mixed religious/civil nature (Rota); grave sins, conscience and theology (Penitentiary); and appeals in religious cases (Signatura). The oldest and most powerful was the Sacra Romana Rota, the highest ecclesiastical tribunal, outranked only by the Pope. The Rota was both a tribunal of appeal for the faithful who had faced a local ecclesiastical tribunal, and a court of first instance for the residents of the Papal States and Rome. By the 1170s, the Rota began to deal with the enormous growth in ecclesiastical cases, which were usually heard by the papacy. Popes began to delegate these judicial duties, assigning each case to a cardinal or a bishop who would hear the case (the auditor) and present the evidence to the pope.[39] In the thirteenth century, the auditors were increasingly allowed to make their own decisions, subject to papal approval, in minor cases such as benefices. In 1307–9, Clement V gave the auditors independent judicial powers, allowed litigants to choose whether the pope or the auditor would decide their case, and the Rota began to act as an autonomous tribunal. The Rota became a stable institution in 1331 with the *Ratio Iuris* bull, which formalized its various procedures and

39. *https://www.newadvent.org/cathen/13205c.htm*, accessed 4 November 2020.

activities (Jedin 1993, 155). More than 80 percent of the cases were litigation over benefices, followed by property disputes (Salonen 2016a, 284). Both clerics and lay people turned to the tribunal, and more than 70 percent of the cases were decided (or dismissed) within a month (Salonen 2016a, 287). These new duties required a large cadre of legal experts, educated at Bologna and other universities, who brought with them Roman law and their professors' scholastic techniques (Clark 1986, 680).

The Penitentiary, or *Penitentaria Apostolica*, developed along with other central administrative offices in the mid-twelfth century (Salonen 2016, 260).[40] The Fourth Lateran Council in 1215 expanded its role, since it redefined many sins as absolvable only by the pope, and reserved many cases for popes and bishops. The office handled matters of absolution and excommunication, and of religious penalties and their lifting. Honorius III (r. 1216–1227) formalized the office, granting it powers to absolve penitents and conferred the power to grant absolutions to legates and bishops (Robinson 2004a, 419–20). With Innocent IV, the expanded college of scribes made the Penitentiary a writing office comparable to the Chancery (Zutshi 2007).[41] The court heard thousands of cases annually, from all over Europe, and increasingly focused on marriage law, the legitimacy of children (especially important for children born out of wedlock who sought to become priests), holding more than one benefice, and ecclesiastical ordinations (Salonen 2016, 287).

Finally, the Signatura emerged from the small coterie of clerks in the Apostolic Camera, the *referendarii apostolici*, who were commissioned to investigate and report on the petitions addressed to the pope. By the mid-thirteenth century, the referendaries examined and referred petitions that could be granted by the pope, and the college of referendaries eventually began to sign papal responses for the pope (Daniel 2009, 633). In the fifteenth century, their numbers grew rapidly and, since the office was a prestigious one, so did the number of sinecures: officials who held the position but did not actually perform any office.[42]

These papal courts sat at the apex of a system of ecclesiastical courts across Europe, which adjudicated cases involving clerical offenders, but also held jurisdiction over marriage contracts (which made up the bulk of cases heard),

40. The Penitentarius had served the popes since the seventh century, but the Penitentaria now became a distinct office.

41. Penitents traveled to Rome, where proctors and then auditors ensured the petition was in the proper format and made the correct references to canon law. Once heard and approved, the scribes composed the official letter, the *datarius* dated it, and after double checking and sealing by a *sigillator*, the case was registered, the fees paid, and the penitent received the official letter (Salonen 2016, 264).

42. Alexander VI (r. 1492–1503) further split the offices into the *Signatura Gratiae* and the *Signatura Justicia*, and Sixtus V (r. 1585–90) limited their numbers in 1586 to 100 and 70, respectively.

as well as wills and property adjudication, ecclesiastical finances, breaches of faith, and defamation cases. They functioned in parallel with the lay courts: in England, for example, inheritance battles moved back and forth between secular courts (land ownership) and church (validity of marriage) (McSweeney 2019, 74). Ecclesiastical justice was attractive: for one thing, it was often faster. Canon law also "gave laymen a discipline that was clear-cut and not very oner- ous; it laid down rules and conditions for all the main occasions and areas of the Christian life—baptism, confirmation, confession, communion, penance, marriage, religious instruction and religious duties, alms, usury, last wills and testaments, the last rites, burial, graveyards, prayers, and masses for the dead" (Southern 1970, 116). Church courts were so popular even in the fourteenth century that around 40 percent of cases in the church courts should have been sent to royal ones: for example, ordinary commercial contracts fell under the rubric of breach of faith (Duggan 1974, 660). The appellate jurisdiction of Rome was recognized and widely used by canonists. By the twelfth century, appeals to Rome had become frequent (Snow 1963, 325).

Secular courts coevolved with ecclesiastical ones. As the church worked out an appeals system, kings copied this template: decisions by local courts could be appealed to royal ones if there was a breach of justice at the lower level (Reynolds 1997, 41). Secular and papal courts expanded in the twelfth century alongside each other: the Rota and the Common Pleas tribunals become prominent in same decade, the 1170s. Much as the papacy developed the system of judges-delegate, twelfth-century English itinerant justices in the eyre traveled to dispense royal justice (and assert centralized royal author- ity). The English judiciary continued to centralize and specialize: the court of Common Pleas was founded in 1178,[43] the King's Bench in the late twelfth century, and the Chancery in the fourteenth.

Kings also sought to limit the expansion of papal jurisdiction, the steady flow of customers paying fees to the church, and the ready system of appeals. By the twelfth century, Henry II resorted to writs of prohibition in England to prevent people from going to church courts and vice versa (Adams [1936] 2017). The king wanted to retain the court fees and the authority, but church courts delivered faster justice than lay ones in several areas, including debt.

French and Spanish monarchs also tried to both limit the reach of papal authority into their lands and reassert jurisdiction. By 1190, Philip II Augus- tus established local royal courts known as *assizes* in France, borrowing from Henry II, as he sought to gain greater control over the towns and regions.[44]

43. The Common Pleas cleaved off from the Exchequer and began to hear ordinary civil litigation on a regular basis around 1195.

44. He also regulated the central court justices who went to localities to hear laymen and ecclesiastics in the assizes. They were to report to the queen and the archbishop, who in turn were to inform Philip three times a year of the state of the kingdom. Subsequent kings retained jurisdiction over serious crimes, with rape and murder judged by the king's

Louis IX (r. 1226–70) and then Philip IV the Fair (r. 1285–1314) centralized and reformed the administration, dividing the royal council into a Chamber des Comptes for the administration of finances, Conseil du Roi for political affairs, and Parlement for legal affairs (Ergang 1971, 59). Parlement was a critical innovation, as a council and the highest court of justice. Clergy and lay judges maintained parity at both the Parlement of Paris and regional parlements (Millet and Moraw 1996, 179). The French judiciary was not as centralized or specialized as the English (or papal), as we will see in the next chapter. Nonetheless, it also challenged clerical jurisdiction: the Parlement constantly intervened to judge the claims of churches to jurisdiction, policed the boundaries of ecclesiastical justice, guarded against the abuse of excommunication and sanctuary, and provided alternative procedures in marriage and wills, all of which "steadily eroded the Church's position" (Harding 2002, 169). The Parlement asserted control over the church: prelates could be judged in Parlement, but were excluded from membership by 1319. Clerical and lay courts competed—and the state was winning.

The Holy Roman Empire

The Holy Roman Empire diverged from this pattern of proliferation and specialization of central administrative offices. Fragmented by the church's divide-and-conquer tactics, the empire was destined to remain a hodgepodge of hundreds of principalities, territories, duchies, and bishoprics. There was no bureaucracy, central executive, or even clearly defined territory—and the cohesiveness of the empire declined further over the Middle Ages (Stollberg-Rilinger 2018, 11). The emperor had few fiscal rights or taxing powers, so no exchequer or other centralized fiscal apparatus arose, and the empire operated without a budget, written bookkeeping, land registers, central financial offices, or even permanent headquarters for the government (Isenmann 1999, 247). The Salians attempted to centralize the administration and introduce taxation in the early twelfth century, relying on episcopal elites, but this met with overwhelming opposition (Zacour 1976, 103). Other efforts to establish such offices failed, since the emperors had neither the resources nor the authority to build an administrative infrastructure.

The finances of the medieval German emperors were precarious. Not only was there no central taxing authority, but there was also no enfeoffment— vacated fiefdoms did not revert back to the monarch, as they did elsewhere. The imperial treasury could not benefit from valuable territorial lordship rights (Stollberg-Rilinger 2018, 21). From the Carolingians onwards, the bulk of the empire was held in benefices: royal possessions that were loaned out to various

---

men, and expanded royal jurisdiction by closely supervising communes (Harding 2002, 125 and 112).

nobles. This allowed the Carolingians to dispense with central taxation, which would have required greater staffing and consolidated centralized institutions (Wilson 2016, 327). After 1250, the kings relied on pledges to nobles: but because they could not repay them, the lands remained permanently alienated, and local princes further gained power. By the mid-fifteenth century, the emperor received almost no revenues (Isenmann 1999, 252). The imperial and free cities, and some of the princely territories were much more capable, collecting taxes and enforcing legislation—but that uneven distribution of capacity itself thwarted the rise of a central and functional imperial government. Even as other European countries shifted to public finance and taxation, the Holy Roman Empire continued to levy irregular, individual taxes (Wilson 2016, 327).

The constant rivalry with the church further enfeebled the medieval imperial administration. Not only did the church initially triumph in the Investiture Conflict, but it also emancipated itself from the emperor. Bishops and abbeys used their political and financial authority bestowed upon them by the church to strengthen their lordship within territories (Stollberg-Rilinger 2018, 21; see also chapter 2). Instead of bishops serving the central state as deputies and judges, German bishops gained *autonomous* powers as secular rulers.[45]

The imperial household and administration did not differentiate or specialize as much as the other European courts. Nor did the few central offices help to concentrate authority. For centuries, the Arch-Chancellor was the only real central administrative office—but largely a ceremonial one, held by the Archbishop of Mainz (Herde 2000, 528; Wilson 2016, 120, 319).[46] Eventually the chancery acquired some political heft, since the chancellor could set the agenda of the imperial diet, which met more often in the fourteenth century (Hughes 1992, 25). Yet despite the lengthy list of rights and privileges of the chancellor, the imperial Chancery was not even formalized as of 1400 and became politically important only in the early modern era (Schubert 1997). It continued to be staffed by the bishops of Speyer well into the fifteenth century, "a further indication of the medieval Empire's reliance on the Church" (Wilson 2016, 323).[47]

45. In contrast, after the Investiture Controversy, the political role of Italian bishops was minimal: more like regular clergy than local powerhouses (Morris 1989, 535; but see Houghton 2018).

46. An earlier post of the Arch-Chancellery existed by 965. The Archbishop of Cologne served as the chancellor for Italy, but the post declined after 1250. The Archbishop of Trier took over the chancellorship for Burgundy in 1042.

47. The Habsburg imperial court chancellery (*Reichshofkanzlei*) arose in the late fifteenth century, but the actual business of the government was channeled through the *Reichshofrat*, the supreme court, established in 1497 to safeguard imperial prerogatives (Wilson 2015, 325). The Reichshofrat became purely a court in 1559, the chancellery re-emerged as a clearinghouse for communication, and the Arch-Chancellor then became the second most powerful official.

Royal justice was but one in a welter of complex jurisdictions and legal domains, which also included ecclesiastical, princely, and territorial jurisdictions. Justice remained local, princes enforced the peace, and local courts were as powerful as the royal (Harding 2002, 99). No permanent legal department existed and no jurists sat on the imperial council as late as Charles IV (r. 1346–78) (Fried 2015, 211). The *Hofgericht* offered a high court for disputes, but it traveled with the emperor, making obtaining justice difficult. With the 1231 Statue in Favor of the Princes (itself a concession by the emperor to fight war in Italy), the emperor surrendered appellate jurisdiction over the subjects of princes, further consolidating princely power (Wilson 2016, 622; Watts 2009, 210). By 1300, a two-tiered judicial system emerged of local courts chaired by mayors that met four times a year and district courts presided over by representatives of the princes. It was only in 1500 that a third superior tier was added, a Hofgericht chaired by a prince or a territorial court (*Landgericht*) with an appointed judge (Wilson 2016, 623).

The absence of central state institutions and the fragmentation of the empire meant the church could fill in the vacuum. Even as rulers elsewhere in Europe challenged and replaced ecclesiastical authority, the papacy expanded its authority in the Holy Roman Empire. By the fifteenth century, "the pope had innumerable prerogatives in the German territories that allowed him to extract large sums of money from their inhabitants. His rights to allocate benefices, sell indulgences, and dispense with canon law gave him recourse to huge financial resources" (Stollberg-Rilinger 2018, 61).

Imperial reformers sought to increase central authority, creating a common treasury, taxation, courts of law, and councils. Early attempts at reform in the 1420s introduced the system of military quotas and tax apportionments known as the *Matrikel*—but most of the funds went to the princes rather than the undeveloped central administration. (The Matrikel tax, first attempted in the 1420s, would not become a reliable source of funding until 1521.) The emperor made no headway in restoring the fisc, and instead the last of these lands were given away in the 1430s (Watts 2009, 302). Emperors themselves were largely absent from imperial diets and uninterested in any reforms that would mean constraint. Attempts in the 1430s to reform the administration, supported by both Emperor Sigismund and some of the prince-electors, foundered: the emperor wanted to centralize authority, while the princes wanted a more collegial government.

Reform only arrived at the end of the fifteenth century. After Maximilian I was elected king in 1493, he turned to the Imperial Diet at Worms in 1495 to raise an imperial tax to fund the expansion and defense of the empire. The estates agreed to a direct, per-capita tax, the Common Penny (*gemeiner Pfennig*), in exchange for a more functional Imperial Diet that would meet annually, the Public Peace (*Reichlandfriede*, which excluded feuds), and the Imperial Circles (*Reichskreise*, a new administrative grouping to uphold the peace). The

Diet also established a new legal framework with the Imperial Chamber Court (*Reichskammergericht*).

Yet even these reforms proved fragile. Institutional differentiation was limited: the new Aulic Council (*Reichshofrat*) was the nerve center of imperial governance, the advisory and executive organ for carrying out both political and legal tasks (Auer 2011, 64). It played only a secondary role as a court to resolve cases dealing with imperial prerogatives, with judges named by the emperor (Wilson 2106, 403). The Common Penny lasted for only a few years. It was to be collected by the clergy, through a mechanism that circumvented the princes (Hughes 1992, 27). Without a profit-sharing motive for the lords, the tax failed (Stollberg-Rilinger 2018, 53). The estates regained control and remained in charge of taxation until the end of empire. Taxes on the basis of the imperial register (*Reichsmatrikel*) ended, and collective quotas were restored. The states once again paid according to their size, exemptions to the nobility were again allowed, and collection and apportionment were left to the states (Hughes 1992, 27).

The reform movement lasted until the 1520s and had some successes: peace, more frequent meetings of the Reichstag, and representation of towns. It did not, however, establish an efficient central administration with a functional chancery, direct centralized taxation, or differentiated royal justice. The legacies of the medieval fragmentation of authority had long-lasting consequences.[48]

The Irony of Church Success

The very resources that the church had earlier provided—literate clerks, able administrators, and institutional models—bolstered secular administrative autonomy and capacity. Yet they also made the church increasingly superfluous. More and more, lay officials answered petitions, kept records, collected and accounted for taxes (including taxing the clergy, as in France or Spain),[49] and administered justice. Monarchs gained enormous revenues from ecclesiastical office, with the active help of the army of clerical legal experts who "showed the king how to use the ecclesiastical treasure according to the rules of ecclesiastical discipline" (Southern 1970, 131).

Secular officials began to displace clerics. As royal courts grew, they hired new lay officials, so that the percentage of clergy decreased. Court administrations saw a "proliferation of lay officials, who cut into the hegemony of the clerical

48. The Imperial Chamber Court, for example, was notorious for the decades, if not centuries, it took to reach judgements. The Aulic court was faster and more efficient, dealing with disagreements on the basis of legal precedent.

49. The Spanish Church was technically exempt from taxes, but still provided 20 percent of royal revenue (Bireley 1999, 75).

bureaucrats who had dominated government since the end of the classical world. Further, as secular schools developed and more of their graduates went to work in the expanding governments of the thirteenth century, many bright young men who might have entered the clergy became lay officials instead" (Gottfried 1983, 145). If in 1272 the English King's Bench comprised nearly all clerics, by 1307 half the sitting officials were temporal (Mundy 2000, 210). In 1300, two-thirds of French clerks and secretaries were clergy, but two centuries later, only 8 percent were (Millet and Moraw 1996, 177). Communal bureaucracy also became more professionalized, with notaries and lawyers replacing untrained nobles in local courts over the thirteenth century (Witt 2012, 360). Laymen entered chanceries very gradually, but the practice became more widespread by the mid-fifteenth century (Millet and Moraw 1996, 176–7).[50] They were aided both by the rise of universities and by new ecclesiastical restrictions on clerical entry.[51] As a final irony, or perhaps a tribute to the influence of the church, as laymen replaced clergy, they reinterpreted secular offices as benefices. Using canon law, they granted themselves life-long tenure, the right to resign in favor of a third party, and naming their preferred successor (Ertman 1997, 80).

Within the church, conflict over office mounted during the thirteenth century. Bishops proved to be a double-edged sword for the church. They were important agents for popes and helped to build the state by providing and diffusing human capital: literacy, education, and legal expertise (see Møller and Doucette 2021). They also clashed with popes over local offices and benefices. New mendicant clergy, the Franciscans and Dominicans, challenged the bishops' authority. They said masses, heard confessions, and granted sacraments with the pope's permission—but not necessarily the local bishop's. Benefices and provisions were another sticking point, becoming the symbols of papal corruption and greed (Pennington 1984, 116). The system helped to fill church coffers, but it also led to widespread resentment of both taxation and the favoritism that accompanied papal provisions.

Empowered monarchs began to use their new administrative capacities to subordinate the church, controlling its resources and limiting its jurisdiction. Royal authority began to dominate the ecclesiastical: churches were organized

50. In the fourteenth and fifteenth centuries, clergy were still a sizeable part of government councils, around 20 percent in England, France, Spain, and even higher in Poland (Millet and Moraw 1996, 183).

51. The Fourth Lateran Council stipulated that monks and canons regular could not study law or medicine (Amundsen 1978, 33). Mundy argues that such laws drove clergy from the ranks of lawyers, judges, and public notaries (Mundy 2000, 209). However, bishops did not uniformly implement or enforce these decrees (Wayno 2018), and vast numbers of clergy continued to serve. The restrictions were further mostly limited to monks, who could still study law and medicine with the 1298 *Liber Sextus* decree, if the majority of their religious house agreed (see chapter 4).

along regnal lines and subject to lay jurisdiction. The laity in France was no longer subject to ecclesiastical courts after 1329, and by "1500 the Church's jurisdiction in France was a shadow of what it had been" (Guenée 1985, 168). After Avignon, rulers also began to tax churches. By the 1470s, the papacy retained control in central and southern Italy, but elsewhere it "surrendered most of its remaining rights of appointment and taxation to the princes of Europe" (Watts 2009, 301). Even clerical institutions were subordinated to building state power. The Spanish Inquisition became a tool for building centralized state authority: it curtailed papal power and regional resistance, going after the rich and collecting considerable revenues from them (Marx 2003, 83, 108).[52] For their part, "kings too had at their disposal an improved machinery of government" (Morris 1989, 451). Secular rulers across most of Europe could expropriate and tax, assume territorial control, keep records, and adjudicate disputes by the fifteenth century.

Conclusion

State institutions were not happy accidents, nor were they the inadvertent and functional consequences of early modern warfare and interstate conflict. Their roots are far deeper and older, reaching back into the eleventh-century reforms of the papal court.

Medieval popes and the innovations of the papal court drove this early state formation, not war or elite bargaining. Secular rulers could copy these models, and the key royal institutions of administration, fiscal management, and the judiciary were all patterned on papal precedents. Not all rulers adopted these templates, either because they could not, as in the Holy Roman Empire, or because they did not need to, as in England. Not all templates were savory ones, as the sale of offices shows. Yet many early state institutions would not have been possible without the patterns or the personnel of the church. Both the timing and the general form of state institutions can be traced back to the influence and precedents of the medieval church.

52. The Spanish and Portuguese inquisitions, set up in 1478 and in 1536 by papal authority and royal initiative, prosecuted apostasy: specifically, the reconversions of *conversos* and *moriscos*. Both inquisitions came under the control of the monarchy (Bireley 1999, 66).

CHAPTER FOUR

Law and Learning

THE LEGAL REVOLUTION of the late eleventh and early twelfth centuries was a monumental step in the creation of the rule of law and a culture of learning in Europe. Ecclesiastical and lay experts rediscovered Roman law and systematized canon law. New universities taught and diffused them. Scholars reinterpreted legal and religious concepts, such as elections or the authority of kings in their own kingdoms. Some of these took on a new life as governing principles. This reinvention introduced concepts of public responsibility and governance and ways to settle disputes and resolve conflict among lords, clergy, and merchants alike (Berman 1983). State formation itself in Europe depended on "law as both the motive and the process by which state institutions grew" (Fukuyama 2011, 271; see Charron, Dahlström, and Lapuente 2012).

The medieval church was critical to the proliferation and flourishing of law and learning in Europe. Religion had a broad impact on the legal order that was accepted both by kings and people (e.g., Maitland 1898; Berman 1983; Berman 1983a; Fukuyama 2011). More specifically, canonists and glossators (legal scholars) systematized, reinterpreted, and adapted Roman law in the eleventh century and canon law in the twelfth. Both would form the corpus of civil law in Europe. Papal reforms of the eleventh century and the new autonomy of the clerical and temporal spheres created demand for jurisprudence: a flood of legal cases followed to sort out the jurisdictional boundaries. Both rulers and popes sought to secure their authority through law: "there was a yearning for power to be legitimated.... Bishops and secular princes alike looked for men who could deploy arguments, based on principles which were objective and rational and had a universal authority. Only the Roman texts could provide such principles" (Stein 1999, 53). The church rationalized and legitimated the use of law. The church also reinterpreted private law into principles governing public political life: it advanced the ideas of the impersonal state, property rights and contracts, corporations, and the very notions of the equitable rule of law and the government as the common good (Zacour 1976, 133; Nelson 2006, 39;

Fukuyama 2011, 271–5; Møller 2017, 277). These medieval innovations shaped the rule of law long before the Reformation or the Enlightenment.[1]

The church also fostered human capital, by supporting a culture of learning, demand for legal experts, and the flourishing of legal expertise and the universities that would provide it. The relationship between human capital—skilled, knowledgeable, educated citizens—and discovery, economic growth, and the flourishing of societies has been so well established as to become a truism (see, for example, Mokyr 1990; Barro 2001; Goldstone 2009; Dittmar 2011; Vries 2013; Rubin 2017). Universities, scholastic exchange, and a vibrant print culture are all critical sources. Yet while many scholars have focused on the early modern "culture of growth" (Mokyr 2016; see also Becker and Woessmann 2009), the university is very much a medieval invention. And here, the legal revolution and the sheer utility of law led to a huge demand for trained experts in jurisprudence. Universities provided the analyses, reinterpretation, and teaching—and the surge in human capital and administrative capacity.

The coevolution of Roman and canon law was critical to these advances. Around 1070, glossators led by the jurist Irnerius rediscovered Justinian's Codex, or the *Corpus Iuris Civilis*, a sixth-century compilation of Roman law under the Byzantine emperor.[2] Several decades later, around 1140, the canonist Gratian, an Italian teacher of theology and a monk, compiled his *Decretum*, an authoritative collection of papal answers to petitions, church teachings, and canon regulations that also used the *Corpus Iuris* (Clark 1986, 676). The medieval scholars who researched and formulated canon and civic law rediscovered and excavated the same sources. The same principles and theories informed both: "as a result of these similarities in method and places of creation, over time canon and Roman law tended to fuse to such a degree that it was sometimes hard to distinguish them" (Herzog 2018, 85).

Three consequences followed. First, law became a key way to resolve disputes. If the church rarely had pikes or bows at its disposal, it readily wielded sharp legal arguments as a weapon. The Investiture Conflict had already relied on legal arguments and justifications: Pope Gregory VII deployed archives

1. Some scholars argue that Protestant Reformation was a definitive break with the dominance of canon law and ecclesiastical justice (Berman 1983a, 29). Others emphasize that new legal syntheses relied heavily on extant canon law and its direct transplantation into the new legal codes (Witte 2018, 586).

2. The emperor Justinian compiled a law code in 534 consisting of the *Digest*, a collection of ancient legal opinions and excerpts from leading jurists, the *Codex* (the body of imperial laws of the time), the *Institutiones* (an introductory text for law students under Justinian), and the *Novellae* (Justinian's own laws, added after the compilation of the rest) (Stein 1999, 34–5; Jordan 2001, chapter 8). The Codex made several innovations: it simplified the logic and language of the law, invoked liberty and equality as an ideal, penalized behavior such as gambling or heresies, and made church property inalienable (Rosen 2007, 127). It was renamed the *Corpus Iuris Civilis* by the glossators.

and canon law to show how his opponents were wrong (Brooke 1978, 11). More broadly, "the eleventh century rediscovery and subsequent application of Roman law was to a large extent an attempt by, first, the Church and, later, secular rulers to find judicial arguments to buttress their positions over investiture and jurisdiction" (Ullmann [1955] 1965, 367–8). Popes had superior documentation and expertise—and this advantage, in turn, led secular rulers to hire more legal experts and build up their legal arsenal. Law instead of theology now justified the adversaries' positions, and rational arguments took the place of biblical exegesis (Tierney 1964, 2). Frederick I Barbarossa had used legal argumentation to claim superiority over the pope in the mid-twelfth century. The subsequent two centuries saw the secularization of the justifications for power—and their grounding in law, rather than theology (Clark 1986).

Second, royal rule became even more closely identified with justice in the twelfth century, in much the same way kingship was identified earlier with order and peace. Medieval political life centered around justice and the "preservation of public morality and the sanctity of property" (Ormrod 1995, 109). Kings stressed their role as dispensers of law and justice, and they did so with the blessing of a reformist papacy that "saw the clear need for a secular arm and urged upon kings the necessity if messy job of policeman. Thus, at a critical stage in its origin, the Western state was associated with law in the most close and important ways" (Kaeuper 1988, 140; see also Guenée 1985, 41; Fukuyama 2011, 274).

Justice changed from a collective communal effort, where feuds and blood money resolved disputes, to a more centralized and hierarchical enterprise. Kings and lords provided a legal order, law courts replaced amorphous local assemblies, and better-trained and specialized judges resolved disputes (Reynolds 1997, 39). Government activity increased as university-trained lawyers and secretaries interpreted and expanded law codes (Morris 1989, 551). Governance itself became increasingly rule-bound: law would trump custom and habit, and law was systematized, formalized, and applied to new domains (Cheyette 1973, 163). Authorities at every level "began to manifest an enthusiasm for lawmaking, a development that played out across both secular and ecclesiastical contexts" (Dorin 2021, 11). After 1150, even if many areas held onto local law, Roman law "dwarfed them all . . . in scale and elaboration" (Wickham 2016, 157).

Across Europe, the result was enormous growth in legal cases and records, courts and judges. An elaborate and centralized system of royal justice encompassed both criminal and civil cases in England, and common law developed in the twelfth century on the basis of royal writs. In France, the Parlement continued to be the supreme court and gained greater institutional autonomy in the late thirteenth century. The Empire was too big and heterogeneous to develop the kind of unitary regime that France and England did, but it, too, made strides on the territorial level. In Scandinavia, medieval law was patterned on church legislation, and "the emergence of public justice, organised by the Church as well as the monarchy, was an important factor in the political centralisation and in the development of the elite" (Bagge 1999, 737; Bagge 2014, 89). Law-books furthered the idea of distinct state administrations.[3]

Third, universities burgeoned as the demand for legal expertise did. The development of law required both a corpus of law and the experts to interpret it, and the church was a major source of both (Tierney 1982; Berman 1983a; Finer 1997; Verger 2003; Oakley 2010). Both popes and kings sought legal experts to staff their offices, and legal training became a valuable qualification. The first university in Europe, accordingly, was a law school. Popes, emperors, princes, and eventually communes competed in founding these centers of learning.[4] The result was the growth of human capital, increased competition between universities, new ranks of lawyers—and eventual displacement of clerical experts by temporal ones, in another case of the church providing the bases for its eventual obsolescence.

Below, I first examine the near-simultaneous rise of canon and civil law. Law became a weapon, kings and popes competed over the delivery of justice, and the church transformed both legal procedure and theory. I then trace the influence of the church on the culture of law and learning, and show how both secular and religious rulers competed to sponsor the rise of universities and the blossoming of human capital. For all the reconstructions and renovations of the European legal edifice, the scaffolding of justice remains fundamentally medieval.

The Rise of Civil and Canon Law

The medieval development of law, both civil (governing temporal matters) and canon (governing the church), rested on the rediscovery of Roman law in the eleventh century, and its subsequent adaption and reinterpretation. Both civil and canon law referred to Roman precedents; both were interpreted and compiled by the same legal experts; both used the same concepts, whether of corporations or of representation; and they were taught at the same universities. Young lawyers learned both canon and civil law, whether at Bologna or at Oxford, and practitioners moved back and forth (Duggan 2010, 392, 403). Irnerius and Gratian, the nominal fathers of the compilations of civil and canon law, worked at roughly the same time in Bologna. The corpus they excavated concerned itself as much with ecclesiastical and religious practice as it did with contracts and property law.[5] Many canonists were experts in

---

3. Harding argues that thirteenth-century state building took place through the production of remarkable cluster of national lawbooks, including works by Bracton, Glanvill, the Sachsenspiegel and other German collections, Castilian *Fuero Real*, Welsh and Scottish law books, the French *Livre de Jostice et de Plet*, etc. (Harding 2002, 191).

4. Civil law began to dominate the curriculum in the mid-fifteenth century (Scott 1998, 365).

5. Justinian's *Corpus* was full of laws dealing with religious practice, heresy, the recruitment of clergy and their hierarchy, the status of bishops, charities, and church property: religious unity in the empire was a major concern (Dębiński 2010, 35).

Roman law, and many legists cultivated canon law. Gratian himself stated that gaps in canon law should be filled with civil law, and Pope Lucius III in his 1185 *Intelleximus* decretal announced that if canon law did not regulate something, the canonists were to use civil law (Stein 1999, 50; Herzog 2018, 51). The mutual dependence and coevolution are perhaps best characterized by contemporary aphorisms: "the Church lives by Roman law," or the slightly less pithy "a legist without the canon is worth little; a canonist without the civil laws nothing at all" (Helmholz 2015, 419).[6] New laws and old traditions blended as well: canon, customary, feudal, and urban laws coexisted, and the medieval *ius commune* combined both canon and Roman civil law with local practices and variations (Helmholz 2015, 412; Zimmerman 2015, 464; Herzog 2018, 58; Scheidel 2019, 361). Some countries, like England, adopted canon law but resisted Roman civil law.

By the thirteenth century, the two systems were on equal footing: distinct yet complementary bodies of legal thought. Royal administrators, curial bureaucrats, and organizers of new orders were all "drawing on common pool of legal doctrines they found both persuasive and useful" (Tierney 1982, 25). Popes and monarchs both relied on the concepts of the ruler as a protector of the realm with a consequent right to tax, the consent of those affected, and new notions of public office as separate from the individuals who occupied the office (Watts 2009, 74ff). A clear distinction between canon and civil law only emerged in the late thirteenth century (Schatz 1996, 88; Stein 1999). Until then, both were taught and applied in tandem.

CIVIL LAW

Much of Justinian's *Corpus*, including the only copy of the *Digest*, was owned by a monastery in Pisa since the 700s. It was eventually copied, and Irnerius began to interpret the manuscripts, along with four main collaborators, together known as the "fathers of the law."[7] By the 1070s, a monk named Pepo was already lecturing on the *Corpus*, and within a decade, students had organized law lectures at what would become the University of Bologna. There, scholars carefully scrutinized and interpreted the Justinian compendium of Roman law, giving rise to a legal science unknown since the third century. Their glosses, or comments, were added to the original body of law, and a succession of glossators added new interpretations until Accursius published his collection in the thirteenth century (Brooke 1938, 390).[8]

---

6. "*Secundum legem Romanam, qua Ecclesia vivit*" (or the more succinct "*ecclesia vivit lege romana*") and "*Legista sine canonibus parum valet, canonista sine legibus nihil.*"

7. They were Bulgarus, Martinus, Ugo, and Jacobus. Their work was continued by Placentinus, Azo, Odofredus, and Accursius.

8. This compilation, widely accepted as definitive, contained over 96,000 glosses (Stein 1999, 48).

Roman law gave a special role and prerogative to the emperors. It favored secular power and rejected the Gelasian principle of the sacred and temporal powers, holding instead that the emperor held both (Stein 1999, 42). The Justinian corpus portrayed imperial prerogative as virtually absolute, so glossators tended to strongly support the emperor (Benson 1982, 361). The absolute rights of the emperor could not be alienated—not even by popes. Roman law further justified the centralization of power, shifted judicial power to rulers away from localities, and distinguished the king as a lawmaker, stimulating huge new judicial and legislative authority (Downing 1989, 227; Watts 2009, 74). Imperial legal experts relied on Roman law to argue for the heritability of imperial power, and its autonomy: "drawing on Roman public law . . . [legal experts] resurrected the *lex regia*: from the people's bestowal of power on the emperor, he inferred that the duly installed ruler cannot be deposed" (Benson 1982, 360).[9]

Not surprisingly then, the Hohenstaufens encouraged and protected the study of Roman law at Bologna. Already by the 1150s, Frederick I Barbarossa and his heirs used Roman law terminology and claimed sovereign rights (Watts 2009, 60–1). They went as far as to follow "the example of Bolognese jurists who inserted extracts from the *Novellae* (*novae leges*) into appropriate places in Justinian's Corpus, [and] decreed the insertion of their own new laws as laws of Roman emperors. As a result, a medieval user of the Corpus might find a law enacted by Frederick I sandwiched between a decree issued by Constantine and issued by Valentinian" (Clark 1986, 675).

At the same time, kingship became more legally constrained. It was increasingly taken for granted that kings ruled by law, a belief that had its roots in theological convictions about the universe itself being subject to law (Berman 1983a, 537). The idea that political authority, whether royal or feudal, necessitated the delivery of justice, and that lords had to provide justice to claim authority, was already firmly entrenched, and at the insistence of the church (Strayer [1970] 1998, 31; Zacour 1976, 129). The new interpretations of Roman law also emphasized the compact between the people and the king, rights of popular resistance, and the conceptual basis for popular sovereignty (Kern [1948] 1985, 141).

Roman law did not penetrate everywhere, or evenly. Before the twelfth century, legal procedures and ideas were very similar in England, France, Germany, and northern Italy, bound by local customs such as feuds, wergild (blood money), and so on (Reynolds 1997). With the legal revolution of the twelfth century, royal law in England and in the rest of Europe diverged in

9. The Roman *lex regia*, or law of kings, saw imperial governance as an irrevocable grant of sovereignty. The fundamental legal principle was that "*quod principi placuit legis habet vigorem*" (that which pleases the prince has the force of law) (Nelson 2006, 38–9). A contrasting interpretation was that sovereignty was not a permanent alienation, but as a revocable delegation, where people could take back their consent much as members of a corporation could (Ciepley 2017, 422).

more or less permanent ways that are still familiar to moderns. French and European law became "more systematic, more learned, more Roman, more codified, while English law royal law was more particularistic, more practical, more Germanic, more oriented to case law" (Berman 1983a, 478). Roman law first diffused into legal practice in Italy and France, eventually making inroads in Spain in the thirteenth century (Post 1943, 212ff), and belatedly, over the course of next centuries, in the Holy Roman Empire. In much of continental Europe, written procedures dominated, with hundreds of professional judges interrogating the parties under oath in the inquisitorial tradition of canon law.

In England, the twelfth century's great achievement was the rise of a distinctive common law, based on writs (orders) issued by the king. Common law comprised both a set of institutions (Court of Common Pleas, royal justices, the use of writs) and legal rules that gave primacy to precedent rather than statute. In contrast to Latin Europe, oral procedure dominated, with lay legal justices of the peace and an adversarial system of accusation and denial by the opposing parties. Henry II (r. 1154–89) created both the Court of Exchequer and the general eyre, the nationwide system of royal judges visiting all counties with both criminal and civil jurisdiction that began in earnest in 1176 after the Assize of Northampton (Brand 2007, 232). Increasingly, litigation required a royal writ, an authorization that allowed legal action. The system of writs vastly expanded royal authority over justice during the later twelfth century—and created common law. Applicants obtained a standard writ (*de cursu*, or of course) that slotted the complaint into an existing category. Writing new writs in effect defined new offences and created new law (which is why nobles sought to limit the king's authority to create new writs in the Provisions of Oxford in 1258). Nonetheless, even in England, Roman law influenced both the procedure and substance of common law (Landau 2004, 138; McSweeney 2019).[10] Bishops pervaded the administration, and English *ecclesiastical* courts relied on Roman law (Landau 2004, 139–40). As a result, "Roman law was seeping in through all the seams, directly through texts and persons, indirectly through the rapidly developing ecclesiastical courts" (Duggan 2010, 401; see also Helmholz 1987, 245; Brand 1992; Harding 2002, 48–9).

Everywhere, the rise of formal justice went hand in hand with the development of more complex governments and the concomitant need for revenue: "kings employed lawyers to argue their need of men and money, and clerks to record the results" (Reynolds 1997, 41). Roman law also clarified how and by whom the law may be changed, which earlier customary law did not specify (Tullberg 2020, 154). Royal courts became the new seat of justice, and the

10. Roman law influenced common law through judges such as Henry de Bracton (1210–86), who took many procedures and some substance from Roman law in his compilation known as *Bracton*. (Guenée 1985, 33; Brand 1992, x). The first treatise on common law was *Glanvill*, completed in the 1180s.

kings sat in judgment along with parliaments. The machinery of justice grew
as plaintiffs appealed to the king when local lords would not provide justice.
This expansion of royal justice also led to a new professional class of lawyers,
as in England in the twelfth and thirteenth centuries (Ormrod 1995, 4). The
papacy abolished the ordeal in the early thirteenth century, further stimulating the growth of secular justice: the ban created a gap filled by juries in
England, Scandinavia, parts of Germany, and by new ranks of juridical professionals in France and in southern Europe (Bagge 2019, 66).

CANON LAW

Efforts to collate and systematize canon law had already begun in the eleventh
century, thanks to the pressure of the Gregorian reform and the Investiture
Conflict.[11] Early medieval canon law was a hodgepodge of Greek law, decrees,
the writings of church fathers, and biblical interpretation. In the mid-twelfth
century, Gratian revolutionized canon law with his *Decretum*. The *Decretum*
systematized "approximately 3,800 canonical texts on the nature and sources
of law, ecclesiastical offices and behavior, church dogma, ritual, religious
orders, and other issues of administration and organization" (Clark 1986, 676).
Instead of simply listing laws, the compilation assembled thematic problems
and answers, along with Gratian's commentary and the resolution of earlier
contradictions. The first version barely referred to Roman law. The second,
published by 1150, referred to Roman law hundreds of times, and handled the
references with sophistication (Radding and Ciaralli 2007, 179; Witt 2012).[12]
This second version (recenscion) of the *Decretum* appropriated Roman law
as useful to the church. The survival of Roman law itself was sustained by the
church: both because it continued to use Latin, and because it used elements
of this tradition (Scheidel 2019, 516).

The *Decretum*, described as "one of the finest works of scholarship during
the whole Middle Ages" (Morris 1989, 401), became a popular legal textbook,
harmonized and systematized canon law, reconciled contradictions among
legal rules, and offered comments and analysis. It was taught first in Bologna

11. Two notable earlier compilations of canon laws were based on biblical, patristic,
and traditional sources. The *Decretum* of Burchard of Worms, published around 1010,
emphasized the reformist canonists and the authority of the pope, answering juridicial
questions more than ethical or theological ones. Around 1090–3, Ivo de Chartres composed
his own collection, the *Panormia*, which distinguished a hierarchy of authoritative texts
and categorized them by indulgences, counsels, preceptions, prohibitions, or dispensations
(Dębiński 2010, 74; Witt 2012). Both continued to be used after the publication of Gratian's
Decretum.

12. The Decretum was traditionally dated to 1140. More recent research shows there
were two versions, one in 1139 and the other before 1150 (Winroth 2008; see also Winroth
2000).

and spread rapidly, reaching as far north as Normandy by 1163 (Peltzer 2008, 67). By 1190, popes regularly cited the *Decretum* in their judgements (Zacour 1976, 137; Robinson 1990, 207).

A true system of canon law came into existence, replacing localized, unclear, and incoherent rules (Helmholz 2015, 397), with several effects. First, the *Decretum* demarcated the boundary between civil and ecclesiastical legal concerns, and between theology and canon law.[13] Gratian's systematization allowed canon law to grow more independent of both theology and civil law, "contributed to rational procedure in episcopal and papal courts, and effectively preempted the fields of family and inheritance law" (Clark 1986, 676). Canon law collections further detailed property rights and denied secular rulers control over church properties (Robinson 2004a, 289).

Second, the *Decretum* and canonical scholarship emphasized papal sovereignty, and the role of the pope as the supreme judge and legislator. Its emphasis on the pope as the "moderator of laws, the dispenser of the canons" gave intellectual basis for papal monarchy (Robinson 1990, 208). The pope became the ultimate arbiter in the church, and "the years 1073–1216 saw the pope firmly established as supreme judge not only of all men but also of the law itself" (Robinson 2004a, 386). New legal procedures facilitated appeals to Rome (Tierney 1964, 98). And, with confession at least once a year made mandatory at the Fourth Lateran Council (Canon 21), the legal system grew even more centralized, since only the pope could grant absolution in some cases.

At the same time, however, Gratian followed Ivo de Chartres in declaring that rulers were bound by law: rulers could change laws, but not disregard them (Clark 1986, 677). Gratian declared that "although a lawmaker could change existing norms in a lawful manner, he could not lawfully disregard them. This new theory varied from the older Roman and Germanic principle that a good emperor ought to observe his own laws as a moral question, but was not legally bound to do so" (Clark 1986, 677). The *Decretum* further argued that while the pope has enormous powers, he is not infallible and cannot violate the standards of faith. Canon law also used Roman terms for power, such as *potestas*, *auctoritas*, and *iurisdictio*, which delineated their appropriate application (Dębiński 2010, 134ff). In outlining these notions of appropriate use of power and authority, "the Church, and the papacy in particular, played a central role both through its claims to power and through its elaboration of the language to describe it" (Canning 2011, 6).

Third, canon law conceptualized the church as a corporation, a collective fictive entity, and the pope as its head, following (and reinterpreting) Roman law (Zacour 1976, 138; Møller 2017, 277). Starting around 1200, canonists

---

13. In its earlier incarnation, Roman law governed the church itself. Christian emperors in Rome ruled the clergy and called clerical councils, and Justinian's code stipulated the governance of churches and rules regarding bishops (Helmholz 2015, 405).

emphasized that the church was a corporation; even if individuals were fallible or sinful, the institutional church was not (Tierney 1982, 20). Canonists explained the "collegial structure of church in terms of Roman law of corporations, and had previously explained the doctrine of papal leadership in terms of the Roman law of sovereignty" (Oakley 2012, 152). Cathedral chapters, for example, were corporations, but so was the entire church (Jedin 1993, 134). The medieval church was thus a body with a collective identity and agency, made up of individual members who nonetheless were distinct (and not personally responsible) for its performance.[14] By analogy, the emperor was greater than any individual (who was subordinate to him), but not greater than the corporate collective from whom his power derived (Tierney 1982, 26). The notion of corporation was then adapted to enable economic investment and to justify parliamentary representation, as chapter 5 shows.

Finally, the adaptation of Roman law and the *Decretum* meant a burst of new legal activity in the church. Ecclesiastical jurisdiction expanded and clarified. The remit of church courts was wide-ranging by the late Middle Ages, encompassing inheritance, family law, many questions concerning contracts and corporations, and of course cases involving clerics themselves (Clark 1986, 680). The church's jurisdiction was extensive, dealing as it did in cases in which the subject matter was a sin, where a cleric was either a plaintiff or a defendant, special categories where Jews or university students were involved, and where moral or theological reasoning was necessary (Wieacker 1995, 51–3). Temporal cases were brought to church courts because of their perceived independence and better ability to enforce sanctions (Kroeschell 1973, 23).

Lawyers became a new force in the church. By the 1160s, legal experts were in high demand. "The church, in fact, was the first important entity to absorb large numbers of learned jurists, and so became the first home for the new legal profession" (Clark 1986, 680). Lawyers had to retrain—they became experts in the new compilations and council statements, since only those who knew the *Corpus* could "hope to interpret and apply the new conciliar statutes in the lately mobilized episcopal courts" (Bisson 2009, 458) The flood of papal decretals also meant that commissions to papal judges-delegate also increased. Clerics trained in Bologna increasingly ran local ecclesiastical courts and "legally trained clerics were natural people for a bishop to employ" (D'Avray 2017, 43). Academic achievement became a criterion for appointment, surrounding bishops with legal experts. By 1150, canon law was an organized discipline, with

14. Both the reform of the church and the twelfth-century commercial revolution led to a proliferation of new corporations, including monasteries, cathedral chapters, collegiate churches, confraternities, universities, guilds, and communes (Tierney 1982, 11). Universitas was the generic term for all these corporate bodies that functioned as "fictious persons" distinct from their individual members: see also chapter 5.

recognized masters, canonical texts, and places of learning (Witt 2012, 4–6). Lawyers overtook religious clerks (Benedictines and other orders) in the papal curia (Robinson 1990, 220).

Even the papacy changed, as legal expertise became a qualification for the highest ecclesiastical office. Canonists replaced theologians. If eleven out of the nineteen popes of the 1073–1198 reformist era were monks, the majority of medieval popes after Gratian were canon lawyers (Clark 1986, 679; Fried 2015, 217ff). Every "notable pope from 1159 to 1303 was accordingly a lawyer" (Southern 1970, 132), with Pope Innocent III as perhaps the most famous of canon lawyers to take up the papal throne.

The assertion of church autonomy, its centralization, and legal reform all went hand in hand. The Investiture Conflict, the Gregorian reform program, and the rediscovery of law were not independent events. The rise of academic Roman law coevolved "closely with a massive expansion of papal government, driven by demand from below, a widespread tendency to fight litigation to the highest possible court, and a desire for authoritative case law" (D'Avray 2010, 134). The twelfth century saw a huge new growth in legal records and papal decisions, in response to new demand for papal justice at the local level (Watt 1999, 125; Witt 2012). And papal power drew on papal legal authority: "popes were powerful because they had, if not a monopoly, then at least a strong hold over various different grants: marriage dispensations, exemptions from episcopal control, crown-givings and so on. Papal government was premised on that" (Wiedemann 2018, 531–2).[15]

Popes became even more powerful and turned to refining canon law (Canning 1983, 18). For Gratian, the canons of councils and papal decrees had equal weight. With Alexander III (r. 1159–81), the authority on which canon law rested shifted: the law was defined by papal decrees, each a response to an ecclesiastical judge in a particular case (Morris 1989, 402). Roman law here provided a formal and rational legal reasoning that the popes closely followed by the mid-twelfth century (D'Avray 2010). The nature of the decretals themselves changed: if for Alexander III they were responses to particular cases, within a few years, with the papacy of Gregory VIII (r. 1187), they became generalized statements of law in decretal form (Robinson 1990, 200; Robinson 2004a, 394). Decretals, in turn, reified papal authority. To adapt to constant new demand and new circumstances, "canon law continued to develop . . . on controversial points of doctrine, liturgy, or discipline, it commonly issued from the papacy as needed in the form of decretal letters (*epistolae decretales*) addressed to one or more bishops or princes" (Clark 1986, 693). By the thirteenth century,

---

15. Schisms, therefore, were highly problematic: the demand for legitimation dropped, not least because even if one pope legitimated a ruler or a petition, the allies of the other did not have to accept that decision.

the papacy asserted itself as the supreme legislator and judge for the church, and assumed responsibility for the codification of canon law.

Popes now turned to assembling their own compilations of decretals. In 1234, Pope Gregory IX (r. 1227–1241), a canon lawyer himself, promulgated his own collection of such legislation, known as the *Liber Extra*. The compendium streamlined and systematized canon law, and "completed the process of establishing papal jurisdiction as supreme over church laws" (Witt 2012, 435). This definitive text included 1971 papal texts, of which Innocent III was the biggest contributor with 596 (Watt 1999, 125). It was prefaced with a bull, *Rex Pacificas*, which declared law as inseparable from morality and Roman imperial law as basis for papal and canon law. *Liber Extra* provided a universal uniform law for the ordering of ecclesiastical society: "it was at once the most effective single act for the realisation of Roman unity and the basis of the new academic discipline of canonical jurisprudence which provided the intellectual formation of ecclesiastical leadership; 'the most important volume ever produced for the government of the Church'" (Watt 1999, 126). Over the course of 1234–1348, following the promulgation of the *Liber Extra*, canon law developed spectacularly in a "golden age of Decretalists," having "grown from a rudimentary and confused jumble of conflicting and often obscure regulations into an all-embracing and intellectually sophisticated legal system" (Brundage 2009, 485; see also Jedin 1993, 131). Despite the rupture of the Reformation, this jurisprudence was durable: *Liber Extra* remained the definitive text of canon law through the twentieth century.[16]

The Influence of Church on State

Canon and civil law influenced each other, much as rulers and popes themselves did. Throughout Europe from the eleventh to fourteenth centuries, a "regular intermingling of the two laws continued and intensified" (Helmholz 2015, 417). Similarly, "frequent interchanges of personnel occurred between the two spheres of government; a medieval king's 'clerks' were also 'clerics,' often holders of ecclesiastical benefices" (Tierney 1982, 10).

Several juridical strategies, concepts and procedures made their way to civil law through clerical reinterpretation, and profoundly influenced notions of the common good and who acted on its behalf. Below, I examine three ways in which the coevolution of civil and canon law shaped the state: through the use of legal arguments in the conflict between clerical and lay authorities, the impact of canon law on civil procedure and substance, and the growth of law and learning.

16. There were several compilations: the *Decretum* was the first, followed by the *Liber Extra*, the *Liber Sextus*, and the fourteenth-century *Clemetinae*. All were put together by the early sixteenth century as the *Corpus Iuris Canonici*, parallel to the *Corpus Iuris Civilis* (Herzog 2018, 85).

THE LAW AS WEAPON

Law was a potent and strategically useful tool, not least because it was malleable and open to interpretation. For its part, the "church attempted to make the notion of law ubiquitous in Western Christendom because law presented a weapon that it was more skilled at wielding than the monarchs were" (Møller 2017, 269; see also Berman 1983a, 95). Such efforts by the church to tilt the playing field in its favor meant that "by constantly contesting and influencing secular rulers, [the church] shaped the administrative, legal, and institutional state" (Canning 2011, 6). The rivalry also took the form of rulers and popes' chartering universities and recruiting bright young lawyers: the law was a powerful resource, and both sides sought to obtain as much as possible.

For the eleventh-century reformist popes, the law would help both to obtain a new, centralized order within the church, and to achieve autonomy from (and an advantage over) monarchical rulers. The Investiture Conflict, and the broader clash between papal claims to autonomy and power and temporal ambitions, made salient the usefulness of law. Accordingly, with the *Decretum*, the papacy created and formalized its own legal system, autonomous of imperial law (Pennington 1984, 2; Dębiński 2010, 73). The reformist quest for uniformity and correctness further led to the systematization of judicial appeals (Reynolds 1997, 41). As the papacy gradually centralized the church, it used law as a tool of internal uniformity and compliance. With the new teaching of canon law in the twelfth century, for example, students were taught that their first duty was obedience to the pope (Brooke 1978, 11).

Popes and rulers relied on legal weapons in their rivalry. It is clear that the *Corpus Iuris* was already well studied (and even used) by 1076, as the struggle began (Radding and Ciaralli 2007, 183, 212, 103). Its "rediscovery" may have been a strategic move by "those who had already known about its existence but now sought to capitalize on it in new ways," those who actively searched papal archives and monastic libraries for legal arguments that would back their claims (Herzog 2018, 77). Throughout its conflict with the empire, the papacy relied on legal arguments to bolster its authority. Church representatives argued that imperial claims over the church were wrong on two counts: "First, the forged Donation of Constantine purported to grant the papacy secular authority over Rome and other territories. Second, an emperor would be insufficiently qualified. It was the pope, successor of Saint Peter, who was entitled to issue laws for and to govern Christian society" (Clark 1986, 665).

The emperors initially struggled to answer, but quickly realized the importance of law and documentation. If Henry IV could marshal some legal arguments against Gregory VII in the 1070s,[17] Frederick I used Roman law less

---

17. Henry IV's arguments misinterpreted the notion of *societas christiana* as a corporate entity and denied the pope's mediatory role as the vicar of Christ. He denied that the

than a century later to defend the unlimited authority of his imperial office, and to keep alive the older notions of a theocratic monarchy that would trump papal power. Both Frederick I, and earlier Henry V (r. 1099–1125), sought the advice of legal experts in their struggles (Fried 2015, 177). At the 1158 Diet of Roncaglia, a catalogue of royal rights and compromises was drawn up for Frederick "with the aid of the greatest jurists of Bologna" (Tabacco 2004a, 430). When the pope suggested "that [Frederick] held his kingdom as a *beneficium* conferred by the pope, he replied that he held it from God alone" (Zacour 1976, 106). Here, interpretations of Roman law supported a strong monarchy, and the compact between people and the king (Kern [1948] 1985, 141). As both sides marshalled legal arguments, the written documentation of contracts, letters, laws, and agreements became widespread. Legal documentation also improved.

By the mid-twelfth century, law was central to the battle over authority. Canon lawyers maintained that the pope remained the only true emperor (Rigaudiere 1995, 21). In contrast, imperial legal experts asserted the independent power base of the emperor. Here, "Roman law dramatically reinvigorated older conceptions of the king and the kingdom" (Watts 2009, 74). It justified the centralization of power, distinguished the king from other lords, and emphasized the king as a lawmaker. Since the absolute rights of the emperor could not be alienated, the papacy worried that the emperor would gain an edge in his quest for hegemony, and non-imperial claims to power would be at a consistent disadvantage.

Legal arguments used both the *Corpus* and the *Decretum*. Emperors had Roman jurists to interpret the law in their favor, while popes could also rely on "newly ordered canon law with a growing international bureaucracy to apply it" (Clark 1986, 681). Indeed, the growth of Roman law and its increasing acceptance were partly fueled by these conflicts: "the wide popularity of the study of Roman law owed much to the political debates of the 11th and 12th centuries about the respective authorities of *imperium* and *sacerdotium*, of prince and priest, of emperor and pope" (Zacour 1976, 135). Thus, Henry II asserted limits on ecclesiastical jurisdiction over clerics and delineated the powers of the crown over the church as part of the Constitutions of Clarendon in 1164 (Harding 2002, 128). In response, his Chancellor, Thomas Becket, appealed to the principles of Gratian's *Decretum*, and once in exile, excommunicated the King's councilors and officials. By the mid-thirteenth century, both sides wielded these powerful weapons: at the First Council of Lyon, for example, the conflict between Innocent IV and Frederick II played out as a performance, as "dueling documents, produced and read out loud before the assembly, took center stage" (Whalen 2019, 165).

---

pope is *a sacerdos regalis*, who because he is priest is also king. In effect, he charged the pope with usurping both kingship and priesthood (Ullmann [1955] 1965, 346) and put himself and other European kings as the pope's equal.

Both Boniface VIII and Philip IV the Fair relied on legal arguments over the boundaries of papal authority in their conflict from 1297 to 1303: "both sides accepted that the church did have power; the questions at issue were how much and of what kind, and where the lines of demarcation lay" (Canning 2011, 12). Philip IV relied on a small army of lawyers, trained in the Justinian Corpus, who were fervent proponents of caesaropapism (Obertyński and Kumor 1974, 210). Boniface's insistence on the legal monism of *Unam Sanctam* made him the captive at Anagni. The expanded jurisdiction of the church courts in the twelfth century also broadened the sphere of conflict, since the royal judiciary had improved its efficiency as well (Morris 1989, 233). In addition to "criminous clerks," [18] another prominent bone of contention was financial: from the later thirteenth century onwards, "the fiscal obligations of clerical subjects to kings, and of laymen generally to the papacy, became a matter of intense dispute" (Black 1992, 43).

Legal reasoning sharpened, and arguments became increasingly sophisticated. The conflict between Boniface and Philip differed from the earlier imperial-papal conflict not only in that the secular protagonist was French rather than German, but also in the far greater complexity and maturity of the concepts deployed. For example, Gregory VII did not use the concept of *plenitudo potestatis*: it emerged in the twelfth century as a way of expressing papal sovereignty (Canning 2011, 11). Once it emerged, however, it diffused beyond the church and was "later deployed by a variety of other rulers in their struggles to claim supreme authority" (Costa Lopez 2020, 235). In the early fourteenth century, during a similar conflict between Pope John XXII and Ludwig of Bavaria, defenders of secular power such as Marsilius of Padua argued that the church, and the papacy in particular, had no power or jurisdiction in this world (Canning 2011, 102). Marsilius further denied that clergy had any authority to enforce law on their own, in effect limiting the spiritual authority of clergy as well (Black 1992, 78). Above all, *plenitudo potestatis* could not apply to the pope: sovereignty lay with the people.[19]

---

18. Under Henry II, English courts asserted the right to judge "criminous clerks" (churchmen accused of felonies or other crimes). The Constitutions of Clarendon in 1164 asserted that once clergy were found guilty and defrocked in ecclesiastical courts, secular courts would punish them as they would a lay man. A subsequent conflict erupted over 1164–70 when Thomas Becket saw this move as an unacceptable attack on the liberty of the church (Mundy 2000, 209; Jordan 2001, 155). For a discussion of "criminous clerks" and the problem they posed for both secular and ecclesiastical courts, see Jordan 2001. The problem of who is responsible for charging, judging, and punishing clerical criminals is not easily resolved, as the abuse scandals in the modern Catholic Church demonstrate.

19. Pope John XXII responded by labeling these views, expounded in *Defensor Pacis*, as heretical. In contrast, in his attacks on the papacy, Ockham accepted *plenitudo potestatis*, but argued it was far more restricted (Canning 2011, 128).

Rulers and popes alike asserted power to *make* law. The Investiture Conflict(s) already developed the ideas that power resides in laws rather than in character, and rules rather than customs. A turning point came when Frederick II created new laws and issued the Constitutions of Melfi in his own name in 1231. The constitutions invoked "the terrible punishment that awaited traitors, heretics, false moneyers and others who undermined the sanctity of the kingdom. . . . Despite his later quarrels with the papacy, Frederick's court was heavily exposed to current legal thinking in Rome, which shared an interest in the issues raised by the key texts of Roman law" (Abulafia 1999, 503). In response, Gregory IX acknowledged that new law could be made, rather than recovered or codified, but insisted on papal influence in the *Liber Extra*.

Secular rulers now had their own legal arsenal, and they used it to further assert their sovereignty. By 1300, rulers had on their side "jurists who could turn to ancient Roman law in defense of the power of monarchs. These lay jurists squared off with clerics who defended papal supremacy and clerical superiority. The end result was the invention—or rediscovery—of a legal basis for royal sovereignty" (Eire 2016, 14), as we saw in chapter 2. In late thirteenth century Naples, jurists "used the historic legatine status of the rulers of southern Italy, the *monarchia sicula*, as evidence for the freedom of kings from day-to-day interference in their affairs. They stressed that the king was not subject to imperial or other authority: he was emperor in his own kingdom" (Abulafia 2000, 503). By the fourteenth century, the development of law, along with the rediscovery of Aristotle and learned interpretations at the new universities led to "political thought that emphasized state sovereignty over people and property, judicial supremacy, autonomy in legislation, certain control of intellectual life in nation" (Jedin 1993, 205).

CHURCH INFLUENCE ON SECULAR LAW

As we saw in the last chapter, kings responded to the growth of papal courts and jurisdiction by reproducing the appeals system, by competing over jurisdiction, and by constraining (however unsuccessfully) access to papal justice. The rise of these parallel and competing judiciaries belies a mutual reliance. Jurisdictional disputes went hand in hand with dependence: bishops relied on the king's officers for the enforcement of ecclesiastical jurisdiction, and the clergy, as sizeable landholders, also "provided much of the civil business of the king's courts" (Harding 2002, 137).

First, royal justice relied on ecclesiastical personnel. Bishops served as judges in temporal courts until about 1300, when secular judges began to take their place. They judged all clerical offenders and "many cases involving the laity: oaths, matrimonial questions, wills and heresy" (Hay 1995, 290). From the late twelfth century onwards, university-trained lawyers occupied high positions in both the church and temporal administrations—which meant that many of these were clergy trained as canon lawyers. Moreover, "the seasoned administrators who framed the royal judgments which gradually replaced agreements and arbitration awards were often churchmen" (Harding 2002, 126).

The booming business of the English courts depended on high clergy as judges.[20] Before the 1250s, the king of England appointed bishops to serve as senior judges—or more commonly, chose bishops from a pool of clerks serving as professional judges (Dodd 2014, 215). In the thirteenth century, most of the justices of the King's Bench and Common Pleas were clerics. After the thirteenth century, professional lay lawyers began to displace the clergy, but bishops continued to adjudicate prerogative or discretionary cases (ones that fell outside of common law and were decided not on the basis of legal precedent but on appeals to fairness and morality). Such cases ranged from piracy on the high seas, to the incompetence of royal ministers, to local banditry. The Court of Chancery relied on university-trained jurists, many of whom were clergy, and who dominated the court as late as the fifteenth century (Millet and Moraw 1996, 178). Bishops adjudicated "a great number of requests and complaints from laymen that were not readily resolvable through common law processes (in addition to a good number of supplications presented by clergy)" (Dodd 2014, 220). In the 1340s, the crown established local peace commissions to replace the overburdened itinerant commissions of judges (the eyre). Prelates were regularly appointed as peace commissioners, involving nearly all dioceses, which meant that "from this point onwards senior clerics were also, at least symbolically, engaged in regular common law processes throughout the kingdom" (Dodd 2014, 236).[21]

Clergy helped to spread Roman law through papal decretals, their episcopal interpretations, and their role as legal experts. Popes inserted Roman law into their decretals even before Gratian's *Decretum*, and by 1120s, "Roman law was an indispensable tool in ecclesiastical courts" (Pennington 2012, 251.) The papacy "decisively started the practical application of Roman principles in the courts of the Church" (Post 1943, 215) beginning with Pope Eugenius III

---

20. English kings delegated royal justice in two ways: first, they used sheriffs and circuit judges. The King's council would act as a clearing house and direct many of the petitions downwards. In 1258, the justices in the eyre could hear complaints without royal writs, and by 1278, justices in the eyre were given permanent powers to hear trespasses on complaint. Second, by 1280, they directed that many of the petitions and bills would be sent directly to the chancellor, justices, or exchequer. Petitions remained the main business of the parliament (Harding 2002, 179–80).

21. If clergy served as lay justices, this also meant that criminous clerks had a higher chance of encountering the milder and more favorable ecclesiastical judges. Clerical participation in justice was thus an insurance policy for the church (Dodd 2014, 226).

(r. 1145–53). In the twelfth and thirteenth centuries, lawyer-popes legislated on a wide variety of topics, including contracts and property rights, through the system of papal courts (Black 1992, 43). Bishops disseminated papal decrees, simplified and altered them, and favored conciliar statues over papal (Dorin 2021; see also Wayno 2018 for the uneven dissemination and freewheeling "reinterpretations" by the bishops of the Fourth Lateran Council canons). The influence of canon law was nearly universal in Europe; it was studied and commented on at most universities across the continent (Black 1992, 6). University graduates traveled back home to serve in bishoprics, parliaments and courts, armed with the latest scholarly analyses. Even in England, the prevalence of clerics as judges meant that courts "frequently, directly or implicitly, adopted the criteria, doctrines, and procedure of canon and Roman law" (Herzog 2018, 109).

Second, canon law changed civil legal procedure. Early medieval law did not distinguish between custom and formal rules (Harding 2002, 191). All cases were between private parties, and there was no distinction between civil and public law (Zacour 1976, 122–3; Bagge 2014, 89). Local nobles, and in some cases juries, adjudicated cases, which were decided by ordeals and trials. In the twelfth century, the church introduced the idea of crimes against God and society, and bishops as judges in distinct, ecclesiastical courts of law (Bagge 2014, 104). Canon law now required legal authorities to initiate proceedings and gather evidence, rather than relying on private actions and trials by ordeal. Trials by ordeal were forbidden by the Fourth Lateran Council: no cleric could "pronounce a sentence involving the shedding of blood, or carry out a punishment involving the same, or be present when such punishment is carried out." The more specific, and gruesome, prohibition was against clergy performing "surgery, which involves cauterizing and making incision, nor may anyone confer a rite of blessing or consecration on a purgation by ordeal of boiling or cold water or of the red-hot iron" (Canon 18).[22] Once the church abandoned ordeals, they were rapidly abolished across justice systems (Zacour 1976, 127).[23] England abolished the ordeal in 1219, France in 1258 (Boucoyannis 2021, 70). Many princes were loath to end the practice: nonetheless, since so many judges were clerics, ordeals died out by the fourteenth century (Jordan 2001, 210).

The impetus for consistent and predictable judicial procedure also came from the church. In lieu of ordeals, the church insisted on new guarantees of legal procedure in the twelfth and thirteenth centuries, partly as a result of the flood of appeals to its own courts. One of the early canonists, Bulgarus, already described the *ordo iudiciarius*, the procedure of investigation and appeal,

22. *https://www.ewtn.com/catholicism/library/history-and-text-1465*, accessed 11 May 2021.

23. For example, they disappeared in Denmark soon after 1215, Norway in 1247, and in Sweden by the 1260s (Bagge 2014, 90). England had already started to introduce juries before the Fourth Lateran Council (Harding 2002, 136).

in 1123–41 (Donahue 2016, 83). Subsequently, Alexander III (r. 1159–1181) insisted on guarantees to litigants that they would face this order, rather than other forms of proof or procedure (Pennington 2016, 135). Appeals to Rome relied on the *ordo iudiciarius*, even where the secular court systems did not, as in England (Donahue 2016, 96; McSweeney 2019, 73). This Roman-canonical amalgam, inspired by the *Iuris Corpus* but created by canon lawyers, was "first adopted by popes and ecclesiastical courts and then taken up by secular jurisdictions, including royal, feudal, and municipal courts" (Herzog 2018, 85).

Third, canon law exercised a considerable *conceptual* influence on secular law. The recurring pattern, illustrated in the next chapter with the notions of consent, representation, and corporations was that of "the assimilation of a text of Roman private law into church law, its adaptation and transmutation there to a principle of constitutional law, and then its reabsorption into the sphere of secular government in this new form" (Tierney 1982, 25). Harold Berman went so far as to argue that as a result, canon law served as a template for modern secular law (Berman 1983a, 4). More specifically, the fundamental legal principle of *pacta sunt servanda* ("agreements must be kept") derived from canon law (specifically, from the canonist Hostiensis, writing in the thirteenth century), as did the principle of restitution in kind (Zimmerman 2015, 464). Earlier concepts in canon law "regarding the inalienability of Church property served as a model for the establishment of an independent and impersonal *fisc*" (Kantorowicz [1957] 2016, 178). Roman and canon law served as the basis for royal legislation, such as Constitutions of Melfi 1231 in Sicily, the Seven Parts issued by King Alfonso X of Castile in 1265, Code of the Realm for Norway in 1274–6, or the Swedish Code of the Realm in 1350.[24] In some cases, the importation was even more direct: in thirteenth-century Hungary, principles of canon law enforced property rights and established conflict resolution procedures for land disputes (Rady 2000, 75). Canon law shaped western law indirectly as well: "the competition between church and state, the tensions within each hierarchy, the development of corporative associations such as universities, all had a beneficial effect of imposing limits on European rulers and encouraging incipient constitutional forms of government" (Clark 1986, 669). Unlike royal, feudal, municipal, or customary, law, moreover, Roman and canon law were seen as universal and applicable across Europe (McNeil 2020, 231).

Thanks to canon law, both office and state acquired more of an impersonal and collective character. The principle of *universitas non moritur* (the corporation does not die) was already familiar from the traditional doctrine of apostolic succession, which emphasized that *sedes non moritur*, "the seat does not

---

24. In contrast, neither England nor France developed a legal code in the Middle Ages. Instead, kings governed by statutes regarding concrete issues, which together with precedent formed common law (Bagge 2019, 65). France codified its laws in 1805, while England never did.

die" (the powers of an episcopal or other see are transmitted intact from one occupant to the next) (Black 1992, 190). The very idea of the state itself as a corporate body with interests apart from its constituent individuals, with rights that take precedence over those of individuals, stems from canon law (Zacour 1976, 130). Power derived from office as impersonal authority rather than the personal property of the officeholder: "around 1200 any competent Roman or canon lawyer could discriminate between ruling and owning, between jurisdiction and holy orders, between making law and finding law, between legislating and judging, between allegiance to a person and allegiance to an office" (Tierney 1982, 30).

Finally, ecclesiastical courts exercised authority over laity. In thirteenth-century England, "church courts were indispensable to the whole community, for in them were settled disputes about marriage-contracts, wills (and thus the descent of moveable property), defamation, and a variety of breaches of faith. At the parish level they enforced a moral discipline over clergy and laity" (Harding 2002, 137). Family and morality were central in medieval life, and "until the fourteenth century, canon law retained a virtual monopoly on legal control of lust and its physical manifestations" (Brundage 2009, 3).[25] Church courts could also deny access: for example, they would not write or enforce wills for heretics (Fourth Lateran Council, Canon 3) or usurers (Second Lateran Council, Canon 27). As late as the sixteenth century in France, church courts had very broad competence, including debt cases. Creditors even demanded excommunication as a penalty for delinquent debtors (Lange 2016, 103). In England, church courts functioned largely as before the Reformation and continued to adjudicate probate law, family law, and some criminal cases. Henry VIII asserted royal control over ecclesiastical matters, but failed to revise canon law itself (Brundage 2009, 572). As a result, "English marriage law remained largely canonical and was even administered by ecclesiastical judges as late as 1867" (Smith 1964, 60).

If the church influenced lay justice, it relied on secular enforcement, for example when it came to religious orthodoxy. In eleventh- and twelfth-century England, the "king's ministers sometimes called in aid the church's power to excommunicate against peace-breakers (though they resented its being turned against themselves), while churchmen looked to the king for the force to make an obdurate excommunicate submit to ecclesiastical discipline" (Harding 2002, 126). In cases of heresy, the churches relied on secular enforcement: "since the fourth century the Church had normally looked to secular authority to generate the fear which had proved itself to be the most effective

---

25. Lay authorities began to control sexual conduct, especially nonmarital sex, after 1300. They assumed greater control after the Reformation (see Van Creweld 1999; Gorski 2003), but even in staunchly Protestant regions, "an astonishing amount of medieval sex law remained intact" (Brundage 2009, 4).

remedy to heresy and it is no accident that in the central middle ages nations with strong rulers had very few problems with heretics" (Riley-Smith 2005, 164). The carrying out of sentences against heretics and apostates lay in secular hands—those found guilty were handed over to temporal authorities so as to not sully the clergy.

Legal coevolution and influence, the struggles between popes and monarchs, and the diffusion of both canon law and personnel into the judicial systems were critical to the rise of constitutionalism and rule of law in Europe. It is to these legal experts that we now turn. Learned and trained, they are emblematic of a broader development: the spread of a culture of learning and human capital that resulted from both church-state rivalry and emulation.

The Rise of Expertise and Human Capital

The rise of law created universities and fostered a new culture of learning. If law was a weapon, then universities were the arsenals. Law schools became universities, trained legal experts fanned out across the continent, and scholasticism and analytical inquiry took the place of grammar and rhetoric. Universities became a critical hothouse for human capital, creating not only trained experts but also favorable ancillary effects, such as widespread literacy, lower transaction costs, and growing markets and trade (Cantoni and Yuchtman 2014). Even the impact of the Protestant Reformation on economic development flowed through literacy and human capital (Becker and Woessmann 2009).

The papacy helped to create human capital by chartering and protecting universities, but could not effectively control how this human capital would be used. The rise of universities was a direct consequence of the rediscovery of Roman law by both canon and civil lawyers, and the eagerness of both papal and imperial sides to use legal arguments to bolster their standing and authority. If the Investiture Controversy created the demand for law and catalyzed its study, universities provided the supply of legal expertise. These students, books, and ways of thinking then diffused across Europe and found a home at royal chanceries and courts. They would eventually supplant clergy as legal and administrative experts.

Over one hundred universities arose by the time of the Reformation in Europe, from Salerno in 950 to Frankfurt Am Oder in 1506. The first universities appeared in Italy, Spain, and England, and then spread (see figure 4.1). Unlike monastic schools, they attracted students from across Europe. Most medieval universities were not planned, nor were they founded initially by powerful donors. They emerged from the spontaneous organizations of scholars eager to learn and their masters,[26] but then went on to gain a charter

---

26. *Universitas* was the guild or society of students and masters, and the *studium generale* the name for the schools of higher learning until the late fifteenth century. It was

FIGURE 4.1. Medieval universities, 1000–1400. Darker dots indicate
earlier founding date.

(Clark 1986). Bologna was founded in 1088 out of an informal assembly of
students eager to obtain training in Roman law. Some arose by splintering:
the University of Paris emerged as an offshoot of cathedral school of Notre
Dame in 1150. Oxford arose when at the height of the conflict between Henry
II and Thomas Becket, the king ordered English scholars at Oxford to return
to England "if they loved their benefices" (Wieruszowski 1966). The move
spurred an exodus in 1167 and the founding of Oxford based on faithful copying of the Parisian templates. Cambridge, in turn, was founded by a faction of
scholars from Oxford.

---

only when the guilds and schools fused that the university label emerged (Wieruszowski
1966). Shortly after 1200, these universities acquired new privileges and formalized their
structure (Morris 1989, 506).

Medieval universities flourished because both secular and religious leaders required legal expertise. Legal arguments and appeals to Roman tradition— and the experts who could make them—became requisite in the disputes between popes, kings, and emperors. Well-trained experts were much sought after, and universities "reacted to political, religious, and economic pressures by providing church and state with the type of officials or jurists needed to promote their respective interests as well as to maintain order and to further other values, and transmitted new ideologies about law and government as well as methods of argument that filtered into and molded the larger culture" (Clark 1986, 656).

Royal demand shot up for competent men of letters: secretaries, jurists, and doctors to help in increasingly complex administration, especially as cities and economic activity expanded. This was even the case in England, where Roman and canon laws were understood as universal by those who taught and learned them. Bishops and archdeacons both employed university-educated canonists (McSweeney 2019, 74). Roman law was taught at both Oxford and Cambridge. An understanding of Roman law was essential to understanding canon law, and "in the face of an assertive Church that was increasingly speaking in the language of law to affirm its rights, the crown may have felt the need to lawyer up" (McSweeney 2019, 76). By the end of the twelfth century, more than 30 percent of English court officials had trained at universities (Verger 1998, 265).

The papal administration also needed more experts. The flood of decretals and the commissioning of papal judges-delegate in the twelfth century required learned expertise: "the papal curia, and especially its evolving chancery (Rota Romana) which handled an increasing flow of disputes sent to Rome, required a large cadre of legally trained assistants, whom Bologna and other newly formed universities educated. These learned jurists brought with them Roman law, and their law professors' scholastic techniques" (Clark 1986, 680). Legal training became central to the careers of both lay and ecclesiastical officials, including the papacy. The College of Cardinals also became dominated by lawyers (Robinson 1990, 211; Brundage 2008, 132, 347; Costa Lopez 2020, 230). Already by the time of Philip II Augustus (r. 1180–1223), 10 to 20 percent of French high clergy had university degrees, as did some officials at the court.

The church also needed more canonists, administrators, and educated preachers to address the new urban classes and to counteract heresy (Verger 1999, 264). By the beginning of the thirteenth century, universities displaced monasteries as the centers of learning. There was huge demand for the training they offered and secular powers were eager to recruit university graduates: "scholars were necessary for the conduct of business; their presence brought repute to a town or kingdom; they provided a storehouse of technical advice, and ensured a succession of future servants of government" (Southern 1970, 278). The development of canon law required "men who were thoroughly acquainted with the content and principles of Roman law and could apply them to a large body of new material" (Zacour 1976, 136). Indeed, "canon law depended on Roman law—minus its ideology—for the proper technical legal tools to systematically organize its own body of rules. Juristic theologians, therefore, frequently studied Roman law to adequately develop their legal skills" (Clark 1986, 694).

The church was especially well disposed to recruiting university graduates: as much as 50 percent of the Avignon Curia graduated from universities. Bologna, in fact, became dependent on the papacy as a source of employment for its graduates (Witt 2012, 386). In contrast, fewer than one-third of German canons were university graduates (Verger 1999, 79). As time went on, the church hierarchy became increasingly well educated: seventy-two out of seventy-nine English bishops from 1388 to 1485 had a university education, with comparable figures in France (Verger 1998, 239). In the papal curia, canon lawyers "vastly outnumbered theologians" (Verger 1998, 239). Such expertise required training: "new legal learning provided its students with qualifications which won them positions of responsibility both in episcopal and princely establishments. Enlightened bishops sent their promising young chaplains to Bologna to acquire at least some knowledge of the new learning, while princes and nobles seeking to legitimate their power sought to ensure that its results were also available to them" (Stein 1999, 53).

For their part, "churchmen were even more eager than secular lawyers to exploit the newly discovered texts" (Stein 1999, 44). Clergy sought to study Roman law for the "training it gave ecclesiastics engaged in the newly revived study of the law of the Church; young clerics, especially archdeacons, were sent to Bologna to study Roman Law as a necessary prelude to the study and practice of Canon Law" (Brooke 1938, 391). Canon law was also taught and studied at Bologna, although scholars had to wait until *Decretum* for an analogously authoritative text.

The demand for legal expertise meant that popes and emperors alike vied to protect universities and grant them new privileges (Brooke 1938, 379; Stein 1999, 53). Popes and kings did not *found* universities—but gave them privileges and protections that inoculated scholars and masters from the predation and persecution they might face from townspeople. Given their need for legal interpretation, trained administrative experts, and new ideas, secular and papal authorities both chartered these new independent corporations, in hope of training and attracting able future administrators and leading clergy (Morris 1989, 507). As figure 4.2 shows, the race was a close one: popes chartered the majority of the universities founded prior to the Reformation: sixty-four were chartered by the papacy, thirty-four by kings or the emperor, and twenty-nine by both. After the Reformation, secular powers emerge as the clear winner.

Emperors and kings encouraged and protected the study of law (Watts 2009, 60–1). Frederick I Barbarossa chartered the University at Bologna with the *Habita* (1158), at the request of Bologna faculty and students, giving

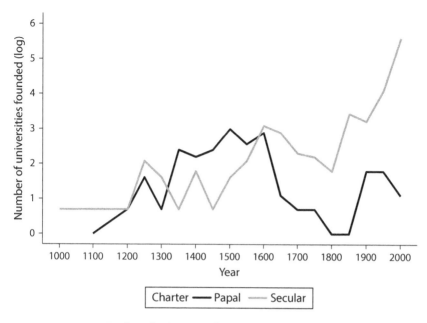

FIGURE 4.2. Number of universities chartered by popes and secular rulers.

students a safe right of passage, and excluding them from prosecution in city courts (Dębiński 2010, 67). The students' privileges also "included immunity from taxes and tolls during the trip to Bologna, freedom from reprisals (liability for debts or damages incurred by a fellow student countryman), and the right to trial before one's own master or bishop" (Clark 1986, 674). Frederick II founded the University of Naples as a center for legal studies and the training of civil servants (Angelov and Herrin 2012, 153). In Paris, the conflicts between town and gown, and the heavy punishments imposed by city authorities, led the masters to turn to King Philip Augustus for redress. Worried that students would leave, Philip chartered the university in 1200 and granted the students full recognition of their clerical privilege, removing them from secular jurisdiction (Wieruszowski 1966, 33).

The papacy also repeatedly intervened to protect universities. Students had the status of clergy, which left them under the jurisdiction of church courts. In 1179, the Third Lateran Council allowed absent clerics to keep their benefices while they were studying. A few years later, in 1181–5, the papacy expanded tuition, or special protection that traditionally covered merchants, peasants, and pilgrims, to students as well (Witt 2012, 366). When the University of Bologna university faced an increasingly hostile commune, the papacy extended its protection in 1224—and in the process, established control (Jedin 1993, 143). Pope Honorius III intervened on at least three occasions (1217, 1220, and 1224) to defend the liberty of students, who periodically left Bologna along with their professors in response to the commune's overweening attempts to control them. When conflict between students and townspeople in Paris (technically, a bar brawl) led to the papal legate and the bishop taking the town's side, the masters stopped lectures and dispersed to England and other towns. By 1231, Gregory IX entreated them to return, redressed their grievances, and conferred new privileges in *Parens Scientarum*. The bull was not simply a local address, but a "full blown mission statement for what we can, by now, call the university, as a key location for learning" (Wickham 2016, 163).

Papal protection of universities also meant the reaffirmation of papal authority. Alexander III introduced the license system, in effect establishing university accreditation. The certifying authority for awarding the *licentia docendi* was the archdeacon of Bologna, rather than the professors, so that the papacy retained control over the law school. In 1292, Nicholas IV reaffirmed that anyone who obtained a degree in Bologna had the right to teach anywhere without further examination (*licentia ubique docendi*) (Witt 2012, 367). By granting these protections, the papacy retained control over universities: masters and students remained clerics, under ecclesiastical jurisdiction. Thus, the papacy granted privileges and liberties that sought to free academics from the control of town authorities—and in the process, upheld papal authority (Verger 1999, 263).[27]

In short, popes and rulers vied to nurture and shelter universities and to reap their human capital. Chartering universities served two purposes: it extended papal and monarchical authority to yet another domain, and it provided both popes and rulers with trained experts who would serve as judges and high state officials. The rivalry between sacred and temporal authorities thus acted as an incentive to charter universities.

Patterns of university foundations show that conflict between these authorities is closely associated with the rise of medieval universities. Figure 4.3 reports the results of mixed-effects random intercept regressions on city-level data with city and year clusters. These models allow the mean of the dependent variable to vary across cities and years, and are appropriate here since universities differ by charter type within cities and years. The dependent variable is the presence of universities with secular or papal charters, split into medieval and early modern eras. The independent variables are measures of

---

27. Church control was uneven. Alexander III's *licentia docendi* system meant that ecclesiastical authorities could control the founding of new schools. Yet the study of law in Italy was a lay venture, and universities multiplied in the thirteenth century, thanks to "the great number of independent burgher communes, all ambitious to outdo each other in political power and cultural ventures" (Wieruszowski 1966, 85). Communes paid for the professors' salaries and tried to supervise and control the universities (Wieruszowski 1966, 87; see also Brundage 1990, 288). In contrast, advanced education in northern Europe was a domain of clergy down to the fifteenth century, and clergy had monopoly over the study of civil law from first half of twelfth century to the thirteenth (Witt 2012, 6).

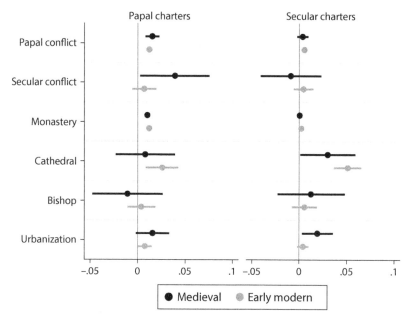

FIGURE 4.3. Papal conflict is associated with universities with both secular and papal charters (ME with city-year level 2 clusters). Horizontal lines indicate 95% confidence intervals. Commune variable not shown.

papal and secular conflict, bishops, monasteries and cathedrals, urbanization and commune status, and status as Protestant after 1500.

Medieval papal conflict is positively associated with the rise of universities, especially those chartered by popes, in both the medieval and early modern periods. Secular conflict is also associated with papal charters, but only in the medieval era. Medieval monasteries show a positive association with papal university foundations, suggesting that the human capital and financial resources of the church supported these.[28] And universities did not come cheap: the wealth of a city (proxied by its size) is positively associated with medieval *secular* university foundations (see Hollenbach and Pierskalla 2022). Cathedrals show little impact in the medieval period, not surprisingly, since almost no universities arose from cathedral schools (the University of Paris is a prominent exception). In the early modern era, however, they (or rather, their resources) are positively associated with the growth of universities. Bishops seem to have no impact on the founding of universities in this specification, but they have a positive association if they are the sole religious factor in the regressions, as Hollenbach and Pierskalla (2022) also argue. (Please see appendix tables A.8, A.9 and A.10 for these and

28. No universities emerged out of monastic schools, which were too isolated geographically and too intellectually conservative (Wieruszowski 1966, 19).

other specifications and robustness tests.) This suggests that broader church demand, rather than bishops alone, enabled universities to flourish.

These results are consistent with the narrative advanced earlier: papal clashes with secular rulers relied on the law and created the demand for legal expertise.

Legal knowledge became a valuable commodity, and both clergy and secular students sought this new expertise. In Italy there were twenty-two universities by 1400, all of them teaching both canon and civil law save one (Salerno, a school of medicine).[29] All ten universities in Spain taught Roman civil and canon law, with the first university, in Palencia, opening up in 1208. Spanish kings founded universities as part of their state-building projects, with papal acquiescence (Wieruszowski 1966, 93). English bishops and high clergy, whether Thomas Becket, Gilbert Foliot, or Peter of Blois, studied Roman law at Bologna in the early twelfth century (Duggan 2010, 395). Oxford and then Cambridge taught Roman law and its concepts and transmitted these notions both through clerks in the royal court and the high clergy in Parliament, shaping common law (Herzog 2018, 95ff).[30]

Popes tried to safeguard their stock of this precious resource and staunch the flow of human capital out of the church. The attractions of secular offices for clergy led the church hierarchy to impose restrictions on clerical legal training and service. To protect the study and practice of canon law, Pope Alexander III in the late twelfth century and then Honorius III in the thirteenth prohibited monks and regular clergy from pursuing the study of *civil* law. The Third Lateran Council ruled in 1179 that "no clerk is to presume to take up . . . the administration of secular judgement under any princes or secular men, so as to become their justiciars." Already by 1163, monks were prohibited from studying civil law or medicine, and by 1219 the prohibition was extended to parish rectors: "clerks were prohibited from serving as lawyers, judges, and public notaries for civil persons and governments, laws that effectively if gradually drove them out of these professions" (Mundy 2000, 209). One justification was that if clergy stopped serving as lawyers, judges, and public notaries for civil persons, they could not get prosecuted in civil courts.

The church also sought to control those aspects of legal training that it saw as unseemly—or favoring secular authority. Since Roman law studies were popular with clerics who pursued their education at Bologna, Popes Alexander III (r. 1159–81), Clement III (r. 1187–91), and Innocent III (r. 1198–1216) attempted to control the emerging university by dealing with student

29. Of the thirty-three other universities in Europe, ten were in Spain and France each, three in England and Germany, two in Portugal and Hungary, and one each in Vienna and Cracow.

30. The influence of Roman and canon law on English law has been debated for more than a century, a controversy begun by Bishop William Stubbs and F.W. Maitland. See Donahue 1974; Duggan 2010; McSweeney 2019.

organizations (Clark 1986, 676). In Paris, Honorius III forbade the study of Roman law in 1219, because he did not want a second Bologna and instead wanted theology to be the dominant discipline at Paris (Wieruszowski 1966). Paris, after all, was the seat of powerful kings who were often not that well-disposed to the papacy (the study of Roman law at Bologna posed no such dangers).[31] At various times, popes also sought to limit the study of disciplines they saw as subversive: logic, Aristotle, and Arab tomes on medicine and science (Morris 1989, 363–6).

These moves had limited success: most clergy were still permitted to take up secular professions, and future bishops and court officials freely obtained an education in Roman law. Moreover, the papal strictures were not observed outside of Italy: in England, Germany, and elsewhere, there were simply not enough professional cadres to fill offices. Even in the fifteenth century, "many secular posts could still be filled by clerics" (Verger 1998, 239). Clergy also continued to learn canon law—and those who were trained in canon law were valuable assets to royal administrations. Trained canonists staffed the chanceries of kings as well as the bureaucracy of the church. For example, most of the middle-ranking administrators at the court of King Edward I (r. 1272–1307) had studied canon law (Tierney 1982, 11).

The flourishing culture of learning, literacy, and new legal and commercial expertise all spilled beyond the walls of the schools. Bologna gave rise to a raft of Italian universities, as communes strove to outdo each other in their political and cultural ambitions. Priests grew more learned: Dominican friars, many of whom had university training, filled the new demand for more sophisticated urban clergy and set up an international system of advanced schools that required three years of university training before permitting their friars to teach (Lawrence 2015, 259–60).[32] By the thirteenth century, reading and writing were common in Italian towns, and "literacy was ceasing to be a monastic monopoly" (Lawrence 2015, 240). Subsequent universities allowed further development in the study and theory of law: "the pinnacle of law's development was seen between the eleventh and thirteenth centuries. Among the causes of those new conditions was the emergence of universities and their particular focus on Roman and canon law" (Dębiński 2010, 82).

---

31. Other French universities then taught Roman law, to keep students from moving to Bologna (Wieruszkowski 1966).

32. Franciscans and Dominicans, founded in the early thirteenth century, entered universities and became university masters, in sharp contrast to the twelfth-century isolation of Cluniac and Cistercian monasteries. This was a problem especially where theology was taught, as at Paris. There, the friars were indifferent to university autonomy and privileges, obeyed only their superiors and the pope, and proselytized intrusively (Verger 1999, 271–2). They demanded to be admitted to the University of Masters and enjoy privileges without committing themselves to the collective interests of the university (Wieruszowski 1966, 48). The pope sided with the friars, but they were expelled anyway.

Universities not only formally propagated knowledge, but they also diffused it informally: for example, the thousands of students at Bologna would lease legal texts and copy them for their own use, thus diffusing the legal training at Bologna throughout Europe when they returned to their home countries (Stein 1999, 53). As several scholars have pointed out (Van Zanden, Burginh, and Bosker 2012; Cantoni and Yuchtman 2014; Fried 2015, 177), universities supported economic activity and growth, through human capital, the formation of networks, and the new legal training they offered.[33] Others caution that we can only talk in general terms about links between the commercial revolution and advancements in education (Witt 2012, 267).

Universities continued to spread. The Great Schism led to the establishment of new universities in Germany and Eastern Europe (see Cantoni and Yuchtman 2014). Paris was loyal to the Avignon papacy, but since Germany remained faithful to the Roman popes, German students left Paris. They founded new universities: Heidelberg was established in 1386 with Pope Urban VI's support; Cologne followed in 1388 and Erfurst in 1379/92. Universities in Buda, Cracow, Prague, and Vienna were all founded in the fourteenth century as well. Yet the schism also meant a new vulnerability for universities: the papacy could no longer guarantee their autonomy, and so towns and states could increase their control of universities. By the fifteenth century, many of these institutions became increasingly secularized and controlled by the state (Verger 1998, 235).

The church actively supported the rise of universities—and thus undermined its own position. The rise of universities ended the church's monopoly on literacy, education, and expertise: knowledge "began to break free from ecclesiastical structures" (Møller 2017, 268; see Berman 1983a, 161–2; Verger 1999, 256; Howe 2016, 204–29). No longer were the clergy the only literate, trained candidates for royal office, who could impart both ecclesiastical values and institutional templates while guarding church interests. Instead, new university graduates now competed with them, often working to enhance the power of the state: "a proliferating class of lawyers—trained at Bologna and other law faculties—promoting rationalism and secularization, labored to reduce the role of the church in government . . . a staff of educated notaries, attorneys, judges, and accountants" (Clark 1986, 679). By the fifteenth century, "the spread of law codes was facilitated by the growing number of advisors trained in secular, especially Roman, law, who increasingly displaced the clerics previously staffing princely chancelleries" (Wilson 2016, 607).

33. Cantoni and Yuchtman argue that universities were critical to resolving the "fundamental problem of exchange" or "the resolution of uncertainty due to highly disaggregated institutions, high costs of transport and communication, and thus high risk of expropriation" (Cantoni and Yuchtman 2014, 839). Yet legal training alone could not resolve these problems: they necessitate a formal system of adjudication and enforcement of such disputes—in short, the state.

Conclusion

The medieval legal revolution essential to the development of the rule of law in Europe was both a clerical enterprise and a lay one. Both canon and civil law drew on Roman law, and they were intertwined in theory and in practice. Canonists and glossators reinterpreted private Roman law, disseminated it at universities, and sent forth graduates across Europe armed with new legal codes and understandings. Law became a potent weapon of dispute resolution, a way to settle both domestic cases and international claims. The church changed how justice was delivered and then provided new templates for what the replacement procedures should look like: a sifting of evidence, the idea of a public crime rather than private conflict, and a system of appeals.

Another medieval innovation was the university. The church's active role in the legal revolution also led it to support formalized education, universities and scholars, and rigorous scholastic inquiry. New human capital spilled beyond university walls, escaping church control, and a precocious culture of learning flourished. In short, the medieval church made it possible for the rule of law and higher education to thrive as they did in Europe.

CHAPTER FIVE

Parliaments and Representation

PARLIAMENTS ARE AMONG the most critical and widely examined of political institutions. These assemblies represent societal interests and make binding policy decisions on behalf of society. They further constrain the discretion of rulers, acting as a check on arbitrary executive rule and expropriation. As a result, parliaments can promote economic growth and build the state by ensuring secure property rights, consent to taxation, predictable investment environments, and the peaceful resolution of conflict (North and Weingast 1989; Weingast 1997; North, Wallis, and Weingast 2009; Stasavage 2011; Acemoglu and Robinson 2019).

The roots of European parliaments reach deep into the Middle Ages, as an impressive scholarship has shown. They first arose and peaked in activity and importance between 1250 and 1450 (Blockmans 1998; Stasavage 2011; Van Zanden, Buringh, and Bosker 2012; Boucoyannis 2015; Møller 2017; Boucoyannis 2021; Møller and Doucette 2021). These early parliaments provided justice: nobles were summoned to parliaments to aid the king in adjudicating disputes and answering petitions. They assented to taxation, if irregularly. They were a long way from democratic representation, but they made possible consent and binding commitments to taxation and foreign ventures. Such councils frequently governed communes (Abramson and Boix 2019; Møller and Doucette 2021)—and less often, assisted the king at the national level (Boucoyannis 2021). Some, as in England, survived for centuries, grew more powerful, and continue to govern their countries today.

This chapter argues that by including the role of religious authorities and templates, we can better understand why parliaments function as they do, and how they could express popular consent and bind entire communities to the decisions of representatives. Forms of consensual governance, such as councils and assemblies, whether the Roman Senate, Germanic tribal councils, or the Viking *thing*, existed long before the church influenced parliamentary development. Assemblies and petitions also existed outside of Europe (see Stasavage 2020; Boucoyannis 2021, chapter 13). But the church provided the institutional templates and voting rules, and above all, the concepts of binding representation and consent, that made European parliaments distinct.

First, earlier church synods and councils provided some of the rules that governed how assemblies functioned. At a time when unanimity and consensus were prized, the church introduced the expedience and efficiency of simple- and super-majority rules. It provided the example of ecclesiastical synods and councils, and their role in adjudicating disputes, settling conflict, and generating governing principles. The church also provided the templates of councils themselves and the *obligation* to attend. Since bishops attended both the church and royal councils, they translated these norms both at realm-level and in local assemblies.

Second, these parliaments concerned themselves both with the provision of justice and with taxation. Church innovations made both of these possible. Church synods had earlier settled disputes and legitimated papal decisions for centuries before the first proto-assembly met in León in 1188. Popes summoned bishops and other high clergy to adjudicate petitions. As we saw earlier, systematic taxation arose first in the church and was then adopted by secular monarchs after the Crusades. The church even made some local assemblies feasible in the first place by fragmenting Europe: parliaments were more likely to thrive in smaller polities (Blockmans 1978, 208; Blockmans 1998, 36–7; Stasavage 2010, 625–6, but see Boucoyannis 2021, 40).

Above all, representation and consent were made possible by church practice and its conceptual innovations. For its own convenience, the papacy adopted the doctrine of corporate representation and pioneered proctorial representation with a full mandate: in other words, an individual could represent a collective constituency, fully empowered to make decisions binding on all (Møller 2017 and 2019; see also Stasavage 2016). Canon lawyers, bishops, and popes reworked private Roman law into public principles of shared, full, and binding decision making: the critical notions of the consent of those affected, the representation of a corporate body or community, and the full power to make binding decisions on the behalf of that community. They adapted concepts used by the church, such as "with full power" (*plena potestas*) or "that which touches all ought to be decided by all" (*Quod omnes tangit, ab omnibus approbetur*, or *Quod omnes*) into rules that regulated first ecclesiastical and then secular assemblies. Church lawyers also developed the notion of legal personhood—the corporation, without which modern contracts, business firms, universities, or voluntary organizations could not exist. Canon theorists even developed a revolutionary doctrine of conciliarism in the fourteenth century, which proposed that a council could overrule and depose a malevolent pope or ruler. The church thus provided the rules and concepts that made it possible for parliaments to function as they did.

This chapter examines the role of the church in the rise of medieval parliaments. The critical contribution of the church was to provide templates and concepts for representation: conciliar examples, voting rules, models of justice and taxes, and the fundamental notions of consent and binding representation. These conceptual innovations proved so powerful that they led to a reform movement within the church itself: conciliarism, which prized assemblies over popes. Conciliarism withered within the church, but survived in secular thought and practice. In the final section, I examine how the same sources that first validated participatory decision-making then rationalized the absolutist turn.

The Golden Age of Medieval Parliaments: 1250–1450

Medieval parliaments peaked in their influence and activity from 1250 to 1450. In the last decades of the thirteenth century, they become widespread, with the rulers of England, Hungary, Sicily, Brandenburg, Scotland, Flanders, and France all establishing assemblies and increasingly formalizing their records and rules (Watts 2009, 235; see also Bisson 1973). "Parliament" first appears in 1236 in the official record in England as a "meeting of the king and his councillors acting as a court of last resort," that had been taking place for decades (Harding 2002, 170; Dodd 2007, 12). We see similar efforts in France in the 1220s, Sweden from the 1250s, Denmark in 1283, and Scotland from the 1290s.[1] Charters of parliamentary privileges were signed in Germany in 1220 with Frederic's *Privilegium*, in England with the Provisions of Oxford in 1258, in Aragon in 1283 with the *Privilegio General*, and in Hungary with the Golden Bull in 1222 (and again in 1351), and in Catalonia in 1305. Even the authoritarian Frederick II summoned parliaments from 1232, as an opportunity for his subjects to "lay grievances before king's representatives before being informed of their tax obligations" (Ryder 1976, 9).

Medieval parliaments varied both in form and in their roots, whether top-down initiatives by kings seeking support or city-state communes organizing their own councils (Blockmans 1978). Meetings were limited by physical distance as much as by monarchical reluctance to call them.[2] They were more

1. Local assemblies carried on these traditions even earlier, as in Italy or in twelfth-century Scandinavia. In Norway and in Sweden, provincial councils were first summoned by the Archbishop of Uppsala and papal legates (Sawyer 2004, 298–9). Bishops and other councillors were also consulted regularly starting in the thirteenth century in Scandinavia and in Poland (Helle 2003, 351). Since kingship was elective, councils were a way of making sure nobles had a say (Ribalta 1996, 21).

2. Many parliaments met less than once a year on average. The English Parliament met as often as three times a year during the fourteenth century, but French provincial estates,

likely to arise where the central rulers were strong and the polities were small (Blockmans 1998, 36–7; Stasavage 2010 and 2016; Boucoyannis 2021). These national assemblies had their roots in the kings' councils (*curia regis*). Their emergence from the king's councils meant that "advice and support, counsel and aid, were intimately linked" (Hudson 2001, 109). These early assemblies prized consensus, rather than debate, conflict, or constraint: they were nothing "like a constitutional body, either licensed to restrain the crown or capable of doing so" (Maddicott 2010, 7). In England, early royal councils were made up of bishops, abbots and *thegns*, older relatives of the king, as well as barons of exchequer and other high-ranking officials (themselves mostly clergy). They allowed the king to present himself as a superior and wise ruler; displayed his standing; and showed off the wisdom, magnanimity, and eloquence of both the king and his advisors (Hudson 2001, 112ff). Parliaments were everywhere dominated by nobles, a privileged minority with the economic and political means to impose its views (Guenée 1985, 191).

What drove the rise of these parliaments? Stasavage (2016) crisply reviews the existing explanations, which focus on war, cities, and ideas. First, parliaments emerged in the face of an external threat or change in military technology (North 1981; Downing 1992; Ertman 1997). Where monarchs mobilized military campaigns, including the Crusades, parliaments became more active (Blaydes and Paik 2016). Rulers needed revenue largely to finance wars and territorial expansion. In this account, parliaments arise as sites of the bargaining between rulers who taxed mobile assets and took out loans, and the nobles, merchants, and cities who provided the wealth (Bates and Lien 1985; North and Weingast 1989).

The balance of domestic power also mattered: most famously, in the canonical account of the English Glorious Revolution of 1688, parliaments enabled credible commitments by constraining the ruler and exchanging these constraints for consensus on taxes and loans (North and Weingast 1989). Margaret Levi argues that a weaker English king was able to tax more than a strong French one in the thirteenth to fourteenth centuries, because parliamentary bargaining led to quasi-voluntary compliance (Levi 1988). Deborah Boucoyannis reverses this perspective and argues that only strong kings could summon parliaments and compel attendance. Parliaments thus emerged where the monarch was strong (McIlwain 1932, 709; Boucoyannis 2015; Boucoyannis 2021).

---

with the exception of Languedoc, did not meet more than once a year, and neither did the Hungarian parliament. The Spanish Cortes met annually from 1295–1312, when the king was in straitened circumstances, but less frequently later in the fourteenth century (Linehan 2000, 625; Blockmans 1978, 196). In Bohemia, Prussia and Poland, diets met frequently in the first half of the fifteenth century, and as often as twice a year or more in the case of Prussian town assemblies (Blockmans 1978, 199). When rulers gained either permanent taxation or independent revenues, the frequency decreased.

Cities are seen as another factor in the emergence of parliaments. Patterns of local representation could shape national-level assemblies (Ertman 1997, 22–3, but see Boucoyannis 2021, 155, 278). In the cities, growing populations accumulated wealth and gained autonomy from local princes and kings. They initially turned to assemblies to govern their cities (Blockmans 1978, 201, 205–8; Poggi 1978, 36–42). Representatives competed to attend, rather than were compelled, as was the case with national assemblies (Møller and Doucette 2021, 66). Urbanized areas had more intensive representation, but the causation has been difficult to untangle. Some scholars have argued that parliaments strengthened cities (Van Zanden, Buringh, and Bosker 2012, 847), while others argue that urbanization led to both economic growth and parliaments (Abramson and Boix 2019). Cities were also relatively small, so that effective local assemblies could meet more frequently and gain powers (Blockmans 1978 and 1998; Stasavage 2010 and 2011).

Ideas are a third powerful influence. Stasavage (2016) emphasizes that the reinterpretations of Roman private and contract law underlay notions of consent and representation. Yet it was not simply "medieval Europeans" and "scholars trained at Bologna" that translated Roman law into principles of representation (Stasavage 2016, 151). Instead, a phalanx of canon and civil lawyers, canonists, and glossators adapted concepts already used by the church in its councils and decision-making, and those found in private Roman contract law. Below, I explore the religious roots of these innovations—and the mechanisms of their diffusion.

How the Church Mattered

Medieval parliaments differed from their modern, and even early modern counterparts, in several ways. Attendance was often obligatory, and representatives were summoned rather than elected. Justice and legitimation were critical roles for parliaments, who processed petitions and settled disputes rather than legislated. Notions of consent and of representation arose, but suffrage and democracy did not: "medieval parliaments did not purposefully strive to become modern representative democracies" (Reynolds 1997, 252). These distinct characteristics all have common origins in church practice and concepts.

Church precedents and its stock of human capital shaped the rise of parliaments in three ways. First, the church lent institutional precedents. Its earlier synods functioned much as national assemblies did: popes summoned clergy, and the councils delivered justice. Summoning instead of election followed earlier church practice, as did majority-decision rules. Second, the expansion of parliaments to representative and legislative roles required principles that the church provided. Clerical reinterpretations of Roman law gave rise to concepts such as consent of those affected, or binding and collective representation.

For example, communal petitions that transformed the English parliament were possible thanks to notions of corporations, fictive persons whose interests could be represented—and that notion came directly from church practice and theory. Third, bishops diffused these practices and norms across Christendom: the king's councils where parliaments originated were filled with clergy and readily adopted ecclesiastical templates, while scholars spread these conceptual innovations across Europe.

Institutional Models

More than a century ago, Otto Hintze argued that "the example of Church Councils in the Middle Ages was also of great importance in the development of assemblies of the Estates into regular institutions" (Hintze [1905] 1975, 318). By the time the first national assemblies began to meet, the church already had centuries of conciliar experience, having pioneered both the papal synods of the pre-reform period, and assemblies of bishops from outside of Rome and imperial territories (Robinson 1990, 122). These ideas, practices, and principles were all notable for "infiltrating at first the ideas of churchmen and the assemblies of the church but eventually moving across to influence secular politics" (Maddicott 2010, 208).

Councils were essential to Christianity: given how far flung the administrative units and the bishops were, it was the only way to arrive at coherent and binding decisions (Black 1992). Originally synods were mostly local Italian affairs, but with Leo IX's Council of Reims in 1049, synods summoned bishops from across Christendom, led and presided over by the unquestioned authority of the pope (Cowdrey 2004, 265). From the time of Gregory VII, the entire western church would take part in the papal synods. They confirmed doctrine, deposed bishops and rulers, condemned heresies, and reformed clerical and lay life. The Fourth Lateran Council further mandated that archbishops hold annual diocesan synods, to ensure consultation and church discipline (Watts 2009, 117). Diocesan synods and councils were critical for two reasons: a bishop had to preside (the same bishops who sat in secular national assemblies), and they could meet frequently: in Champagne alone, nearly seventy such meetings are documented over the course of the eleventh to mid-twelfth century (Demouy 1990, 111-2).

The church pioneered practices of summoning and approval at papal councils that would be adopted by secular rulers.[3] Attendance for archbishops,

3. Earlier papal synods were called to regulate the local business of the church in Rome. The more general papal councils only emerged in the twelfth century, with the Council of Reims in 1119 and the First Lateran Council in 1123, so known because they assembled clergy from across broader Christendom and because their canons applied to the whole church (Robinson 2004, 396).

bishops, and abbots who were summoned was mandatory. Failure to come to Rome or to attend a local council called by legates meant automatic excommunication (Blumenthal 2004, 29). Post-reform councils were attended by clergy from every part of Christendom, and their conciliar decrees were binding on the whole church. That said, despite language suggesting consultation and shared decision-making, their main role was to *approve* rather than to debate proposed reforms. The curia drafted reform decrees and new canons, but clergy's role was only to affirm them (and once in their parishes, enforce them).

Similarly, early parliaments were summoned rather than elected. Attendance at parliaments was a legal obligation, not a right, and emerged where the king was strong enough to compel attendance (Boucoyannnis 2015, 307–8). Failure to show up was a signal of conflict with the summoning ruler (Blockmans 1998, 33). Given their potential for collective action and opposition, kings hesitated to summon parliaments and chose carefully who would attend (Blockmans 1998, 35). Once there, the kings turned to the barons for advice and aid, often summoning only the magnates whose particular cooperation was required. In England, Edward I summoned anywhere from fifteen to two hundred barons, along with fifty to one hundred bishops and abbots, and eventually, two knights from each county whom the sheriff might see chosen. In France, Philip IV first summoned barons and procurators of clergy and communes to deliberate in 1302 and 1308, in his conflict with Boniface VIII, and the attendance of town representatives made possible the great assemblies (Harding 2002, 232).[4]

These practices of summoning and approval were first transmitted through joint participation: bishops took part in assemblies summoned by the kings, and rulers took part in ecclesiastical councils (Mitteraurer 2010, 130). Early synods in the Holy Roman Empire met twice a year, concurrently with the royal council. Emperors presided over councils of imperial bishops, sometimes with papal participation. Indeed, rulers had called imperial councils to regulate ecclesiastical affairs in the empire before the Gregorian reforms, and the pope and emperor jointly chaired some, as in 1022, 1027, 1049, and 1055 (Robinson 1990, 122; Blumenthal 2004, 26; Summerlin 2016). Not surprisingly, then, royal councils by the twelfth century looked like church synods and were dominated by clergy and their concerns (Reynolds 1997, 295ff).

MAJORITY RULES

Majority rules were also adopted from church practice. Specifically, the rule of the *maior et sanior pars* (the greater and better part) would come to mean the consent of the majority as the consent of the corporation. *Maior et sanior*

---

4. For the difference in parliamentary structure, and the summoning on the basis of territory versus estate, see Salter and Young (2018).

pars referred to those individuals who would be better judges of a candidate or an issue (Monahan 1987, 139). Subsequently, however, it was reinterpreted to simply mean the more *numerous* part: the majority. Once again, medieval canon lawyers and legists adapted and extended a concept in Roman *private* law to new, *public* domains.[5]

The earliest electoral formula, whether in communes or the early church, was unanimity. Medieval life itself was saturated with consensus, which was prized as by far the best way to achieve a decision: feudal contracts relied on mutual consent, guilds and fraternities chose leaders by consent, and kings summoned assemblies to consent to taxation. The church chose its bishops and popes (in the ideal if not in practice) by unanimous consent and election (Tierney 1982).[6]

Consensus and unanimity gave way to qualified majorities beginning with the Gregorian reforms of the late eleventh century. Papal and episcopal elections became more important than ever, both as a way of asserting autonomy from secular authorities and as a way of ensuring centralization of power within the church. Gregory VII introduced the concept of the *sanior pars* into canon law, where it stayed until 1917. Subsequently, papal schisms led to the adoption of supermajority rules. Several papal elections in the mid-twelfth century resulted in disputed results, with multiple candidates claiming to be winners. In response, the landmark Third Lateran Council of 1179 reinterpreted canon law and formally replaced unanimity with the greater and better part as the criterion for papal and episcopal elections (Black 1992, 166; Peltzer 2008, 39). Specifically, a two-thirds supermajority was decisive, a rule that begat two centuries without papal schisms (Schwartzberg 2014, 59). The Fourth Lateran Council in 1215 further specified that the election of chapter canons would take place with the agreement of the "greater or sounder part of the chapter" (Canon 24). This majority was sometimes specified as two-thirds, although the Dominican order used a straightforward majority principle since the 1220s in its governance (Monahan 1987, 142; see also Møller and Doucette 2021, 135). The numerical majority alone became decisive: at the 1274 Council of Lyon,

---

5. Bracton went even further and argued that the *maior pars* of magnates and prelates represented the community of the realm (Monahan 1987, 136).

6. Electoral principles were established in the early Church: Pope Leo I (450–64) declared, in reference to episcopal elections, that "he who governs all shall be elected by all" (Monahan 1987, 86). The doctrine of canonical election was largely forgotten when secular powers became accustomed to filling local episcopal offices, but the principle re-emerged in western Francia in the ninth century, and many bishops were elected until the centralizing policies of the thirteenth-century papacy (Benson 1968; Monahan 1987, 88). They were abandoned during (and by) the Avignon papacy in the fourteenth century, largely for financial reasons: the popes wanted to ensure they would get the annates and other taxes from the bishoprics (Schatz 1996, 99).

two-thirds was now considered the *sanior* part (Peltzer 2008, 48). Boniface VIII further confirmed the majority principle (Guenée 1985, 182).

From there, as with other aspects of representation, clerical reinterpretations shaped secular parliamentary procedures: "majority voting, when the optimum of unanimity could not be achieved, was introduced, partly on the model of ecclesiastical procedures derived from the early church" (Black 1992, 166). Secular assemblies also adopted super-majoritarian voting, for example in the Italian communes (Schwartzberg 2014, 49–53). "Secular assemblies began to count their votes," as at Rhens in 1338 or in adopting the Golden Bull of 1356 (Guenée 1985, 182). While the majoritarian principle traveled to parliaments, elections themselves did not. The election of bishops and popes served as a weak precedent for the election of kings: it was generally rejected, except in Sweden, Norway, Poland, Hungary, and the Holy Roman Empire, where the monarch was relatively weak and the nobles powerful.[7]

LEGITIMATION AND JUSTICE

Medieval church councils and early parliaments served to legitimate rulers and to mete out justice. Gregorian reform meant new decrees and canons, and their legitimation by huge new international councils that involved the whole of Western Christendom (Schatz 1996, 96). The new papal monarchy had to be broadly acknowledged and celebrated. At least fifty councils were held during the height of the reform era, from 1049 to 1198, and they served to legitimate papal power, emphasizing his prestige, power, and authority (Summerlin 2016, 175). Subsequently, councils served to acclaim new popes, to resolve papal crises and schisms, and to demonstrate papal authority.

Much as with their parliamentary successors, the main role of papal councils until the late twelfth century was judicial activity, resolving internal disputes (Summerlin 2016, 181). Over the course of the eleventh and twelfth centuries, major cases (*maiores causae*) were adjudicated at papal synods, including the abdication and deposition of bishops,[8] heresy, dispensations in cases of consanguinity, simony, questions of faith, the canonization of saints, and appeals to the pope (Robinson 2004, 375–6). This adjudication also made the synods the site of papal reform efforts, which were then disseminated by the attendees when they returned home. The councils themselves deposed kings and emperors and imposed other ecclesiastical penalties on wayward rulers. As part of the reform movement, numerous bishops and abbots were

---

7. In Poland and in Hungary, the free election of monarchs took place later, in 1374 in Poland (Jadwiga) and intermittently starting in 1395 in Hungary (Sigismund).

8. The *appointment* of bishops was exclusively the province of the pope, but their deposition and excommunication were adjudicated at councils. There was some debate over papal powers here (see Robinson 2004, 374, 378).

deposed and excommunicated at councils (Cowdrey 2004, 265). Eventually, given the amount of business on the conciliar agenda, committees of papal advisers would prepare documents and cases for the entire council to approve (Blumenthal 2004, 32). The much more frequent diocesal synods also resolved a myriad of local, smaller cases.

Petitions played a key role in expanding the papal administration and changing the role of the councils. Demands for justice and adjudication flooded the Curia in the twelfth century, as we saw in chapter 3. Appeals from clergy against their superiors, canons against bishops, and monks against abbots, were frequent. The councils often found in favor of the plaintiffs, "provoking fury and indignation among the episcopate everywhere, but especially in Germany" (Blumenthal 2004, 29). (The angry bishops, of course, then appealed to the papal curia, reifying its juridical authority.) Both papal interventions and new cases brought by litigants were increasingly rerouted to the courts at the papal curia, which meant that "night and day the curia resounded with the chatter and shouting of advocates" (Robinson 200a, 380). Beyond these courts, consistories of cardinals in the thirteenth century gradually absorbed the judicial functions of the synod. The solution to the new demand was thus to divert the petitions to existing institutions, create new ones, and delegate justice to a system of judicial deputies.

These roles were important precedents for secular parliaments. Medieval parliaments legitimated monarchs and resolved disputes, only turning to consent and representation over time. Parliaments recognized and endorsed kings, especially when dynastic succession was in question.[9] Dynastic discontinuities, in fact, offered opportunities for subjects to raise their claims in national parliaments—and where there were no dynastic disputes, parliaments were weaker (Blockmans 1998, 47,61). Thus, the first parliament was summoned when Alfonso IX summoned clerics, religious orders, cities, counts and nobles in León in 1188 to support his ascension to the throne. Royal elections in Sweden also strengthened parliaments (Blockmans 1998, 46).[10] In France, King Louis VIII held meetings to receive oaths of fealty from prelates, nobles, and cities in Languedoc after taking possession of that territory in 1226, to consolidate and legitimate his rule. Parliaments also played a fundamental role in legitimating the claims of rival powers: "popes appealed to councils to judge a king, kings to councils or parliaments to chide and judge a pope" (Black 1992, 45). The English Parliament, for example, spent much of

9. As Rubin (2017) points out, such legitimation became increasingly costly over time, as it involved concessions of both authority and revenue to the nobles.

10. Where the royal elections involved only the great princes (the empire) or magnates (Poland and Hungary), the election of monarchs did not strengthen the parliament (Blockmans 1998, 47).

its time on relations with the papacy in the mid-thirteenth century (Maddicott 2010, 160).

Yet the main role of medieval parliaments was to dispense justice. Much as the church councils had done, medieval parliaments initially served as both councils and courts of justice, and the growth of royal jurisdiction reflected the growing demand for order and civil legislation (Kaeuper 1988). Parliaments addressed petitions and requests for resolving disputes, punishing wrongdoers, and enforcing the king's laws. And here, "rulers had a duty to address petitions, one that echoed the practice of the Pope" (Boucoyannis 2021, 53). French and English parliaments both functioned as high courts and councils into the late thirteenth century (1250–75). Petitions were also central to royal justice in Hungary (Rady 2000, 100ff) and in Poland.[11]

Justice led state institutions to expand and multiply. Where the ruler delivered justice through the parliament, more petitions and requests inevitably followed. The administrative apparatus grew in response. Following papal precedent, petitions to the English parliament were first sent by individuals about personal grievances and cases after 1275, reaching more than 500 in 1305 and then 2,000 to 4,000 only decades later (Ormrod 1995, 68; Harding 2002, 189). Edward I (r. 1272–1307) encouraged his subjects to petition the crown, "particularly as a means of complaining against the malpractices of his own ministers and local agents, together with his formal guarantee that all petitions received in parliament would be granted a response before the session ended" (Ormrod 1995, 33). By 1280, so many petitions flowed into the English court that they were directed to the Chancery, Exchequer, Justices, and Justices of the Jews (Maddicott 2010, 295–6). Property rights and the resolution of landholding disputes were the chief concerns (Harding 2002, 132). The result of this opening up of royal courts to oral plaints and informal petitions was the "bill revolution" of the 1290s (Harding 2002, 181). Parliaments also adjudicated property disputes and personal cases against nobles, giving them an incentive to attend.

In contrast, in the Holy Roman Empire, justice and legislation did not fuse. Emperors asserted legislative authority with the peace ordinances (*Landfriede*) of 1152 and 1235, but continued to rely on local nobles enforcing the peace as provincial judges, and the local courts (*Landgerichte*) remained powerful (Harding 2002, 99). Decentralized rule in the empire meant that "it was only during the difficulties of Louis of Bavaria with the pope in 1338–44 that the king sought the active support of all his subjects" (Blockmans 1998, 43).

---

11. Polish and Hungarian kings served as judges by the fourteenth century. The Hungarian king Béla III expressly directed in the last quarter of the twelfth century that plaints be directed as written petitions, "as in the Roman curia and the Empire" (Rady 2000, 100).

As a result, the Imperial Diet (formally the Reichstag as of 1489) could not be described as a national assembly, or even a formalized institution, until at least 1470 (Blockmans 1998, 3). Ecclesiastical and temporal princes were obliged to meet irregularly at the court of the emperor (the meetings were known as the Hoftage, or the King's assemblies).[12] Both the invitations and the agenda were at the emperor's discretion, and so the meetings could not provide the kind of consent that regularized parliaments with fixed memberships could. As a result, these meetings also did little to deliver justice or bind the empire together. Instead, the Diet served largely as an "ad-hoc, ceremonial, and courtly assembly" (Stollberg-Rilinger 2018, 115). *"Sitz und Stimme,"* or a seat and a vote in the Imperial Diet, denoted status but not the ability to deliver justice, represent communities or make binding commitments (Stollberg-Rilinger 2018, 18). There was no majority voting until 1497, and even then summons to the diet meant assent to its conclusions. The Diet acquired a fixed membership in 1521 based on estates (Wilson 2016, 408), but the emperor and the princes no longer attended. It was only in 1663, centuries after others, that a permanent institution was finally established, with the emperor as "an essential, integral part of the diet" (Härter 2011, 123). Ecclesiastical precedents and templates could only be taken up by rulers who had the capacity to do so.

CONSENT AND TAXATION

Papal councils turned to legislation over the twelfth century, though their role was largely limited to acclaim rather than the creation of new legislation. Starting with the First Lateran Council in 1123, popes summoned the clergy to pass ambitious new legislation. Hundreds of clergy from all over Christendom attended, and their presence was mandatory. In the 1140s and 50s, both popes and canonists such as Rufinus and Gratian further linked councils to the making of law (Robinson 2004, 396). Critically, by the end of the thirteenth century, the advisory and judicial role of the earlier synods disappeared, and instead the councils focused on the new statutes and approving reforms. Already in the eleven councils of Urban II (r. 1088–99), "consultation and debate tended to be replaced by the more monarchical procedure of promulgation of decrees by the pope, followed by acclamation by the bishops" (Robinson 2004, 397).

Taxation led to new forms of representation and consent. Before 1217, cathedral chapters were not represented at church councils (Kay 2002, 96). Once the clergy began to be taxed at the end of the twelfth century, however, canon

12. Regional assemblies, known as Landtage, were also held, but dominated by the princes (Ozment 1980, 185). See Carsten (1959) on the regional assemblies, and especially their early modern activity.

law made it clear that a bishop could not make major commitments without consulting his clergy. Pope Innocent III pioneered binding representation when he summoned procurators with full power from the six cities of the March of Ancona to meet with him in the Curia in 1200 (Post 1964, 88, Guenée 1985, 175). Given his background as a law student at Bologna, it is "not surprising that the chancery of Innocent III was fully acquainted with the Roman terminology and meaning of corporate representation" (Post 1943, 229). These principles were now to be expanded to the entire church.

The turning point came in 1215, when Innocent III widely summoned clergy to the Fourth Lateran Council. The council would discuss property rights and taxation—matters that touched the chapters directly. Accordingly, the pope called for church chapters to send suitable representatives to the council, as several decisions regarding the chapters would be made there (Kay 2002, 97). Innocent III himself also sent legates as full representatives to the Cortes of Lérida in 1214, to resolve royal succession in Aragon (Post 1964, 88; Møller and Doucette 2021, 112). Reaffirming the right of clerical representation, Honorius III issued the decree *Etsi membra corporis* in 1217, which "firmly established the chapters' right to be heard through their representatives at ecclesiastical assemblies. The decision has great significance in the growth of western parliamentary institutions because it fostered the development of the theory of, as well as the practice, of political representation" (Kay 2002, 98).

The Fourth Lateran Council also served as a precedent for *limiting* taxation, specifically on ecclesiastical taxes on the clergy. The clergy would tax itself only when necessary, and "among the laity this must have created a desire for analogous treatment" (Marongiu 1968, 38). The newly empowered clergy used their powers: the Council of Bourges in 1225 sharply rejected papal plans for general taxation of the church, while Lyon in 1245 heard complaints about papal provisions from the barons of England (Watts 2009, 117). As early as 1225, church chapters refused to pay taxes because they were not consulted (Stasavage 2020, 118–9). From 1300 on, councils asserted their rights to govern with the pope, as opposed to assenting to his plans.

Initially, secular assemblies also had little to do with either taxation or constraining the monarch. In twelfth-century English assemblies, for example, "general taxes were at most only rarely and barely linked with consent" (Maddicott 2010, 103), largely because until 1162, the only direct tax was the geld, which fell mostly on the peasantry and thus required no sanction. Indeed, "the old theory—that representative institutions developed because princes needed financial subsidies and accordingly took the initiative in summoning assemblies—is simply at variance with the facts. Defence of their own concerns, not financial policy, was the original function of the assemblies" (Blockmans 1978, 202; see also Boucoyannis 2021, chapter 6). Even as the

English Parliament assumed a political role in the fourteenth century, "if the series of parliamentary petitions, statutes, and judicial commissions are taken together, local justice and not taxation is seen to be the first great subject of political discussion between the king and the people" (Harding 2002, 185). Only a minority of parliaments served to assent to taxes (Dodd 2007, 131). Even after 1295, only one-quarter to one-third of sessions dealt with taxation (Boucoyannis 2021, 45).

Yet taxation mattered because it required consent. English nobles were taxed and so had good reason to insist on monitoring and agreeing to levies, even if they were a minor part of the agenda.[13] Taxation was largely dependent on cooperation: with no standing army or police force, even the highly organized English central administration could not simply enforce taxes by force (Ormrod 2000, 285). As a result, taxation required both acquiescence— and notions of representation, where those in the Parliament could bind their constituencies to parliamentary decisions. Magnates and prelates assented to taxes in exchange for reaffirmation of their rights and privileges. As royal taxation expanded, the role of the magnates shifted from barons of the king to "spokesmen for a broader collective" (Maddicott 2010, 142).

The church provided not only a template, but also active support. In their role as members of Parliament, bishops insisted on the representation they experienced in papal councils and local synods. Already in England between 1220s and 1250s, representation was broadened to include knights and burgesses, and behind this shift "lay the dual influence of frequent requests for taxation, chiefly royal but also papal, and of clerical insistence on the inability of great men to bind their inferiors to taxation's payments without some extended form of consent. The magnates were no longer see as fully representative of the realm" (Maddicott 2010, 218).

As taxation expanded, parliaments increasingly became the site of both representation and conditional consent—and refusal.[14] Taxes impinged on all subjects, and the men who sanctioned the taxes were seen as standing in for— representing—their communities. The English crown formally summoned lay and ecclesiastical tenants in chief, and also knights (1254), townsmen (1265), and clergy (1297) to the national assemblies (Guenée 1985, 175). Representation expanded, if democracy did not. English knights of the shire representing the counties were present at parliament by the 1220s, but were formally summoned

13. The payment of taxes by the nobility was a peculiar feature of English system, creating strong incentives for English barons to attend parliament (Maddicott 2010, 430). Parliaments in Léon and in Aragon by the early thirteenth century also bargained over taxes. In contrast, French nobility did not have to pay taxes (but voted on them) and received a formal exemption from direct taxation in 1384.

14. For example, over 1237–72, the English Parliament refused all nine royal requests for additional taxes (Mitchell 1951, 94).

as such in 1254 (and until 1918) (Maddicott 2010, 199 and 207).[15] City representatives (burgesses) were summoned by Simon Montfort for the parliaments of
1258 and 1265. The short-lived Provisions of Oxford of 1258 further systematized
representation, introducing a regular national assembly.[16] In other words, if the
royal "compellence of the nobility generated the *institution* of parliament . . .
compelling attendance from the Commons, on the other hand, generated the
practice of 'representation'" (Boucoyannis 2015, 307). Similarly, in Iberia, the
clergy, barons, and towns were summoned regularly from 1280 onwards, debat-
ing privileges, preservation of peace, justice, approval of statutes, and taxes,
since "extensive warfare against Castile made Aragonese kings highly dependent
on their corts" (Blockmans 1998, 50).

This expansion of parliamentary representation increased its authority. By
the 1250s it was clear that the English lower clergy and knights would reject
a request for taxation unless it was credible: that is, unless they had a say in it
(Maddicott 2010, 195), and by 1327, their full inclusion became the norm. The
new understanding of consent shifted from a few magnates to a far broader
body of shire and town representatives (Ormrod 1995, 32). In 1295, Edward I
summoned knights and burgesses to the celebrated "Model Parliament."
Instead of being summoned to assent to decisions already made by the king
and the barons, however, the Commons was now summoned with the *plena
potestas*, the "full power" to represent their communities and to assent to taxation in their name, decisions made at the Parliament itself. By the end of the
reign of Edward III (r. 1327–77), the Commons was the only body that could
impose taxation (Ormrod 2000, 292).

As a result, the English Parliament transformed into a "major political
institution" over the course of the fourteenth century (Ormrod 2000, 295).

---

15. The dominant unit of representation in England was the shire, since towns were
not as powerful or autonomous. In contrast, in Spain, Scotland, and few French regional
assemblies, the local electing body was the town. (Maddicott 2010, 408). France failed to
develop any clear or consistent units of representation.

16. After his victory at the Battle of Lewes in 1258, Simon de Montfort and his allied
barons stripped Henry III of his powers. The 1258 Provisions of Oxford included the representation of towns, called for Parliament to meet thrice a year, and established a privy
council of 24 barons. The council made all decisions, in consultation with Parliament.
English clergy backed de Montfort and the Provisions of Oxford (Maddicott 1996, 354).
The 1259 Provisions of Westminster reformed courts and taxation laws, and established
laws of mortmain: the perpetual ownership of land by a corporation. While the provisions
of Oxford were reversed, those of Westminster remained, but not before de Montfort and
the Second Barons' War of 1263–7 tried to force Henry to abide by both. The subsequent
1279 and 1290 Statutes of Mortmain required the authorization of the crown before land
could pass perpetually into a corporation, an important change since the church owned
enormous tracts of land in perpetuity. Westminster also granted the lower aristocracy the
right to occupy the most important administrative positions. Barons and knights became
royal justices and administrators, gaining decisive influence over the kingdom's policies
and finances (Ozment 1980, 183; Fried 2015, 297).

Individual petitions seeking redress and justice were replaced by petitions filed in the name of the community—first at the behest of the nobility and then, as early as 1315, in the name of the "community of the realm," affected by everything from river obstructions on the Thames to abusive magnates (Dodd 2007, 130). Thanks to these communal petitions, the English Parliament began to acquire a legislative role, since kings answered communal petitions with new laws regarding property rights, landholding, and administration (Harding 2002, 172). By the 1370s, the Commons had become the focal point for legislative activity, since filing a petition through the Commons ensured it would be heard by the king (Ormrod, Dodd, and Musson 2009, 13). Nearly all legislation of the fourteenth century had petitions as their origin (Boucoyannis 2020, 56). Members could now defend the interests of their communities and implicitly link aid to the king to these interests (Kaeuper 1988, 289).[17] In fact, the king himself could be targeted, as in the "Merciless Parliament" of 1388.[18]

While taxation led to the expansion of representation in both the church and the English Parliament, it failed to do so in France. Unlike either the high clergy or English barons, French nobles were exempt from taxation, so they had less of an incentive to attend or monitor. The French Parlement functioned as a central high court, but any political and legislative roles were devolved to the Estates General and provincial assemblies, which met rarely.[19] As a result, Parlement was overrun with judiciary business, and monarchs had no forum where they could obtain consent to systematic and universal taxation. French kings instead had to improvise, relying on tax farming, expropriation, and indirect taxes. When Philip IV finally called a national assembly, the Estates General, for their first meeting in 1302, it was largely a propaganda exercise designed to legitimate the king and to shore up support for the monarchy in its conflict with the papacy: "the formidable influence of the Church explains the king's urgent search for support" (Blockmans 1998, 51). Taxation was not decided at the next meeting in 1308, either. Instead, the French monarchy largely relied on indirect taxes,[20] which made the French king independent of the estates—and less likely to call an assembly (Blockmans 1998, 52). After

17. Parliament also made consent to taxation conditional on relief of grievances. By the end of the fourteenth century, Parliament waited to assent to taxes until the last day of the session, when the crown's responses to petitions were read out (Ormrod 1995, 36).

18. In 1387, a group of judges decided the king could call and dissolve parliaments as he pleased. In response, the 1388 Parliament impeached Richard's Chancellor, Michael de la Pole, and convicted him of treason, exiled the judges to Ireland, and imprisoned clerks in a "ruthless and wholesale elimination of Richard's household" (Barron 2000, 315).

19. Notoriously, for example, the 1779 meeting of the French Estates General was the first since 1614.

20. Indirect taxes largely escaped the notice of the estates and parliaments: for example, the salt taxes (*gabelle*) went uncontested by the French estates general in 1355, as did their increase in 1435 and from 1440 onwards, the introduction of the taille. Philip IV also expropriated Jews, Templars, and clergy.

1275, then, the French and English parliaments diverge: the French Parlement continued to administer justice, while the English turned to lawmaking, taxation, and representation.[21]

The English Parliament was unusual in its growing power, and the French in its relegation to judicial activity. In the Holy Roman Empire, power was too fragmented and local nobles for national assemblies to function. The emperor called assemblies fairly frequently, with over forty meetings between 1314 and 1400 (Wilson 2016, 404). Yet they had no power to tax, did not function as the highest court in the land, and could withhold men and money, but had no active prerogatives (Scott 1998, 349). The seven electors were the only members of the diet with real power: others had little to say and tended to attend only sporadically.[22] Similarly, taxation did not expand national representation or administration elsewhere: regional rather than national assemblies continued to make decisions in France, Scandinavia, and Poland.[23] In Hungary, nobles exempt from taxation rarely insisted on approving taxation, instead finding it "cheaper to empower the king for years in advance, rather than spend weeks at the diet" (Bák 1998, 721).

Parliamentary Principles

Concepts essential to modern parliamentary practice have their roots in church practice, theory, and interpretations of canon and Roman law (Møller 2018). Foremost among these are the notions of consent and binding representation, first developed by the church in the twelfth century, and then applied at the councils of the early thirteenth. Canonists intensely theorized representation in the church, as a "regular, inherent, and sanctified part of it as no other organization" (Black 1992, 169). These are indelibly part of secular parliaments, even if these "forms and procedures derived from ecclesiastical concepts and models have been introduced on such a broad basis and over so long a period of time that they simply have become part of the generally accepted way of handling these matters" (Monahan 1987, 135). Ecclesiastical interpretations and practices gave counsel and consent new justification, meaning, and domain of application.

Taken together, the notions of consent, binding representation, and the corporation make possible modern representative democracy. Of course, these

21. The English Parliament could pivot to legislature because specialized courts, such as Common Pleas (founded in 1178), King's Bench (also late twelfth century), and Chancery (mid-fourteenth century), were in place (Harding 2002, 185). See chapter 3.

22. The secular princes only appeared as a corporate body, a curia, alongside the electors in 1487 (Scott 1998, 349).

23. The Polish Sejm arose independently of the regional *sejimiki*, the regional assemblies. Its rise is traditionally dated to 1386 and the Act of Union with Lithaunia. (See Górski et al. 1966).

principles were often more aspirational than descriptive: actual political practice often did not mirror high theory. Indeed, the "theory of government by consent . . . was fully formulated by the early fourteenth century; the practice of government by hierarchy, status, and degree continued to flourish in the 17th" (Tierney 1982, 52; see also Reynolds 1997). Nonetheless, modern democratic representation relies on these concepts.

QUOD OMNES TANGIT

Among the most important concepts was that of consent, or *Quod omnes tangit, ab omnibus debet comprobari,* or "that which touches all, should be approved by all." The principle originated in the church, when canon lawyers expanded the precedent that acts of popes and bishops required the approval of councils (Nelson 2006, 39). It was first used by Pope Innocent III in 1200 to summon representatives from cities in the Papal States. Frederick II then used it in 1231 to convene Italian city representatives (Tierney 1982, 24; Stasavage 2016; Stasavage 2020, 127). Implied at the Third Lateran Council in 1179, it was expressly cited at the Fourth in 1215 (Guenée 1985, 174). By the end of the thirteenth century, the principle appeared regularly in the writs of summons to secular assemblies (Tierney 1966, 13) and "permeated the atmosphere everywhere" (Guenée 1985, 174). *Quod omnes* became "the commonest justification for parliaments and was used both by kings and Estates, to express both the duty and the right to consultation" (Black 1992, 166). Thanks to *Quod omnes,* popular consent, rather than divine sanction or coercion, would legitimate political decisions.

Quod omnes began as a technicality of Roman contract law, referring to the consultation of those affected by a contract or a will: for example, all heirs of a will must be consulted. The relevant actor expressing approval was the individual, rather than a community or a corporation. The principle was already found in the Justinian code of 531. Interest in the principle developed in canonical circles in the eleventh century in connection to the election of bishops, and by the mid-twelfth century Bernard of Clairvaux wrote of "an ancient rule" that everyone affected by an episcopal election should participate in it (Monahan 1987, 99). Canon lawyers then reinvented the principle, from private contract law to a public rule: "a matter that 'touched' a whole community could be approved by a representative assembly acting on behalf of all" (Tierney 1982, 25).[24] By 1200, the phrase was used in general church councils, at the Fourth Lateran council in 1215, and at subsequent ones. By the thirteenth century,

24. These interpretations were critical, since *Quod omnes* was highly malleable: William of Ockham, for example, used it to justify individuals calling councils, consent as a one-time event, imperial autonomy, and the principle that those who benefit ought to pay (Nederman 2021).

Quod omnes implied supermajority rule, rather than unanimous consent (Post 1964, 72; Schwartzberg 2014, 57–8).

Parliamentary assemblies followed ecclesiastical councils in adopting the principle. It was already used by the English king Henry III in 1225 (Maddicott 2010, 209), and it spread across Europe by the mid-thirteenth century (Monahan 1987, 100). It was pervasive: "every major work on law and political theory written around 1300 contains at least some passing reference to consent" (Tierney 1982, 42). *Quod omnes* became a standard formula legitimating "inevitable political choices where broad support for difficult demands was needed" (Blockmans 1998, 49–50). Thus, "in 1244 the Emperor Frederick II had quoted it in the summons of a great assembly of ecclesiastical and lay princes, as Rudolf of Habsburg had to do in 1274" (Blockmans 1998, 49–50). In 1254 in England, "these clerical practices were adopted as a model for the representation of the laity," with the representation of shires and towns (Maddicott 2010, 210). King Edward I's writ of summons for the 1295 Model Parliament used the *Quod omnes* formula, and it became "used invariably from 1294 to 1872" (Tierney 1982, 24). Philip IV, in summoning the French Estates General in 1302, also relied on the formula (McIlwain [1973] 1932, 57). Characteristically, the Imperial Diet of the Holy Roman Empire did not use this template. It was only in the sixteenth century that new reforms sought to make all of the Reichstag bound by its decisions (Stollberg-Rilinger 2018, chapter 3).

Quod omnes was used by popes and kings alike to deflect requests for money as much as to justify them. Thus, in the 1220s, Pope Honorius III proposed to fund the papal curia by imposing a tax on the prebendal income enjoyed by cathedral chapters. The proposal was discussed and rejected at the Council of Bourges in 1225. Undaunted, Honorius tried again: the papal nuncio brought the same proposal to Henry III, but was told that king could not settle the matter because of the strictures of *Quod omnes*. The English prelates, in turn, deferred a decision because the king and magnates were not present. The nuncio went away empty-handed (Maddicott 2010, 209). Bishops also insisted that lower clergy could not be taxed without their consent: clerical representatives were summoned both to episcopal synods and to the English parliament (Maddicott 2010, 216–7).

What was meant by consent in the medieval practice of *Quod omnes*? Consent was *not* a limit on royal action, an assertion of popular sovereignty, or a constitutional principle in the twelfth or thirteenth centuries. It was a form of legitimation. The traditional limitations of being bound by law, rather than consent, served to constrain medieval executives (Monahan 1987, 110 and 263). Even as assent to taxes was sought by the king, there was little talk of constraining rapacious monarchs, as analyses of early modern parliaments would have. Medieval kings were supposed to be limited by law, custom, and consultation with bishops and nobles who spoke on behalf of the collectivity (Reynolds 1997, 22). In this setting, consent and consultation delineated just kings from tyrants: "the twelfth century already held firmly to the doctrine that the just ruler ruled for the good of his people, the tyrant according to his own will" (Harriss 1975, 23).

BINDING REPRESENTATION

If *Quod omnes* demanded that the affected parties be consulted, the principle of proctorial representation made that consultation feasible. Representatives would be chosen by the communities whose consent was needed. They could then make binding decisions on behalf of that community. Such representation did not imply full suffrage, secret ballots, or democratic procedure—what was critical was that an individual could stand in, evaluate proposals, and commit to decisions, all on behalf of his community. With the ecclesiastical notion of *plena potestas* (full power), representatives were endowed with the power to make choices and agreements on behalf of their communities, who would be bound subsequently by these decisions.

Proctorial representation was originally an ecclesiastical concept, with "little mention of proctors or syndics of corporate communities other than churches" until the twelfth century (Post 1943, 212). So long as ecumenical councils and episcopal synods focused on justice and acclaim, no representation was necessary. Taxation, however, required the consent of clergy and canon chapters. Consulting all chapters in a kingdom or Christendom was impractical—but canon lawyers were ready with a solution. Procuration, or representation by proxy, was a principle found in both Roman and canon law. Originally, a procurator was an agent who could act on behalf of another in contracts or lawsuits, a legal substitute who attended court and handled the case. Christian clergy had already benefited: Emperor Valentinian III (r. 425–55) gave clergy the privilege of employing a procurator in secular courts (Snow 1963, 324). By the ninth century, the right of an ecclesiastic to be represented in court was extended to representation in church assemblies (Snow 1963, 326).

Reasoning by analogy, collectivities could be represented by individuals. In the canonistic tradition of consultation and corporatism, each ecclesiastical unit was already considered a body or a corporation (Watts 2009, 117). It was a short step from private representation to corporate, and these "precedents provided by church councils suggested, again, that groups were represented by individuals who then consulted together as a group" (Black 1992, 165). Just as with *Quod omnes*, canon lawyers refashioned the notion of proctorship: an individual proxy could now act on behalf of a group and represent that community in councils or assemblies. Proctorial representatives would now travel to the council on behalf of their chapters and monasteries, and make binding decisions their constituents could not revoke.

To represent, a proctor needed *plena potestas*, or the full power to commit their communities to decisions or royal requests. Without this power, consent was reversible and representation undermined. Here, Roman law lacked an adequate doctrine of agency applicable to public life: the problem with *potestas* in Roman private law was that the delegation to an agent and his powers were revocable (Tierney 1982, 26).[25] Yet again, twelfth-century canonists stepped in and translated *plena potestas* from a doctrine of papal power to a concept of representation. They likened *plena potestas* to the binding power of attorneys. They then elaborated it as an irrevocable power of representatives acting on behalf of a group, which was then obliged by the acts of the representatives even if it did not grant full consent to them ahead of time (Post 1943, 211; Tierney 1982, 24; Monahan 1987, 123). Centuries before Burke, representatives were empowered to act as trustees rather than delegates.

Proctorial representation diffused within the church. Eugenius III (r. 1145–53) had decided that abbots and monks of Clairvaux were not compelled to take oaths in court, but could instead hire an agent. Innocent III used the concept in 1200, and proctors represented chapters at the Fourth Lateran Council in 1215. The next pope, Honorius III, made proctorial representation a church statute in 1217 with *Etsi membra*. The development of canon law and increase in litigation at the church courts and appellate jurisdiction in Rome also escalated the demand for proctors. "By the middle of the thirteenth century . . . proctorial representation had become the law and custom of the western church" (Snow 1963, 327). Clients relied on proctors to petition the papacy and represent their interests. Monasteries had proctors in various departments at papal curia, in effect acting as lobbyists representing a monastery's interests (Zutshi 2007, 15; Bombi 2009, 74). Chapters also employed proctors, or representatives, when carrying lawsuits to the Roman curia (Kay 2002, 97). Such representation was so wildly popular that one diocesal council at end of fourteenth century saw none of the clerics attend in person: all sent proctors (Snow 1963, 327).

The ecclesiastic use of proctorial representation grew rapidly in the twelfth to thirteenth centuries when demands by secular rulers to tax the clergy multiplied. Popes insisted on clerical consent, and "out of these conflicting demands evolved a system of consent by proctorial representation" (Snow 1963, 330). Thus, when Henry III received papal permission in 1226 to tax clergy in England, he sent forth a letter requesting a grant of one-twelfth or one-fifteenth. The Salisbury chapter recommended a national assembly with proctorial representation. Archbishop Langton agreed and convoked a national council in London in October 1226 of bishops, abbots, higher clergy—and proctors representing the collegiate and cathedral chapters. Such national

25. The phrase was preserved in the Justinian code, appears as early as the sixth century in papal correspondence, and again in the eleventh-century Gregorian reforms; but in these instances, it referred to the full power of the papacy, its full authority over a given decision or domain (Schatz 1996, 89).

councils became the standard practice for securing subsidies from the clergy and were held again in 1267, 1269, 1272, and later (Snow 1963, 330).

The clerical innovation spread to secular monarchies through the canon courts, and from ecclesiastical assemblies to "those secular councils and parliaments to which clerics were summoned" (Snow 1963, 331). For rulers, binding representation made assent to new powers and requests, and especially to taxation, more expedient.[26] Frederick I Barbarossa summoned proctors from Italian towns such as Pisa, Como, Lodi, Milan, and Genoa as early as 1154, and at the subsequent meeting of the Diet of Roncaglia, although they did not take part in the formal deliberations. After 1210, "the system of corporate representation by agents given full powers grew steadily" (Post 1943, 224, 231). The 1214 Lérida assembly in Aragon marked the first time proctorial representation was used at a secular assembly (Kagay 1981, 70; Møller and Doucette 2021, 111). In Spain, proctorial representation formalized after 1250, though an earlier, looser version of proctorial representation functioned as early as the middle of the twelfth century (Post 1943, 224). Frederick II summoned proctors as well, and after 1250, proctorial representatives served in the Kingdom of Sicily and in the Papal States, and the practice had been established in Spain, England, and France (Post 1943, 231). Representatives with explicit *plena potestas* were summoned to the English Parliament in 1268, the Estates General of France in 1302, and the Cortes of Aragon in 1307 (Post 1964, 91; Stasavage 2020, 130).

In England, the proctorial representation of the shires by knights after 1220 "was almost certainly one derived from clerical precedents" (Maddicott 2010, 215). Henry III also hired Master Simon to represent him in several ecclesiastical disputes involving the papacy in the 1230s, and he sent six proctors to represent the crown and barons at the Council of Lyon in 1245, and then again to the papal curia. Barons were given proctorial powers to negotiate with Louis IX in 1261, and a few years later, the supporters of Simon de Montfort appointed baronial proctors to confer with the papal legate in Boulogne (Snow 1963, 333). The English crown included proxy clauses to summons to the parliaments of 1255, 1282, 1294, and 1295.[27] Thus, by 1300, the system of corporate representation by delegates given full powers flourished throughout western Europe, adopted from church precedent.

26. This is also why individual towns and estates would resist proctorial representation with full powers, as in the Cortes of Castille, or the French Estates General in 1302, necessitating lengthy bilateral negotiations between Philip IV and the towns to obtain taxes (Stasavage 2020, 130).

27. Proxies were officially mentioned in summons to the parliament in 1316, and by 1371 they were both recognized by the crown and used by peers (Snow 1963, 334). From 1294 to 1872, every summons to the English Parliament referred to full powers (Stasavage 2020, 208).

UNIVERSITAS

Finally, much like the concept of a procurator, the notion of a *universitas*, a corporation that could be treated as a person, began its modern life in the second half of the twelfth century. The corporation was a fictional person and could thus "sign contracts, own property, and negotiate with other corporations" (Edelstein 2021, 152), but its members retained voting rights. Prior to 1150, the notion of corporate representation was virtually nonexistent, and the only model of governance a personal one. By 1170 to 1200, however, a literature on corporations and their representatives began to flourish, and after 1310, knowledge of corporate representation became widespread (Post 1943, 216; Monahan 1987, 115). A watershed was Azo's famous *Summa Codicis* (1209), which addressed corporations and their representatives extensively (Post 1943, 214).

The notion of a fictive person or universitas was first commonly used by the papacy as part of its eleventh-century quest for autonomy (Post 1943, 229; Snow 1963, 329; Berman 1983a; Greif 2006, 309). The canonist reinterpretation of universitas was that the approval of corporation *as a whole* was required, not that of each single member (Tierney 1982, 24) This new refashioning of *universitas* as a fictive person meant that the relevant agents in expressing consent in the *Quod omnes* formula were corporations, not individuals. The universitas model allowed the exercise of highest authority by a rector, who was above the individual members, but not above the *universitas* itself, as he was the corporation's agent (Schatz 1996, 105). In medieval corporatist theory, members retained both individual identity and a corporate one.

The fiction of a corporation was a useful one: it made both representation and forms of economic activity possible. Communal petitions in England presupposed a corporation to represent. Impersonal trade and entrepreneurial risk-taking were both made feasible and efficient by the corporation (Greif 2006.) Universities established themselves as corporations of students and masters, often in the face of hostile local authorities (Dębiński 2010, 67). Cathedral chapters, monastic orders, universities, cities, and the church itself became increasingly theorized as corporations. By 1250, English barons thought of themselves not only as members of a feudal hierarchy but also of a corporate entity, the *universitas regni* (corporate body of the realm), subject to the law. Parliament itself began to be seen as a corporate body, and when described as *universitas regni*, the kingdom was a corporation, which in turn implied "consent, tacit of express, of all members" (Black 1992, 166; see also Tierney 1982, 21) By the fourteenth century, the corporative model both justified and stimulated the growth of parliaments and assemblies, communal self-governments and universities, and religious orders (Schatz 1996, 104).

Diffusion Mechanisms

These innovations could diffuse through several channels: university masters who traveled back home to serve at courts; papal decretals and their episcopal interpretations; and above all, high clergy who returned from papal councils to communes, parliaments, and courts armed with new concepts and new directives. They were familiar with church procedures, whether compelled attendance or supermajority rules, and parliamentary concepts such as *Quod omnes*. Bishops could thus smooth the way for functioning assemblies. Møller and Doucette accordingly find that episcopal towns—where a bishop was present—had a higher rate of self-government and assemblies than non-episcopal towns (Watts 2009, 99; Møller and Doucette 2021, 78).

Above all, bishops actively participated in assemblies at all levels, ensuring that church interests would be represented, new reinterpretations of Roman law could be disseminated, and ideas from ecumenical councils and canonical exchanges could inform deliberations. Bishops and other high clergy were represented in all medieval parliaments at the insistence of the church (Hintze [1905] 1975, 308). In France, bishops attended council meetings held in the tenth and eleventh centuries, and clergy was represented as an estate in the Estates General as well as in many regional assemblies (Fawtier 1963; Maddicott 2010, 381). Twenty percent of the council of Louis XI were bishops (Millet and Moraw 1996, 183). Clergy served in the Parlement, which both monitored clerical activity and enforced the royal protection of the church (Harding 2002, 169). Prelates were only excluded in 1319 (but still retained their places in the king's council). English high clergy served in the king's council and then in the Parliament. During the tumultuous years of Henry III's reign, bishops saw themselves as both the guardians of lawful government and a constraint on kings—and with the rise of Simon de Montfort's council, as partisan supporters of the conciliar government (Ambler 2017, 7).[28] Lower clergy left the parliament in the 1330s, but the House of Lords still had about forty to one hundred secular nobles and fifty ecclesiastical magnates.[29] As late as the sixteenth and seventeenth centuries, 15 to 17 percent of Spanish state council members were clerics, and in Poland all bishops in the kingdom had a seat in the Senate (Millet and Moraw 1996, 183). Finally, although no national assemblies existed in the Holy Roman Empire until 1470, German kings held assemblies at which they judged and legislated with the help of both clergy and

---

28. Around half of the episcopate (eight bishops) worked with Montfort to seize the government from Henry III and create the new council in 1258 (Ambler 2017, 7).

29. The representation of lower clergy in the English Parliament ended in 1337. The lower clergy fought for the right *not* to attend, which would have legitimated the king's full legal competence and encroachment on their autonomy (Denton and Dooley 1987, 88).

secular lords (Mitterauer 2010). The ecclesiastical princes served together in one chamber of the Imperial Diet, while other bishops, princes, counts, and barons sat in the second and the cities in the third (Stollberg-Rilinger 2018, 27).

To see how bishops are associated with the rise and activity of parliaments, and what their relative importance is to war and cities, we turn to broader empirical regularities. Figures 5.1 through 5.3 present two different dependent variables: a dummy variable for the presence or absence of an assembly in a given city-year, and a measure of parliamentary activity that codes the number of years per century that parliament met. The data comes from Van Zanden, Buringh, and Bosker (2012), who code parliaments as independent legal bodies with city representatives (not just clergy or nobles). To compare the impact of cities, war, and ideas as the catalysts of parliaments, I use data on city population (log of urban populations from Bairoch, Batou, and Pierre 1988) and self-governing communes (Dincecco and Onorato 2016), warfare sites (Dincecco and Onorato 2016), and the presence of bishops. Bishops precede the rise of parliaments, ameliorating the worry that medieval parliaments led to the influence of bishops and universities.[30] Secular authorities did name bishops after the Reformation, and so I include a variable for a given city or state becoming Protestant.

As figure 5.1 shows, bishops are closely associated with medieval parliaments, as are communes. This relationship is consistent with the importance of ecclesiastical human capital, and with Møller and Doucette's argument about the importance of earlier self-governance (Møller and Doucette 2021; see also Abramson and Boix 2019). Both of these relationships switch directions in the early modern period when we also include Protestantism: bishops and communes are now *negatively* associated with the rise of parliaments. In the early modern period, secular conflict and larger urban populations are not associated with the presence of parliaments (see table A.11 in the appendix). This is not surprising: in Protestant areas, bishops became servants of the state (and many states became absolutist).

When it comes to parliamentary *activity*,[31] both secular conflict and commune status are initially closely associated, as figure 5.2 shows. As predicted by the bellicists, secular conflict and parliamentary activity are even more strongly correlated in the early modern period, when expensive war made taxation—and parliamentary consent—all the more important.

30. The first parliaments were established in the late twelfth century, long after bishops settled in cities (dating back to the Roman era), and universities were founded in the eleventh century. Larger cities were more likely to receive bishops, so I control for urban population.

31. The activity variable here measures the years that a parliament met in a given century, from Van Zanden, Buringh, and Bosker 2012, 840. The unit of observation is a city-year.

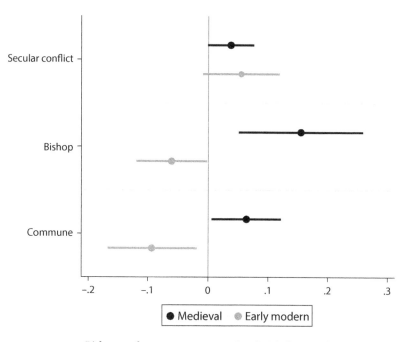

FIGURE 5.1. Bishops and communes are associated with the rise of medieval parliaments, city-level data (OLS regressions with city and year 2FE). Horizontal lines indicate 95% confidence intervals.

Once we include bishops in these models, however, this relationship changes. Figure 5.3 shows that in the *medieval* era, bishops are far more closely linked to parliamentary activity than are either war or commune status. The results are consistent with the active participation of bishops in medieval parliaments and the diffusion of the canonical concepts of consent and representation. In the early modern era, however, once we control for the Protestant status of a city, this relationship disappears (see table A.12 in the appendix). Bishops no longer matter to parliamentary activity, and neither does war nor commune status. Once again, this is consistent with the argument that the bishops mattered because they diffused papal templates and concepts—in Protestant areas, bishops could no longer serve that role, and instead served the monarchical state. They no longer had a way to either diffuse ideas from Rome or promote local conciliar activity.

These analyses suggest that we need to include religious authorities in our explanations of the rise and activity of parliaments, especially in the medieval period. Much of the existing scholarship has focused on the importance of cities and communes for the rise of parliamentary activity (Van Zanden, Buringh, and Bosker 2012; Abramson and Boix 2019; Møller and Doucette 2021). This analysis shows that religious factors are just as powerfully linked. If bishops served both as local administrators and emissaries of the church, they may well have fostered the rise and activity of parliaments by providing

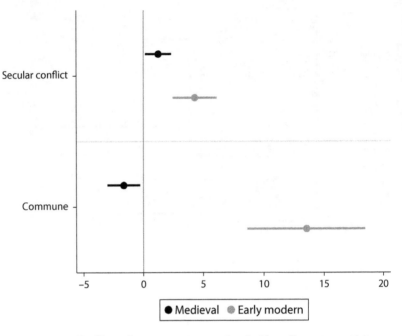

FIGURE 5.2. Conflict and communes are associated with parliamentary activity, city-level data (OLS regressions with city and year 2FE). Horizontal lines indicate 95% confidence intervals.

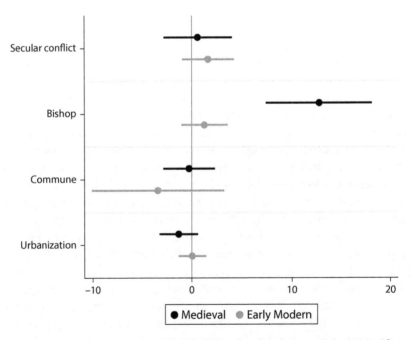

FIGURE 5.3. Bishops are associated with medieval parliamentary activity (OLS with 2FE). Horizontal lines indicate 95% confidence intervals.

conciliar ideas, fostering human capital, and employing the same clerks and lawyers that would facilitate parliamentary activity.

Conciliarism

The late fourteenth century saw the rise of conciliarism, a movement that represented the "ecclesiastical fusion between representation and consent" (Møller 2019, 219). This school of thought postulated that councils have supremacy over the pope, since reform required consent, and the whole church is represented in the great councils. It became particularly prominent during the Great Schism (1378–1417), though conciliar ideas had a longer history.[32] None of its proponents "wished to deny the divine origins of papal supremacy, but rather . . . to limit it" (Gordon 2000, 35).

The irony of the conciliar movement is twofold. First, a movement designed to bring about greater collective governance instead paved the way for absolutism both within the papacy and the monarchy, and the supremacy of secular rulers over the church. Second, conciliarism indirectly promoted the spread of the Protestant Reformation: a papacy suspicious of councils delayed a response to the Lutheran challenge until it was too late.

Conciliarists held that a representative council has primacy over the pope; it can override the normal authority of pope, judge and sentence him, and even depose him (Black 1998, 78). Jean Gerson, chancellor of the University of Paris from 1395 to 1418, argued that God intended his church to be governed by councils. His version of conciliarism explicitly saw kings and popes as both bound by the views of their counselors (Watts 2009, 384). Marsilius of Padua argued that consent legitimated government, and William of Ockham claimed that final authority lay with councils (Tierney 1982, 40; Black 1992, 172). Along with Conrad of Gelnhausen, Henry of Langenstein, and Pierre d'Ailly, they laid down the "basis for deposition of the schismatic popes, election of new one, and ongoing conflict over direction of Church" (Watts 2009, 292).

The result was a ferment in both the church and temporal polities: by 1400, the "whole Western Church was engaged in trying to replace papal monarchy with conciliar government, and almost every country from Scandinavia to Spain and from England to Hungary had produced constitutional documents stating that the ruler was under the law and had experimented with representative assemblies seeking to give effect to that principle" (Tierney 1966, 6). Conciliarism proved very popular in Germany and Central Europe,

---

32. In the early thirteenth century, the more radical of church thinkers thought "the pope could be corrected and even deposed by a council if his conduct endangered 'the state of the church'" (Tierney 1966, 12). By 1200, the pope himself was bound by canons of General Councils, but there was no conflict with papal primacy: the pope himself was the presiding head of a General Council.

while it was disliked by Italians (where university theology was in the hands of mendicant friars who were dependent on papal protection) and ignored in England and in Spain, which were too independent and too preoccupied with ferreting out Moriscos, respectively (Black 1992, 6; Gordon 2000, 45; Kłoczowski 2000, 70–1).

Conciliarist influence peaked with the Great Schism, and the search for its resolution (see chapters 1 and 2). The "era of the councils" began, as councils at Constance (1414–8,) Siena (1423–4), and Basel (1431–9) proclaimed supreme authority over the pope (Watts 2009, 193). Constance finally ended the schism under the leadership of Emperor Sigismund and Gerson, who preached, galvanized cardinals, and led the council to depose Pope John XXIII in May 1415 (Gordon 2000, 37).[33] Two new decrees asserted new conciliar powers: *Haec Sancta* declared that the council was superior to the pope in matters of faith and reform, and *Frequens* declared that councils must be summoned regularly and frequently (Black 1992, 170, Schatz 1996, 104).[34] Put in familiar political terms, this was an "ambitious attempt to make church councils superior to the papal head, that is, to demote the latter to the role of a form of prime minister of the church subject to a parliament in the form of regularly convened church councils" (Møller 2021, 927).

Yet at the Council of Basel (1431–9), conciliarism was defeated. The council initially suspended Pope Eugenius IV, who bitterly opposed the conciliar movement (Gordon 2000, 43; Black 1998, 71). As the council bogged down in arcane debates between curialists and conciliarists, however, Eugenius persuaded secular rulers of the dangers of conciliar radicalism, and regained the upper hand (Fried 2015, 491; Wickham 2016, 241).[35] Kings and princes now saw conciliar ideas as a potential threat. Pope Pius II (r. 1458–64) then issued the *Execrabilis* bull in 1460, which condemned conciliarism and prohibited the review of papal decisions by councils (Hay 1995, 318). Conciliarism retained supporters at the University of Paris and among German and French nobles, but it was spent as a force within the church (Gordon 2000, 45).

Conciliarism had unanticipated consequences for both secular politics and religious rivalries. First, by creating alternative authorities to popes, the conciliar movement allowed rulers to exploit the divisions within the church and emerge triumphant. Several kings posed as defenders of ecclesiastical

---

33. The Council brought together 33 cardinals, 47 archbishops, 145 bishops, 93 suffragan bishops, 132 abbots, 155 priors, 217 doctors of theology, 361 doctors of both canon and Roman laws, 5300 simple priests and scholars, 3,000 merchants . . . and over 700 "harlots in brothels" (Oakley 2003, 21).

34. The next council would come in five years, the one after that in seven, and then in ten-year intervals. When Julius II failed to summon one, a breakaway met in 1511 in Pisa. The pope then placed both Pisa and Florence under interdict, denounced the council, and called the Fifth Lateran Council (1512–7) to condemn it further.

35. The king of England and the duke of Burgundy had already brought their churches under secular control and had nothing to gain from clerical liberty.

liberties, even as they extended their jurisdiction over the church within their domains. In France, England, Poland, Aragon, and some German principalities, rulers forbade appeals to Rome, required permits to publish church edicts, allowed appeals to state authorities against church punishments, and nominated bishops as late as the nineteenth century (Górski et al. 1966, 132; Schatz 1996, 111).[36]

Second, even as it was defeated within the church, conciliarism continued to shape *secular* constitutional theory (Figgis [1906] 1960; Oakley 1972; Tierney 1982; Oakley 2003). Conciliarists formally distinguished between the religious and secular spheres, and advocated separating the two different kinds of authority (Oakley 2015, 18). They also drew a distinction between the individual and the office, using an earlier notion of the "seat does not die" (*sedes non moritur*). This distinction both allowed the church councils to depose the popes without undermining the papacy and may have formed the basis for modern bureaucracy (Black 1992, 190; Møller 2021, 927). Conciliarism has been likened to an ecclesiastic League of Nations: a short-term failure that spawned long-term changes in thought and practice (Wickham 2016, 441ff).

Third, instead of transforming the church, the conciliar turn inadvertently contributed to the success of the Reformation. The conciliar episode made popes skeptical of further experiments in reform. Curialists worried that a reforming council would strip popes of powers and continued to deny the popularity of the reforms (Brundage 2009, 562). After the Reformation began, their reluctance to hold councils "prevented the summoning of any council till it was too late" (Hay 1995, 312). The sack of Rome in 1527 by the troops of Charles V concentrated the minds of the papal hierarchy, but no coherent plans for reform formed until the 1545–63 Council of Trent.[37] Even then, the third phase of the council was delayed by the new pope, Paul IV (r. 1555–59), for fear of a conciliar challenge. It was only in 1561 that his successor, Pius IV (r. 1559–65), reconvened the council. It introduced strict procedures regarding the appointment of bishops and cardinals, annual visitations, synods, the education and training of clergy, and penalties for clerical marriages and concubines. These moves strengthened the church, but it did little to stem the Protestant advance.

The Church and the Absolutist Turn

If the church shaped the golden age of medieval parliaments, it also influenced the "absolutist turn" of the 1500s. While England, the Netherlands, Sweden, and Switzerland continued to have active parliaments that met relatively

36. For example, with the Concordat of Bologna in 1516, Pope Leo X conceded all major ecclesiastical appointments to Francis I (r. 1515–47) in exchange for disavowing conciliarism (Bireley 1999, 16).

37. The Roman Inquisition was established by Pope Paul III in 1542 in response to the Protestant threat (Bireley 1999, 66ff). By 1580, however, the church was more concerned with hunting down witches than prosecuting Protestants.

frequently, in other countries, such as France, Spain, and Denmark, parliaments faded away. New sources of revenue, whether indirect taxes in France or Denmark, or the flood of silver and other colonial wealth to Spain, made assemblies superfluous. The centralizing power of princes, and their ability to play off estates and corporations against each other, also contributed (Blockmans 1998, 64). Holding assemblies was expensive, and rulers grew more financially secure. Meanwhile, once clergy and nobility were freed from taxation, as in France and Spain, they paid little attention to parliamentary decline (Guenée 1985, 187).

This absolutist turn, however, also had its religious aspects. The defeat of the conciliarist movement coincided with the beginnings of an absolutist resurgence in Aragon, Castile, France, and parts of Germany, and a decline in their representative assemblies. In response to conciliar ideas, a new generation of papal and secular monarchists of the mid-fifteenth century, such as Jean Bodin, developed ambitious new theories of monarchy as critical to peace and social order. Pointing to the Great Schism, these theorists argued that plurality bred discord and destabilization, while papal (and secular) monarchies meant unity and stability.

Absolutists also seized on alternative interpretations of Roman law. They used the notion of *maior et sanior pars* to deny power to the undeserving majority of common people (Tierney 1982, 24; Schatz 1996, 105). Conciliarists used the concept of the corporation to argue that the collective power of the church trumped the pope: their monarchical opponents argued that that people transferred power once and for all to the monarch, the corporate *persona ficta* (Edelstein 2021, 160). At the end of the fourteenth century, concepts of *quod principi placuit legis habet vigorem* (what is pleasing to the prince has the force of law) and *princeps legibus solutus est* (a prince is not bound by laws) replaced the dominant ideas of medieval rulers as constrained by law and obligation (Rigaudiere 1995, 27–8). Medieval interpretations of Roman law included these ideas, but now they would underpin the absolutist model of the sixteenth century. The *princeps* became the source of all authority and undivided sovereignty, giving rise to both royal absolutism and papalism (Schatz 1996, 105).

The Reformation itself empowered rulers: Protestants gained territorial churches and property, while Catholics extended secular authority into ecclesiastical sphere (Jedin 1993, 729). Reformation involved "a close cooperation between church and state, and a blurring of the boundaries between religious and mundane concerns" (Eire 2016, 590). The spread of the religious reforms, and their acceptance, often required political sponsorship of kings and princes, as in England, Sweden, Poland, Hungary, Norway, and some parts of the Holy Roman Empire.[38]

---

38. The debates over whether the English Reformation was a "bottom-up or a "top-down" affair have been extensive. A.G. Dickson's *The English Reformation* (1964) points

Where kings already controlled the church, they saw little need to involve parliaments in asserting control.[39] In France, the King neither implemented the Reformation nor did he initially prosecute the dissenters (Reid 2000, 214). There was little point in doing so, given his control over the church. In Castile and Navarre, a powerful Inquisition had been prosecuting *moriscos* and *conversos* since 1478. It was running out of steam (and targets) by the 1520s, and quickly turned its considerable expertise to prosecuting Protestant heresy on behalf of the monarchy (Coleman 2000, 299). Both Charles V (who now ruled Castile and the Crown of Aragon) and his son Philip asserted more absolute power in Spain, partly in the name of defending the faith, and fully supported the Inquisition's campaign (Coleman 2000, 304).[40] The price of such protection was ecclesiastical support for the absolutist project (Härter 2011, 117).[41] Thus, where absolutist kings protected Catholicism, Luther's teachings "fell on stony ground" (Pettegree 2000, 3). More broadly, the papal goals of a counter-Reformation coincided with the interest of Catholic dynasties in centralizing their state. These twin processes took off in the Catholic countries in earnest in the 1570s, after the delayed reforms of the Council of Trent, and lasted until 1700 (Hsia 2005, 77).

In contrast, where kings needed parliamentary support to carry out their religious reforms, as in England and in Sweden, the Reformation reasserted the rights of national assemblies. The canonical example is England, where Henry VIII rejected papal supremacy and set out to reform doctrine through parliamentary legislation (Parish 2000, 225). In Sweden, King Gustav Vasa formalized the parliament and included representatives of nobility, clergy,

---

to Lollardy or the dissent of John Wycliffe in the fourteenth century as evidence of an existing push for the Reformation. However, Geoffrey Elton's *Reform and Reformation: England 1509–1558* (1977) points to political elites; Eamon Duffy's *Stripping of the Altars* (1992) paints a picture of vibrant Catholic piety, devotion, and practice in pre-Reformation England; and Jack Scarisbrick's *The Reformation and English People* (1984) also argues that on the eve of the Reformation, the English Catholic Church was both popular and woven into the fabric of everyday lives.

39. Rubin (2017) argues that Protestant parliaments were dominated by merchants who promulgated institutions that favored both their interests and overall economic growth. Catholic countries, in contrast, continued to rely on religious legitimation, with the Inquisition, for example, as a sop to the church in Spain. Yet many parliaments were dominated not by growth-oriented merchants but by agrarian nobles, mercantilists, clergy, and nascent partisan interests (see Carruthers 1990 and Stasavage 2002). Further, the Spanish monarchy protected the church, rather than vice versa.

40. The Spanish Church had also undergone extensive reform, thanks to local efforts such as those of Archbishop Francisco Jiménez de Cisneros of Toledo (1495–1517), who forced clerical reforms, cleaned up the Franciscan order, sponsored the publication of devotional texts, and established the University of Alcalá (Eire 2016, 120).

41. Charles V also extracted the rights to all bishop appointments from Pope Adrian VI (r. 1522–3), which "gave the Spanish crown virtual control of the administration of the Church" (Ergang 1971, 141).

towns, and peasants, in part to obtain consent for the Reformation. At the Riksdag of Västerås in 1527, the parliament dismantled the economic and political power of Catholic Church (Grell 2000, 272). In Bohemia after the Hussite revolution, the clergy lost their place in parliament, and the Habsburgs had to contend with a powerful assembly, fiercely protective of its powers, that could levy taxes, sanction new legislation, and confirm royal appointments (Murdoch 2000, 194).

In the Holy Roman Empire, the fragmentation of territorial authority meant that individual princes often decided the outcome. They usurped episcopal powers: bishops handed over land to the princes in exchange for protection and lost their ability to appoint and control clergy (Dixon 2000, 149). A prince's decision to implement the Reformation meant greater control over land and resources and new investments in the state apparatus: visitations, converting chapters into districts, appointing new clergy and overseeing their annual synods, establishing consistories to monitor moral discipline, and the takeover of church assets (Dixon 2000, 159; see also Gorski 2003). The Reformation also strengthened the claims of towns and princes against the emperor (Grell 2000, 258). In short, the Reformation was a political process: religious reform depended on secular implementation and enforcement.

Conclusion

Representative assemblies in Europe owe much to the church. Debates over the origins and roles of parliaments tend to neglect that parliaments did not rise *ab novo*. They relied on the existing rules and the conceptual innovations of the church. The church provided the precedents of mandatory summons and majority rule; new concepts of consent, binding representation and parliamentary supremacy; and the clergy who served in parliaments and propagated church ideas. As a result, bishops are closely linked to parliamentary presence and activity.

The church also influenced the activity of parliaments in subtler ways. For example, prominent analyses have noted that smaller polities were more likely to have active assemblies, since representatives did not have to travel far and could engage in active oversight and decision-making (Stasavage 2010, 2016). Other analysts argue that only strong monarchs could call effective national assemblies (Boucoyannis 2021). Yet a major force behind the variation in both fragmentation and royal power was the church, as we saw in chapter 2.

By the fourteenth century, the conceptual innovations of consent and binding representation took hold in both church councils and national assemblies. Despite the absolutist turn, these concepts lived on, preserved in conciliar thought, providing foundations for future parliamentary consensus, representation, and accountability.

Conclusion

THE CHALLENGE AND example of religious authority galvanized state formation in Europe. The medieval church sought to ensure its own autonomy and power, and in the process transformed the political terrain of Europe. Papal ambitions and ecclesiastical influence help to explain several puzzling developments, such as the persistent fragmentation of Europe, the precocious development of state institutions such as chanceries and fiscal offices, the rapid spread of law and universities, and the rise of concepts of representation and binding consent.

First, the territorial fragmentation of Europe was no accident, but a result of deliberate church policy designed to neutralize the threat of the Holy Roman Empire. As we saw in chapter 2, the fragmentation of territorial authority took off as the church gained power after 1100. Popes used a variety of tactics to destabilize and to fragment the rule of monarchs they found hostile. The success of these relied on the good will and cooperation of other rulers, which is why wars by proxy, crusades, or alliances were so much more effective than excommunications. The differentiation of religious and lay authority in the Investiture Conflict, and new ideas of monarchs as sovereigns free from external superiors, also reinforced the atomization.

This fragmentation persisted long into the modern era, into the nineteenth century, contrary to accounts arguing that early modern war consolidated states. The splintering of political authority endured because local notables gained power at the expense of the emperor. The constant forays of the emperors outside of Germany, and the distraction of papal conflict, allowed these princes, dukes, and bishops to claim authority. They could stymie imperial efforts to centralize power and obtain even more concessions from the emperors. In Italy, self-governing cities became competing republics. As a result, the fragmentation of authority in Germany and Italy was durable and lasted long after its catalyst, the Catholic Church, had lost its wealth and organizational reach.

As intense as this rivalry was in the Middle Ages, its goal was to delineate spheres of influence rather than eliminate any players. The conflict was about autonomy and jurisdiction, rather than mutual destruction. In many accounts, this constructive fragmentation of Europe was critical to subsequent economic and political development in Europe, characterized by efficiency-enhancing competition and the absence of an overweening, overly powerful emperor who could stifle growth (North and Thomas 1973). Kings and popes were counterweights to each other, in ways that rulers in other settings, whether the Islamic Caliphate or the Ottoman, Byzantine, and Chinese empires, never faced (Bendix 1978, 47).

Second, the church also provided models for institutions of taxation, courts, and parliaments that developed long before early modern war or bargaining supposedly made them necessary. Rivalry and fragmentation were themselves not enough to create new institutions of governance. They provided the incentive, but not the means. Instead, innovations at the papal court were the source of both institutional templates and governing concepts. Medieval secular rulers borrowed and adapted ecclesiastical techniques of taxation and answering petitions (a key role of governments at the time), and the division of labor within the court offices. Bishops and clergy, stationed in royal courts in faraway lands, transmitted these church templates: everything from the art of formal letter writing to methods for tax collection to a system for answering petitions. This emulation of ecclesiastical models explains the similar division of labor, institutions, and operating procedures across the European royal courts.

The rivalry between secular rulers and the papacy interacted with this emulation. Where domestic authority was fragmented, as in the Holy Roman Empire, rulers were unable to use these models to consolidate authority and establish new institutions of central governance. At the other extreme, in England, where the papacy counted on rulers to stay out of the conflict and made all kinds of concessions to that end, kings were free to centralize power and develop new institutions as they saw fit, the system of common law being perhaps the most salient example.

Third, the church contributed to the primacy of law and to the culture of learning in Europe. The rediscovery of Roman law during the Investiture Conflict, and the systematization of canon law a few decades later, meant that law could be a potent weapon in the conflict between the papacy and secular monarchs. Popes and emperors sought out legal arguments and competed for the experts who would ferret them out. This reinforced the notion of the law as a dispute resolution mechanism, and the idea that rules, evidence, and precedent mattered more than ordeals, sworn promises, or status. We also see competition over jurisdiction and cases, since there were parallel court systems, one lay and one ecclesiastical.

The huge new demand for legal expertise led to the rise of new law schools and universities during the Investiture Conflict. Nearly all these new institutions

taught both Roman and canon law on an equal basis. Two consequences followed: first, both of these corpuses permeated European civil law, along with
local, customary, manorial, and urban law. Second, as popes and emperors
vied to found, fund, and protect universities and their students, they catalyzed a surge of learned expertise that would make possible credible contracts,
property rights, trade, and economic growth. The papacy and the emperors
invested in this human capital partly to be more efficient competitors. In the
process, they generated enormous positive externalities that neither antici-
pated: the primacy of law and an ethos of learning, the very foundations of the
Enlightenment and the "culture of growth."

Finally, conceptual innovations of the church made possible the dis-
tinctly European versions of representative assemblies. Councils and assemblies are widespread, found across different cultures and historical periods,
whether the Vikings in the ninth century or the Huron in the seventeenth.
But what gave life to European parliaments, and what made them different,
were the notions of consent and representation. These concepts, in turn, have
their direct roots in the church, as do early notions of corporate governance,
the summoning of parliaments, and majority decision rules. This was the
church's contribution: to transform medieval parliaments into representative bodies that could make decisions on behalf of the commonwealth, as we
saw in chapter 5. Here, some church thinkers went even further and advocated for conciliarism, the notion that the collective decisions of the assembly
should trump the executive, whether pope or king. These ideas went nowhere
within the church, and in fact, inadvertently hindered a speedy response to the
Reformation—but secular theorists would pick up and adopt these.

Many of the distinct features of European state development—the multitude of sovereign statelets, rule of law, autonomous universities, and national
representative assemblies—thus have sacred foundations: the powerful medieval church. Its assertion of autonomy and authority led to conflict with many
European kings, emperors, and princes. At the same time, its administrative
advances, conceptual innovations, and the network of bishops and clergy all
across Europe offered new patterns and resources for building state institutions. These were still embryonic administrations, but key aspects of the rule
of law, taxation, and parliaments had been established long before early modern conflict and bargaining would give them center stage.

Subsequent state formation in the early modern and modern periods
was based on these earlier advances. As a result, the purported *causes* of state
formation (wars necessitating taxes, which then necessitate bargaining) may
in fact be the *consequences*. For example, early modern warfare relied on the
medieval fragmentation of territory for both its protagonists and its lengthy
course. This fragmentation not only created the space for new communes,
ambitious princes, and regional politicians—but these actors then ensured
that the fragmentation would be sustained and defended. In face of these

vested interests, early modern war did not neatly reduce the number of European states or consolidate them—that would have to wait until the nineteenth century. By the same token, both parliaments and universities, critical to accounts of elite bargaining and the economic takeoff in the early modern era, were both medieval innovations, nurtured by both religious and secular actors. The vast stores of human capital and legal expertise diffused across Europe, making contracts and impersonal exchange both possible and viable. The very autonomy of church and state, seen as critical both to the Reformation and to subsequent political development in Europe, has its roots in the eleventh century. Rather than early modern war necessitating taxation and bargaining, then, the development of state capacities in the Middle Ages made it possible for stronger states to tax and to bargain—and then to wage war more effectively and efficiently.

Many ecclesiastical concepts and institutions of governance took on a life of their own. Secular rulers adopted these precedents for their own ends, in a case of "institutional conversion" that subverted the church. They justified, fueled, and legitimated secular governance, and in the process, rendered the church increasingly obsolete. Pronouncements such as *"rex in suo regno imperator"* were meant to hinder imperial ambition, but were then used to question papal authority as well. Human capital flourished with the investments of popes and kings, only to escape the walls of courts and universities, and the control of the church. The church lent models for legal arguments, documentation, petitions, and taxation: secular rulers used these to assert their autonomy from the church and consolidate their power.

European state development was so distinct because the church itself was unusual: unlike other religious denominations, it became a centralized hierarchy, with a powerful papacy at its apex. The church was the most powerful and influential actor in medieval Europe, one that commanded wealth, human capital, and spiritual authority like no other. Elsewhere, the state developed without the challenge of a monumental religious rival. The autonomy of the church was critical. Not only did independence serve as the incentive to fragment Europe and conceptualize sovereignty, but it also made it possible for the church to then shape the European state.

To see why this autonomy was so important, we only need to look to Byzantium, after the schism of 1054 split the one church into western and eastern churches. The story of the church in the West is the one we have just visited: reformist popes gained ecclesiastical independence from the overweening secular authority of the Holy Roman emperors and local landlords, competed with rulers for authority, and shaped state formation. In contrast, in Byzantium, a church with the same roots was powerless to shape the state. The Byzantine empire was in a more advantageous starting position: it was a centralized tax state with a budgetary capacity unmatched in Europe until 1204 and the capture of Constantinople (Angelov and Herrin 2012, 150). Byzantium had a fixed court and capital since 330, long before the western empire did. Yet during the schism, the church did not become independent: instead, the Byzantine emperor assumed nearly complete authority over the church. As a result, Byzantine emperors called church councils, shaped theological pronouncements, and taxed the clergy, exercising political authority over the church (Dagron 2003, 282ff). In effect, the situation was reversed: the emperor shaped how the church would develop. Without the example of the autonomous church, there were no new templates to adopt. Instead, eastern emperors preserved Roman administrative offices, such as the praetorian prefect. Offices, hierarchies, and ceremonies multiplied. Specialization, when it occurred, did not follow western trajectories: medieval Byzantine justice and finance offices were fused at all levels, for example, as were military affairs and justice, with military commanders acting as judges (Magdalino 1994, 95–6).

This is not to claim that the church somehow determined the course of European state development. Church models were not always emulated (despite repeated exposure), as clearly demonstrated by the growth of common law in England, the refusal of most monarchies to adopt elections as a way of choosing their kings, and the rejection of chastity at all levels of society. Theological prohibitions against usury were widely ignored in practice, in both ecclesiastical and lay courts (Dorin 2015; North 1990, 105). Some precedents were unsavory and reeked of corruption, such as the sale of offices, nepotism, or the sale of indulgences. The institutional church was a strategic actor, developing clear goals and tactics in light of others' actions—but it could also badly miscalculate. Popes as politicians were all too fallible, as shown by Boniface VIII's overreach with Philip IV, the competing antipopes of the Great Schism, and the delayed response to the Reformation for fear of a conciliarist resurgence. The papacy also faced weaknesses inherent to its religious organization: controversies over succession, internal divisions and schisms, and finances that never quite covered its ambitions (Bagge 2019, 125).

So what does this European trajectory tell us about state formation more broadly? For one thing, war may be one path of state formation, but it is neither necessary nor sufficient, not even in Europe. It is not necessary, because institutions attributed to war, such as taxes and parliaments, arose long before the demands of the military revolution of the sixteenth and seventeenth centuries. If anything, these costly conflicts undermined state capacity, by leading monarchs to sell offices, honors, and economic privileges such as tax collection or monopolies (Brewer 1989, 17–9). War meant venality, not state building, even in early modern Europe. War is also not sufficient: despite hundreds of years of warfare, the Holy Roman Empire did not consolidate into a national state, nor was it able to centralize its institutions. Stability and relative peace, rather than the chaos of war, made nascent state institutions possible. States made war—and war could unmake states.

The broader point here is that we need to be more careful in our analyses of state formation. First, we need to problematize European state development before exporting its truisms to other areas. Not only is European state development not a precedent for other states—its own history is far more complicated and attributable to different forces than we thought. State institutions did not arise simply because war necessitated them or elites agreed on them: rather, clergy diffused institutional templates that were then adopted, adapted, and legitimated.

Second, no single cause is responsible for state formation. Multiple processes and dynamics coexist in the same broad episodes of state building. It is not simply that state building differed across geographical and historical contexts—it is that we see multiple, distinct mechanisms within the same context, in this case post-Carolingian Europe. The European state did not simply arise out of armed conflict or domestic negotiations: the fragmentation of territorial authority and the emulation of ecclesiastical models also shaped the state in foundational ways. Moreover, these mechanisms interact: fragmentation meant that some rulers could not emulate and build central state institutions, as successive Holy Roman emperors found out. Emulation also involved adaptation and reinterpretation, bricolage and reassembly, not simply a straightforward transferal of resources or templates.

Third, culture and ideology also build states. Such influence has been held responsible for the backwardness of the Middle East after 1000, and for the scientific and economic advances in England but not in China after 1650 (Kuran 2011; Goldstone 2009). Cultural forces mattered just as much in medieval Europe. The church played such an outsized role in European state development partly because of its wealth and political ambitions, but also because it was a fundamentally *religious* organization, one that could offer salvation and legitimation, eternal life and temporal glory. Kings may have claimed to have been appointed by God, but none would dare to promise the forgiveness of sins or the hope of heaven. When the papacy developed its comparatively sophisticated bureaucracy, taxation, and justice regime, these templates were taken up by rulers not just because they were efficient, but because they were authoritative, stamped with the imprimatur of the Holy See.

The literature on institutional adoption has emphasized that local, endogenous solutions are often more efficient and effective than those imposed by high-modernist governments (see Scott 1998). Yet the case of medieval emulation of the church suggests that institutional models from central, high, and far-off authorities can be successfully replanted if they are both familiar and legitimate, transmitted by brokers such as bishops, with dual authority in both spheres. The church could thus foster institutions critical to subsequent economic development, constitutionalism, and representative government, including the rule of law, the separation of church and state, universities, and parliaments. Europe took a long and fitful road to get there, but its peculiar trajectory would not have been possible without rivalry with the church and the secular adoption of institutional solutions with their roots in ecclesiastical practice and administration.

The final irony of European state development is that democratic and secular institutions can have their roots in an authoritarian and religious organization. Not surprisingly, many modern analyses have focused on how the Catholic Church stymied economic growth and how the Reformation freed Europe to pursue knowledge, reason, free markets, and property rights. Yet in the picture that emerges from this book, the medieval church, in all its secular ambition and spiritual monopoly, also brought about the separation of church and state, learning, universities, and human capital, the primacy and rule of law, and the concepts of representation, consent, and sovereignty. The most secular of state institutions can have the most sacred of foundations.

Data and Robustness Tests

THE ANALYSES IN this book rely on historical data. The usual caveats apply: data reaching back to the tenth century is scarce, it may be missing systematically thanks to subsequent destruction of documents and archives, and it is unlikely to be fully reliable, as both medieval sources and their secondary collations rely on estimates. The empirical analyses are thus suggestive rather than definitive. Consistent with the theory advanced in the book, the results on many church-related variables tend to be more robust in the medieval period; for example, sensitivity tests suggest that the impact of papal conflict or bishops in the medieval era is much less likely to be overwhelmed by the effects of unobservables than in the early modern era. If the church was a powerful player in the Middle Ages, its impact was diluted in the early modern era, when its domination of politics ceased.

I compiled three sets of data. The first collects data on city-level variables and developments. The data spans the years 1000 to 1850 and includes all European states for a total of 31,969 state-year observations (not all observations contain all variables). It builds on several existing sources of data from Abramson (2017); Bosker, Buringh, and Van Zanden (2013); Blaydes and Chaney (2013); and Dincecco and Onorato (2016). Data on fragmentation and territorial boundaries comes from MPIDR (Max Planck Institute for Demographic Research) and CGG (Chair for Geodesy and Geoinformatics, University of Rostock), and the Historical GIS Files from the Mosaic Census Collection (University of California, Berkeley). Data on communes and urbanization (specifically, the log of the city populations in a given year) come from Bairoch, Batou, and Pierre (1988) and Dincecco and Onorato (2016). I compiled data on monasteries, bishoprics, and cathedrals from the Mapping Past Societies project, formerly the Digital Atlas of Medieval and Roman Civilizations (Harvard University), augmenting these with new data on monasteries and bishoprics, especially in Eastern Europe. The data on dioceses comes from the Digital Atlas of Dioceses and Ecclesiastical Provinces in Late Medieval Europe (Stanford University.) I compiled data on over 600 European universities and their charters founded using de Ridder-Symoens (2003), Wieruszowski (1966), the History of Economic Thought compendium and university websites.

I collected data on papal conflict: the involvement of popes in wars by proxy, direct armed conflict, and armed conflict by allied rulers and against other rulers. These data come from Dupuy and Dupuy (1993), *The New Cambridge Medieval History* country chapters, and the existing database of involvement in armed conflict from Brecke (2012), augmented and recoded to include papal involvement as well as conflict before 1400. To measure secular conflict, I rely on indicators of interstate conflict from Dincecco and Onorato (2016), who code conflict sites and combatants in medieval Europe. The city-level data is the basis for the analyses in chapters 4 and 5.

The second data set aggregates some of this data into state-level variables, relying on the shape files from Abramson (2017). It, too, spans the years 1000 to 1850 and includes all European states for a total of 30,173 state-year observations (not all observations contain all variables). This allows us to examine how fragmentation and communes developed within state borders. A version of this data set combines the city and state data sets into a raster data set with 100km × 100km grid cells, for the fragmentation and commune analyses in chapter 2. I also use the state-level data for the robustness tests in the Appendix, using the number of borders within a given distance of state centroids.

The third data set collects data on ruler duration and excommunications, adding excommunication data from *The New Cambridge Medieval History* and the *Catholic Encyclopedia* to an existing data set used by Blaydes and Chaney (2013), who rely on data on dynasties, rulers, and the duration of rule from Morby (1989) and Bosworth (1996). The state, raster, and ruler duration data sets are all used for the analyses in chapter 2.

I estimated two sets of models. OLS (ordinary least squares) regressions with 2FE (two-way state/city and year fixed effects) allow us to eliminate time- and place-invariant structural variables that could confound the relationship between the influence of the church and the dependent variables. I also use ME (mixed effects) models that take into account the nested nature of the data (e.g., different kinds of universities within cities and states measured over years). These more flexible hierarchical linear models take into account the correlations across observations (or more precisely, between their error terms) and allow us to model both state- and city-year effects.

Dependent Variables

Fragmentation measures the number of political authorities over a given territory. It consists of three measures: the number of state boundaries within a 100km × 100km grid cell, the number of state boundaries within a radius of a city centroid (100, 250, 500 km) and the number of states over time within the 1900 state boundaries of Europe. Since both Italy and Germany unified in the 1870s, this allows us to compare the consolidation of territorial authority over time: the greater the number of states, the higher the fragmentation.

Commune status and urbanization have been used as a proxy for both political and economic development, given their importance to trade, taxation, and self-government (Bosker, Buringh, and Van Zanden 2013; Becker and Woessman 2009; Cantoni and Yuchtman 2014; De Long and Shleifer 2018). The data here, from Bairoch, Batou, and Pierre (1988) and Dincecco and Onorato (2016), consist of a continuous variable for the logged population of all cities and a dummy variable for commune status.

Universities were initially founded to teach Roman and canon law and, much less often, medicine. They are thus a useful proxy for the supply of the teaching of Roman law in a given area. Both popes and secular rulers chartered universities, giving them privileges, legal protection, and accreditation to teach in other universities. Data on university foundations and charters comes from de Ridder-Symoens (2003), Wieruszowski (1966), and the universities' own websites.

Parliaments are a critical institution of council and consent to taxation by the monarchs (see Van Zanden, Buringh, and Bosker 2012; Stasavage 2010 and 2014). I measure whether one existed or not in a given year in a given city, using data from Van Zanden, Buringh, and Bosker (2012). Parliamentary activity consists of the number of years in a given century that parliament met. It is a useful indicator of the authority of the parliaments: if members attend, then the ruler needs their council and consent. This measure is taken from Van Zanden, Buringh, and Bosker (2012).

The variables used in the analyses and their sources are summarized in table A. Table B summarizes the descriptive statistics.

Table C presents the results of Chow tests for structural breaks in panel data, which compare the coefficient estimates from the pooled data set to the subset of data from the medieval period: 1350 CE and earlier. We can reject the null hypothesis (H_0=all coefficients are stable over time), since the p-values are 0.000 in all cases except communes. (Since most communes were founded around the eleventh to twelfth centuries, and very few leave the data set, the medieval data subset and the pooled data set do not differ substantively.) The 1400s were not an economic, cultural or political rupture (Wickham 2016, 4), but this periodization differentiates between the era when

Table A. Summary of variables used

Variable	Description	Source
fragmentation	# of states within a 100, 250, and 500 km radius of city centroid	MPIDR [Max Planck Institute for Demographic Research]; CGG [Chair for Geodesy and Geoinformatics, University of Rostock] Historical GIS Files, Mosaic Census Collection[a]
	# of states existing within the 1900 boundaries of Europe	
commune	city achieved commune status	Bosker et al. 2013
university	university within 5km of city center	Bosker et al. 2013; de Ridder-Symons 2003; Wieruszowski 1966; History of Economic Thought [HET];[b] university websites
parliament	existence of parliament in city	Van Zanden et al. 2012
parliamentary activity	share of years in a given century when parliament met	Van Zanden et al. 2012
Religion		
bishop	city is a seat for a bishop or archbishop	DARMC [Mapping Past Societies, formerly Digital Atlas of Roman and Medieval Civilizations];[c] Bosker et al. 2013; own coding
diocese	boundaries of a bishop's jurisdiction	Digital Atlas of Dioceses and Ecclesiastical Provinces in Late Medieval Europe[d]
monastery	monastery within 5 km of city center	DARMC; own coding
cathedral	cathedral within 5 km of city center	Bosker et al. 2013; own compilation
crusade by 1200	four waves of crusade mobilization by 1200	Blaydes and Paik 2016
excommunication	excommunication status of a given ruler	New Cambridge Medieval History, New Catholic Encyclopedia (1911)[e]

Conflict

secular conflict	conflict within 50km × 50km area of city in past 150 years with secular rulers as combatants	Dincecco and Onorato 2016
papal conflict	conflict with pope as combatant, war by proxy, alliance, political crusade	Brecke et al. 2000; *New Cambridge Medieval History* country case studies; own compilation; Dupuy and Dupuy 1993

Controls

commune	city achieved commune status	Bosker et al. 2013; Dincecco and Onorato 2016
urbanization	log of city population	Bairoch et al. 1988
papal charter	university chartered by pope	de Ridder-Symons 2003; university websites; HET
secular charter	university chartered by secular ruler	de Ridder-Symons 2003; university websites; HET
trade access	proximity to river	Dincecco and Onorato 2016
agricultural potential	soil quality	Dincecco and Onorato 2016
Protestant	city Protestant status in 1600	Cantoni 2012

[a] https://censusmosaic.demog.berkeley.edu/data/historical-gis-file, accessed 18 June 2020.

[b] https://www.hetwebsite.net/het/schools/studium.htm, accessed March 2021.

[c] https://www.darmc.harvard.edu, accessed January–February 2020.

[d] https://doi.org/10.25740/rh195hm5975, accessed April 3, 2022.

[e] https://www.newadvent.org/cathen/, accessed June 11, 2021.

Table B. Descriptive Statistics

City-level data					
Variable	Mean	Std. dev.	Min	Max	N
urbanization	2.04	0.94	0.00	7.71	9,340
university	0.01	0.08	0.00	2.00	28,639
parliamentary activity	13.71	25.34	0.00	100.00	6,787
bishop	0.38	0.49	0.00	1.00	6,760
monastery	0.57	2.18	0.00	87.00	28,639
cathedral	0.05	0.25	0.00	3.00	28,639
papal conflict	1.06	2.69	0.00	18.00	20,889
crusade by 1200	1.34	2.45	0.00	16.00	13,248
secular conflict	0.27	0.44	0.00	1.00	6,760
commune	0.30	0.46	0.00	1.00	6,760
secular charter	0.00	0.05	0.00	1.00	28,639
papal charter	0.00	0.06	0.00	2.00	28,639
agricultural potential	0.73	0.23	0.01	1.00	6,760
trade access	0.55	0.50	0.00	1.00	6,760

State-level data					
Variable	Mean	Std. Dev.	Min	Max	N
papal conflict	.0099	.11	0	3	31969
secular conflict	.13	.29	0	1	786
fragmentation: # of states within 100km	23.629	16.16	0	65	31795
within 250km	78.04	49.49	1	192	31795
within 500km	150.22	72.76	1	235	31795
within 1900 borders	120.759	79.21	1	207	31218
commune	3.75	10.19	0	104	7773
primogeniture	.66	.47	0	1	2338
parliaments	1.50	10.30	0	269	31796
urbanization	1.84	11.67	0	422	31796
monasteries	41.62	211.38	0	5247	31796
bishoprics	10.07	68.72	0	1385	31796

Raster data, 100km × 100km grid cells					
Variable	Mean	Std. Dev.	Min	Max	N
# of state boundaries	1.83	2.44	1	33	105111
secular conflict	.25	.997	0	13	6123
papal conflict	.066	.31	0	9	105111
communes	.31	.80	0	9	6123
primogeniture	.65	.47	0	1	67482
parliaments	.49	1.36	0	14	105111
urbanization	.53	1.44	0	35	105111
HRE	.93	.26	0	1	105111
Protestant	.72	.41	0	1	18034

Table C. Chow tests for structural breaks around 1350

Estimates of:	F statistic	Prob >F
fragmentation	$F(2, 781) = 24.21$	0.0000
communes	$F(4, 501) = 1.93$	0.105
universities	$F(7, 2741) = 6.12$	0.0000
parliaments	$F(6, 2560) = 17.94$	0.0000
parliamentary activity	$F(6, 2561) = 87.37$	0.0000

the papacy was most powerful politically and the period when its political influence had weakened.

Regression Results and Robustness Tests

This section reports the specific results that are presented graphically throughout the book. I include several robustness tests and different model specifications (different dependent variables, both fixed effects and mixed effects models, additional control variables). I also include Oster sensitivity tests (available for the two-way fixed effects OLS regressions but not for the hierarchical ME regressions) and placebo tests, to reduce the possibility that unobserved factors swamp the effect of the included observable variables or that the outcomes are overdetermined.

Figure A.1 reports the results of the same grid cell data regressions as in Table 2.1, but without subsetting for the medieval and early modern periods (model 1 in Table 2.1). Results for the control variables (Holy Roman Empire status and Protestant status) are left out. Papal conflict is a strong predictor of fragmentation.

Table A.1 reports the results of placebo tests: future papal conflict (150-year lead) does not predict past fragmentation at any point. The other variables all retain their previous associations with fragmentation.

Table A.2 provides another robustness test for the results in table 2.1. The proxy for fragmentation here is the number of states within a 100 km radius of the centroid of a state. All models control for the state being part of the Holy Roman Empire (HRE dummy variable). Papal conflict is strongly correlated with this measure of fragmentation in the medieval era, more so than secular conflict. The relationships survive adding two controls: parliaments and city populations (model 2). Once we add communes and primogeniture (model 3), however, these relationships wash out. There is no significant predictor of fragmentation in the early modern period (models 4–6). The coefficients on parliaments, urbanization, communes, and primogeniture are all in expected direction, but at low statistical significance. The Oster sensitivity tests for

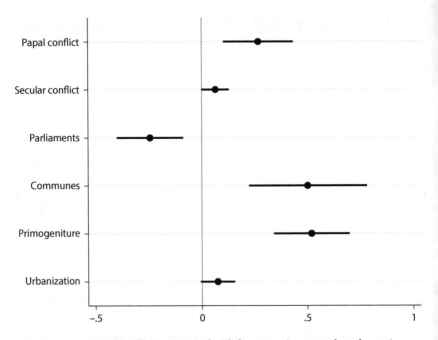

FIGURE A.1. Papal conflict is associated with fragmentation even when alternative explanations are included over the entire 1000–1800 time period (OLS regressions with state and year 2FE). Horizontal lines indicate 95% confidence intervals.

Table A.1. Papal conflict placebo (150-year lead) is not associated with fragmentation, cell grid 100km × 100km data (OLS regressions with state and year 2FE)

	Medieval					Early Modern			
	(1)	(2)	(3)	(4)	(5)	(6)	(7)	(8)	(9)
papal conflict lead	0.000	0.000	0.000	0.000	−0.009	0.089	0.103	0.119	0.213
	(.)	(.)	(.)	(.)	(0.037)	(0.360)	(0.338)	(0.333)	(0.328)
secular conflict	0.000	−0.040	−0.062	0.038	0.036	0.284*	0.284*	0.323*	0.565***
	(0.048)	(0.047)	(0.045)	(0.036)	(0.023)	(0.138)	(0.143)	(0.150)	(0.163)
parliaments		−0.141***	−0.275***	−0.139**			−0.566	−0.669	−1.318*
		(0.040)	(0.063)	(0.044)			(1.022)	(1.032)	(0.640)
urbanization		0.716***	0.353**	0.052			0.148	0.185	0.121
		(0.134)	(0.122)	(0.079)			(0.147)	(0.148)	(0.151)
communes			0.661***	0.298**				−1.254	−1.641*
			(0.133)	(0.111)				(0.643)	(0.685)
primogeniture				−0.047					0.518
				(0.077)					(0.273)
Protestant						−0.835	−0.901	−0.946	−0.293
						(0.704)	(0.728)	(0.763)	(0.741)
HRE	−0.221	−0.198	−0.330	−0.076	0.435***	0.915**	1.019***	1.017***	0.567*
	(0.166)	(0.156)	(0.177)	(0.183)	(0.107)	(0.306)	(0.296)	(0.300)	(0.235)
constant	2.028***	1.881***	1.919***	1.939***	1.506***	4.513***	4.529***	5.271***	4.582***
	(0.040)	(0.050)	(0.053)	(0.056)	(0.039)	(0.566)	(0.655)	(0.786)	(0.792)
N	1650	1650	1650	1081	3662	548	548	548	486
adj. R^2	0.753	0.777	0.794	0.823	0.968	0.971	0.971	0.971	0.980

* $p < 0.05$, ** $p < 0.01$, *** $p < 0.001$

Table A.2. Papal conflict is associated with fragmentation, 100km centroids using state-level data (OLS regressions with state and year 2FE)

	Medieval			Early Modern		
	(1)	(2)	(3)	(4)	(5)	(6)
papal conflict	2.143***	2.070***	0.641	1.448	1.587	·
	(0.490)	(0.507)	(1.650)	(0.926)	(0.992)	(.)
secular conflict	1.123	0.946	-2.191	3.030	3.053	5.271
	(1.249)	(1.279)	(3.138)	(1.828)	(1.843)	(4.791)
parliaments		-0.074	-0.018		0.091	0.046
		(0.040)	(0.047)		(0.059)	(0.034)
urbanization		-0.108	0.262		-0.055	-0.020
		(0.136)	(0.195)		(0.035)	(0.018)
communes			-0.183			0.011
			(0.176)			(0.074)
primogeniture			-0.591			-1.331
			(0.774)			(1.689)
HRE	-0.465	-0.406	1.884	-2.004	-1.985	-0.987
	(0.892)	(0.915)	(1.423)	(1.552)	(1.577)	(0.987)
constant	9.653***	9.993***	0.703	21.764***	21.720***	5.700**
	(0.646)	(0.722)	(0.987)	(1.203)	(1.168)	(1.565)
$\partial = 0 = \beta$ for papal conflict	-1.93	-1.94	-.58	-.98	-1.08	·
N	235	235	33	250	250	42

* $p < 0.05$, ** $p < 0.01$, *** $p < 0.001$

able A.3. Papal conflict is associated with fragmentation using different specifications, state-level ata (OLS regressions with state and year 2FE)

	Medieval			Early Modern		
	(1)	(2)	(3)	(4)	(5)	(6)
	250km	500km	1900 borders	250km	500km	1900 borders
apal conflict	7.840***	24.738***	7.474*	2.235	3.935	6.704
	(1.594)	(4.492)	(3.374)	(1.542)	(2.554)	(6.266)
cular conflict	2.700	7.348	0.504	6.718	4.174	3.086
	(5.083)	(11.760)	(9.464)	(3.742)	(4.229)	(3.205)
nstant	29.078***	65.714***	37.621***	71.202***	145.389***	87.452***
	(0.410)	(0.950)	(0.754)	(0.800)	(0.907)	(0.447)
	235	235	231	250	250	693
j. R^2	0.830	0.833	0.764	0.953	0.950	0.917

$p<0.05$, ** $p<0.01$, *** $p<0.001$

papal conflict suggest that the effect of unobservables would have to be nearly twice as high, and run in the opposite direction, to swamp out the effects of the observables.

The models in Table A.3 test whether the association between papal conflict and fragmentation is robust to other specifications of fragmentation. If we examine the number of states within a 250km and 500km radius of the centroid of a state, papal conflict continues to be strongly associated in the medieval period (models 1 and 2). The relationship is robust to specifying fragmentation as the number of states at a given point in time within the 1900 borders of Europe (model 3). In the early modern period (models 4–6), however, papal conflict no longer displays the same strong relationship.

Table A.4 reports the results of placebo tests for the results in Table A.2 using the 100km state centroid data: future papal conflict (150-year lead) does not predict past fragmentation in the medieval period, in contrast to the early modern.

Table A.4. Papal conflict placebo (150-year lead) is not associated with fragmentation at 100km, state-level data (OLS regressions with state and year 2FE)

	Medieval			Early Modern		
	(1)	(2)	(3)	(4)	(5)	(6)
papal conflict lead	−0.720	−0.555	0.012	2.453**	2.374*	0.000
	(1.439)	(1.379)	(0.904)	(0.881)	(0.920)	(.)
secular conflict	1.120	0.967	−1.503	3.062	3.087	5.271
	(1.271)	(1.302)	(3.877)	(1.832)	(1.847)	(4.791)
parliaments		−0.064	−0.005		0.090	0.046
		(0.038)	(0.056)		(0.059)	(0.034)
urbanization		−0.136	0.249		−0.055	−0.020
		(0.121)	(0.188)		(0.035)	(0.018)
communes			−0.192			0.011
			(0.179)			(0.074)
primogeniture			−0.888			−1.331
			(0.826)			(1.689)
HRE	−0.222	−0.223	1.824	−1.982	−1.955	−0.987
	(0.837)	(0.873)	(1.513)	(1.546)	(1.568)	(0.987)
constant	9.570***	9.970***	0.833	21.732***	21.689***	5.700**
	(0.615)	(0.691)	(0.832)	(1.200)	(1.165)	(1.565)
N	235	235	33	250	250	42
adj. R^2	0.838	0.843	0.069	0.905	0.904	0.792

* $p < 0.05$, ** $p < 0.01$, *** $p < 0.001$

Table A.5. Mediation analysis: papal conflict is mediated by primogeniture

	Medieval	Early Modern
Average Causal Mediated Effect (ACME)	.16 (.14–.17)	.09 (.08–.10)
Direct Effect (DE)	.32 (.26–.37)	.9 (.81–.98)
Total Effect (TE)	.48 (.42–53)	.99 (.89–1.07
% of TE mediated	**33%** (.30–.38)	**9%** (.08–.09)

Table A.5 shows the results of mediation analysis (Imai, Keele, and Tingley 2010), which decomposes the total effect of papal conflict and primogeniture into the direct effect of papal conflict, the average mediated effect of primogeniture, and the percentage of the total effect mediated by primogeniture. (See chapter 2, page 65.)

Table A.6. reports 100km x 100km grid cell data results for the rise of communes in Figure 2.8 (models 2 and 5). Papal conflict, bishops, and fragmentation are positively associated with the rise of communes in the medieval era, but not in the early modern. Once we add parliaments and urbanization as controls, papal conflict disappears (model 3), but bishops and fragmentation continue to be associated with communes.

In the early modern period, secular conflict is positively associated with communes, but this relationship falls out once we include bishops, fragmentation, and the other control variables.

Table A.7 reports the results of a robustness test for the results in Table A.6: a placebo (papal conflict with 150-year lead into the future) does not predict the density of communes in either the medieval or early modern period.

Table A.6. Papal conflict, bishops, and fragmentation are associated with medieval communes, 100km×100km cell grid data (OLS regressions with state and year 2FE)

	Medieval			Early Modern		
	(1)	(2)	(3)	(4)	(5)	(6)
papal conflict	0.133***	0.119***	0.051	−0.166	0.103	0.134
	(0.030)	(0.027)	(0.028)	(0.081)	(0.067)	(0.071)
secular conflict	0.041	0.038	0.036	0.375***	0.022	0.015
	(0.038)	(0.033)	(0.031)	(0.064)	(0.016)	(0.017)
bishop		0.395***	0.186**		0.000	0.000
		(0.075)	(0.057)		(.)	(.)
fragmentation		0.148***	0.110***		−0.008	−0.004
		(0.028)	(0.023)		(0.006)	(0.006)
parliaments			0.207***			0.101
			(0.047)			(0.079)
urbanization			0.438***			0.041***
			(0.055)			(0.009)
constant	0.213***	−1.109***	−0.691***	0.220***	0.338***	0.246***
	(0.008)	(0.203)	(0.154)	(0.018)	(0.011)	(0.043)
N	1650	1650	1650	3656	3665	3665
adj. R^2	0.479	0.567	0.707	0.391	0.965	0.966
$\partial = 0 = \beta$ for papal conflict	−1.40	−1.58	−1.95	−2.91	−2.94	−3.66

* $p<0.05$, ** $p<0.01$, *** $p<0.001$

Table A.7. Papal conflict placebo (150-year lead) is not associated with communes, 100 km × 100km grid cell data (OLS regressions with city and year 2FE)

	Medieval			Early Modern		
	(1)	(2)	(3)	(4)	(5)	(6)
papal conflict lead	0.000	0.000	0.000	0.021	0.021	0.008
	(.)	(.)	(.)	(0.014)	(0.014)	(0.013)
secular conflict	0.044	0.041	0.037	0.023	0.023	0.016
	(0.038)	(0.033)	(0.031)	(0.016)	(0.016)	(0.017)
bishop		0.391***	0.183**		0.000	0.000
		(0.076)	(0.057)		(.)	(.)
fragmentation		0.150***	0.111***		-0.005	-0.001
		(0.028)	(0.023)		(0.007)	(0.007)
parliaments			0.211***			0.089
			(0.047)			(0.080)
urbanization			0.437***			0.040***
			(0.056)			(0.008)
constant	0.230***	-1.089***	-0.681***	0.323***	0.332***	0.247***
	(0.008)	(0.204)	(0.154)	(0.005)	(0.013)	(0.044)
N	1650	1650	1650	3662	3662	3662
adj. R^2	0.475	0.564	0.706	0.964	0.964	0.966

* $p < 0.05$, ** $p < 0.01$, *** $p < 0.001$

Table A.8. Religious factors are associated with papal university charters, city-level data (ME random intercept regressions with city-year level 2 clusters)

	Papal university charters		Secular university charters	
	Medieval	Early Modern	Medieval	Early Modern
papal conflict	**0.015***	**0.012***	0.004	**0.006***
	(0.004)	(0.002)	(0.003)	(0.001)
secular conflict	**0.039***	0.007	−0.009	0.005
	(0.019)	(0.006)	(0.016)	(0.005)
monastery	**0.010***	**0.012***	0.000	**0.002***
	(0.001)	(0.001)	(0.001)	(0.001)
cathedral	0.008	**0.025****	**0.030***	**0.051***
	(0.016)	(0.009)	(0.015)	(0.007)
bishop	−0.011	0.004	0.012	0.006
	(0.019)	(0.008)	(0.018)	(0.007)
commune	0.001	0.005	0.012	**0.015***
	(0.016)	(0.007)	(0.015)	(0.006)
urbanization	0.015	**0.008***	**0.019***	0.004
	(0.009)	(0.004)	(0.008)	(0.003)
constant	−0.050*	−0.030**	−0.036	−0.019*
	(0.021)	(0.009)	(0.019)	(0.008)
sd (city)	−9.355***	−36.724***	−9.227***	−33.118***
	(0.295)	(0.756)	(0.058)	(0.820)
sd (year)	−20.091***	−2.893***	−22.344***	−2.814***
	(4.259)	(0.065)	(1.400)	(0.048)
sd (residual)	−1.827***	−1.914***	−2.045***	−2.127***
	(0.115)	(0.015)	(0.041)	(0.015)
N	705	2756	705	2756
adj. R^2				

* $p<0.05$, ** $p<0.01$, *** $p<0.001$

Table A.8 shows the results of mixed-effects regressions on city-level data graphed in figure 4.3. Papal conflict, monasteries, and cathedrals are predictors of university foundations. Note that bishops and communes are not strong predictors.

Table A.9. Bishops and communes are associated with universities if no other religious variables are included, city-level data (ME random intercept regressions with city-year level 2 clusters)

	Papal university charters		Secular university charters	
	Medieval	Early Modern	Medieval	Early Modern
secular conflict	**0.056****	−0.006	−0.003	−0.002
	(0.017)	(0.007)	(0.015)	(0.005)
bishop	0.014	**0.027***	**0.032***	**0.021***
	(0.016)	(0.008)	(0.015)	(0.006)
commune	**0.028***	**0.026***	**0.027***	**0.023***
	(0.014)	(0.007)	(0.012)	(0.006)
urbanization	**0.023****	0.004	**0.017***	0.002
	(0.008)	(0.004)	(0.007)	(0.003)
constant	−0.047*	−0.008	−0.040*	−0.008
	(0.019)	(0.010)	(0.017)	(0.008)
sd (city)	−9.348***	−29.723***	−9.369***	−29.522***
	(0.090)	(0.980)	(0.070)	(0.909)
sd (year)	−19.360***	−2.880***	−19.165***	−2.914***
	(1.539)	(0.069)	(1.277)	(0.052)
sd (residual)	−1.822***	−1.831***	−2.017***	−2.099***
	(0.036)	(0.014)	(0.032)	(0.014)
N	802	2871	802	2871
adj. R^2				

* $p<0.05$, ** $p<0.01$, *** $p<0.001$

Table A.9 reports the results of the same ME model as in Table A.8, but drops several religious variables: papal conflict, monasteries, and cathedrals. If these are absent, bishops and communes are strongly and positively associated with universities, consistent with Hollenbach and Pierskalla (2022).

Table A.10 reports the results of a robustness test for the results in Table A.8. OLS with two-way city and year fixed effects shows the same relationship: papal conflict is positively associated with the formation of universities. I use monasteries, urbanization and cathedrals as controls because they may lead to the "treatment" (papal conflict). The Oster sensitivity tests suggest the result least likely to have been swamped by unobservables is the impact of papal conflict on papal charters of medieval universities, as predicted by the theory.

Table A.10. Papal and secular conflict are associated with university charters, city-level data (OLS regressions with city and year 2FE)

	Papal charters		Secular charters	
	Medieval	Early Modern	Medieval	Early Modern
papal conflict	**0.023***	**0.010***	**0.010***	0.003
	(0.009)	(0.005)	(0.004)	(0.002)
secular conflict	**0.090***	0.008	−0.013	0.013
	(0.040)	(0.009)	(0.030)	(0.007)
bishop	**−0.094***	0.009	0.215	0.021
	(0.038)	(0.023)	(0.233)	(0.011)
urbanization	0.016	−0.001	0.015	**0.008***
	(0.021)	(0.004)	(0.014)	(0.004)
monastery	0.015	**0.012*** **	0.004	0.002
	(0.010)	(0.002)	(0.006)	(0.002)
cathedral	−0.021	0.030	0.072	**0.045** **
	(0.045)	(0.017)	(0.045)	(0.016)
constant	−0.037	−0.009	−0.186	−0.028*
	(0.077)	(0.015)	(0.153)	(0.012)
N	551	2686	551	2686
adj. R^2	0.461	0.276	0.520	0.248
$\partial = 0 = \beta$ for papal conflict	50.3	.10	−.50	.02

* $p < 0.05$, ** $p < 0.01$, *** $p < 0.001$

Table A.11 reports the results graphed in figure 5.1 (models 4 and 9). Bishops and communes are closely tied to the presence of medieval parliaments, and the strong correlation to bishops survives the inclusion of controls for city size. In the early modern period, however, bishops are negatively correlated to the rise of parliaments, and once we include universities, that relationship drops out. Oster sensitivity tests suggest that unobservables overwhelm the effect of observable factors in the early modern period.

Table A.12 reports the results graphed in figure 5.2 (models 2 and 6), which show a strong correlation between war, commune status, and parliamentary activity. Figure 5.3 shows that this relationship in the medieval era disappears once we include bishops (models 4 and 8). The effect of bishops in the early modern period disappears once we control for a city's status as Protestant, however. Oster sensitivity tests suggest that unobservables overwhelm the effect of observable factors in the early modern period.

Table A.11. Bishops are associated with medieval parliaments, city-level data (OLS regressions with city and year 2FE)

	Medieval				Early Modern				
	(1)	(2)	(3)	(4)	(5)	(6)	(7)	(8)	(9)
secular conflict	0.036	0.082	0.037	0.074	−0.010	0.002	−0.010	0.055	0.014
	(0.019)	(0.067)	(0.019)	(0.067)	(0.010)	(0.011)	(0.010)	(0.032)	(0.054)
bishop			0.155**	0.290**			−0.002	−0.060*	0.020
			(0.053)	(0.108)			(0.024)	(0.029)	(0.087)
commune	0.069*	0.117	0.063*	0.121	0.075*	0.015	0.075*	−0.093*	0.112
	(0.029)	(0.069)	(0.029)	(0.066)	(0.035)	(0.022)	(0.035)	(0.037)	(0.111)
urbanization		−0.014		−0.010		0.004			0.036
		(0.044)		(0.044)		(0.006)			(0.036)
university				0.062					0.081
				(0.108)					(0.059)
Protestant								0.000	0.000
								(.)	(.)
constant	0.270***	0.287*	0.216***	0.076	0.796***	0.794***	0.797***	0.402***	0.092
	(0.006)	(0.115)	(0.019)	(0.150)	(0.018)	(0.018)	(0.020)	(0.032)	(0.092)
N	2460	319	2460	319	2460	1852	2460	288	377
adj. R^2	0.506	0.524	0.509	0.541	0.832	0.857	0.832	0.873	0.731
$\partial = 0 = \beta$ for bishop	n/a	n/a	.80	1.35	n/a	n/a	.004	.01	.08

* $p<0.05$, ** $p<0.01$, *** $p<0.001$

Table A.12. Bishops are associated with medieval parliamentary activity, city-level data (OLS regressions with city and year 2FE)

	Medieval				Early Modern				
	(1)	(2)	(3)	(4)	(5)	(6)	(7)	(8)	(9)
secular conflict	0.909	1.148*	0.923	0.598	2.084	4.293***	2.153	1.749	1.635
	(1.833)	(0.447)	(1.839)	(1.744)	(1.141)	(0.937)	(1.142)	(1.154)	(1.306)
bishop				12.739***				16.168**	1.266
				(2.698)				(5.588)	(1.160)
commune		−1.612*	−0.521	−0.288		13.548***	7.849*	7.707*	−3.437
		(0.671)	(1.672)	(1.316)		(2.502)	(3.629)	(3.659)	(3.351)
urbanization	−1.617		−1.549	−1.331	6.827***		6.508***	6.475***	0.044
	(1.049)		(1.115)	(0.989)	(0.926)		(0.952)	(0.952)	(0.700)
Protestant									0.000
									(.)
									[.]
constant	6.398*	1.571***	6.461*	−2.720	11.919***	20.766***	8.117**	0.986	5.797*
	(2.732)	(0.095)	(2.673)	(3.025)	(2.331)	(1.357)	(2.803)	(3.717)	(2.836)
N	336	3075	336	336	1852	2460	1852	1852	254
adj. R^2	0.126	0.186	0.122	0.271	0.629	0.636	0.630	0.633	0.518
$\partial = 0 = \beta$ for bishop	n/a	n/a	n/a	−3.47	n/a	n/a	n/a	−.15	−.02

* $p<0.05$, ** $p<0.01$, *** $p<0.001$

REFERENCES

Abramson, Scott. 2017. "The Economic Origins of the Territorial State." *International Organization* 71, no. 1: 97–140.

Abramson, Scott, and Carles Boix. 2019. "Endogenous Parliaments: The Domestic and International Roots of Long-Term Economic Growth and Executive Constraints in Europe." *International Organization* 73, no. 4: 793–837.

Abulafia, David. 1999. "The Kingdom of Sicily under the Hohenstaufen and Angevins." In *The New Cambridge Medieval History*, Vol. 5, edited by David Abulafia. Cambridge: Cambridge University Press, 497–521.

Abulafia, David. 2000. "The Italian South." In *The New Cambridge Medieval History*, Vol. 6, edited by Michael Jones. Cambridge: Cambridge University Press, 488–514.

Acemoglu, Daron, and James A. Robinson. 2012. *Why Nations Fail.* New York: Crown Business.

Acharya, Avidit, and Alexander Lee. 2018. "Economic Foundations of the Territorial State System." *American Journal of Political Science* 62, no.4: 954–66.

Acharya, Avidit, and Alexander Lee. 2019. "Path Dependence in European Development: Medieval Politics, Conflict, and State Building." *Comparative Political Studies* 52: 2171–2206.

Adams, Norma. 2017. "The Writ of Prohibition to Court Christian" (1936). *Minnesota Law Review* 20. https://scholarship.law.umn.edu/mlr/2017

Ambler, Sophie-Thérèse. 2017. *Bishops in the Political Community of England, 1213–1272.* Oxford: Oxford University Press.

Amundsen, Daniel. 1978. "Medieval Canon Law on Medical and Surgical Practice by the Clergy." *Bulletin of the History of Medicine* 52, no. 1: 22–44.

Anderson, Greg. 2018. "Was There Any Such Thing as a Nonmodern State?" In *State Formations*, edited by John Brooke, Julia Strauss, and Greg Anderson. Cambridge: Cambridge University Press, 58–70.

Anderson, Karen. 2014. *Fields of Blood: Religion and the History of Violence.* New York: Alfred Knopf.

Anderson, Perry. (1974) 2013. *Lineages of the Absolutist State.* Verso Books.

Angelov, Dimiter, and Judith Herrin. 2012. "The Christian Imperial Tradition–Greek and Latin." In *Universal Empire: A Comparative Approach to Imperial Culture and Representation in Eurasian History*, edited by Peter F. Bang and Dariusz Kołodziejczyk. New York: Cambridge University Press, 149–74.

Arendt, Hannah. 1958. "What Was Authority?" *NOMOS* 1: 81–112.

Arnold, Benjamin. 1989. "German Bishops and their Military Retinues in the Medieval Empire." *German History* 7, no. 2: 161–83.

Auer, Leopold. 2011. "The Role of the Imperial Aulic Council in the Constitutional Structure of the Holy Roman Empire." In *The Holy Roman Empire 1495–1806*, edited by R.J.W. Evans, Michael Schaich, and Peter Wilson. London: Oxford University Press, 63–75.

Bagge, Sverre. 1997. "Medieval and Renaissance Historiography: Break or Continuity?" *The European Legacy* 2, no. 8: 1336–71.

Bagge, Sverre. 1999. "The Scandinavian Kingdoms." In *The New Cambridge Medieval History*, Vol. 5, edited by David Abulafia. Cambridge: Cambridge University Press, 720–42.

Bagge, Sverre. 2014. *Cross and Scepter: The Rise of the Scandinavian Kingdoms from the Vikings to the Reformation.* Princeton: Princeton University Press.

Bagge, Sverre. 2019. *State Formation in Europe, 843–1789: A Divided World.* New York: Routledge.

Bairoch, Paul, Jean Batou, and Chevre Pierre. 1988. *Population des villes européennes de 800 à 1850: banque de données et analyse sommaire des résultats.* Geneva: Librairie Droz.

Bák, János. 1998. "Hungary: Crown and Estates." In *The New Cambridge Medieval History,* Vol. 7, edited by Christopher Allmand. Cambridge: Cambridge University Press, 707–26.

Baldwin, John. 2004. "The Western Franks: Crown and Government." In *The New Cambridge Medieval History,* Vol. 4, edited by David Luscombe and Jonathan Riley-Smith. Cambridge: Cambridge University Press, 510–29.

Barraclough, Geoffrey. 1954. "The English Royal Chancery and the Papal Chancery in the Reign of Henry III." *Mitteilungen des Instituts für Österreichische Geschichtsforschung* 62: 365–78.

Barratt, Nick. 2001. "The English Revenue of Richard I." *English Historical Review* 116, no. 467: 635–56.

Barratt, Nick. 2007. "Finance and the Economy in the Reign of Henry II." In *Henry II: New Interpretations,* edited by Christopher Harper-Bill and Nicholas Vincent. Woodbridge: The Boydell Press, 242–56.

Barro, Robert, J. 2001. "Human Capital and Growth." *American Economic Review* 91, no. 2: 12–7.

Barron, Caroline M. 2000. "The Reign of Richard II." In *The New Cambridge Medieval History,* Vol. 6, edited by Michael Jones. Cambridge: Cambridge University Press, 297–333.

Barzel, Yoram, and Edgar Kiser. 1997. "The Development and Decline of Medieval Voting Institutions: A Comparison of England and France." *Economic Inquiry* 35, no. 2: 244–60.

Bates, Robert H., and Da-Hsiang Donald Lien. 1985. "A Note on Taxation, Development, and Representative Government." *Politics & Society* 14, no. 1: 53–70.

Bean, Richard. 1973. "War and the Birth of the Nation State." *Journal of Economic History* 33, no. 1: 203–21.

Becker, Sascha and Ludger Woessmann. 2009. "Was Weber Wrong? A Human Capital Theory of Protestant Economic History." *Quarterly Journal of Economics* 124, no. 2: 531–96.

Bendix, Reinhard. 1978. *Kings or People: Power and the Mandate to Rule.* Berkeley: University of California Press.

Benson, Robert L. 1968. *Bishop-Elect: A Study in Medieval Ecclesiastical Office.* Princeton University Press.

Benson, Robert L. 1982. "Political *Renovatio*: Two Models from Roman Antiquity." In *Renaissance and Renewal in the Twelfth Century,* edited by Robert L. Benson and Giles Constable. Cambridge, MA: Harvard University Press, 339–86.

Berend, Nora. 2004. "Hungary in the Eleventh and Twelfth Centuries." In *The New Cambridge Medieval History,* Vol. 4, edited by David Luscombe and Jonathan Riley-Smith. Cambridge: Cambridge University Press, 304–16.

Berman, Harold. 1983. "Religious Foundations of Law in the West: An Historical Perspective." *Journal of Law and Religion* 1, no. 1: 3–43.

Berman, Harold. 1983a. *Law and Revolution: The Formation of the Western Legal Tradition.* Cambridge: Harvard University Press.

Bireley, Robert. 1999. *The Refashioning of Catholicism, 1450–1700.* Houndsmills, Basingstoke: MacMillan & Co.

Bisson, Thomas. 1994. "The Feudal Revolution." *Past & Present* 142: 6–42.

Bisson, Thomas. 2009. *The Crisis of the Twelfth Century*. Princeton: Princeton University Press.

Black, Anthony. 1992. *Political Thought in Europe 1250–1450*. Cambridge: Cambridge University Press.

Black, Anthony. 1998. "Popes and Councils." In *The New Cambridge Medieval History*, Vol. 7, edited by Christopher Allmand. Cambridge: Cambridge University Press, 65–86.

Blaydes, Lisa. 2017. "State Building in the Middle East." *Annual Review of Political Science* 20: 487–504.

Blaydes, Lisa, and Eric Chaney. 2013. "The Feudal Revolution and Europe's Rise: Political Divergence of the Christian West and the Muslim World before 1500 CE." *American Political Science Review* 107, no. 1: 16–34.

Blaydes, Lisa, and Christopher Paik. 2016. "The Impact of Holy Land Crusades on State Formation: War Mobilization, Trade Integration, and Political Development in Medieval Europe." *International Organization* 70, no. 3: 1–36.

Bloch, Marc. 1961. *The Feudal Society*. Chicago: University of Chicago Press.

Blockmans, Wim P. 1978. "A Typology of Representative Institutions in Late Medieval Europe." *Journal of Medieval History* 4, no. 2: 189–215.

Blockmans, Wim. 1998. "Representation (since the Thirteenth Century)." In *The New Cambridge Medieval History*, Vol. 7, edited by Christopher Allmand. Cambridge: Cambridge University Press, 21–65.

Blum, Ulrich, and Leonard Dudley. 2001. "Religion and Economic Growth: Was Weber Right?" *Journal of Evolutionary Economics* 11: 207–30.

Blum, Ulrich, and Leonard Dudley. 2003. "Standardised Latin and Medieval Economic Growth." *European Review of Economic History* 7, no. 2: 213–238.

Blumenthal, Ute-Renate. 1988. *The Investiture Controversy*. Philadelphia: University of Pennsylvania Press.

Blumenthal, Ute-Renate. 2004. "The Papacy, 1024–1122." In *The New Cambridge Medieval History*, Vol. 4, edited by David Luscombe and Jonathan Riley-Smith. Cambridge: Cambridge University Press, 8–37.

Boase, T.S.R. 1933. *Boniface VIII*. London: Constable and Co.

Bombi, Barbara. 2009. "Petitioning between England and Avignon in the First Half of the Fourteenth Century." In *Medieval Petitions: Grace and Grievance*, edited by W. Mark Ormrod, Gwilym Dodd, and Anthony Musson. York: York Medieval Press, 64–81.

Bonner, Elizabeth. 2003. "Charles VII's Dynastic Policy and the 'Auld Alliance': The Marriage of James II and Marie de Guelders." *Innes Review* 54, no. 2: 143–4.

Bonney, Richard, ed. 1999. *The Rise of the Fiscal State in Europe, c. 1200–1815*. Oxford: Oxford University Press.

Bosker, Maarten, Eltjo Buringh, and Jan Luiten Van Zanden. 2013. "From Baghdad to London: Unraveling Urban Development in Europe, the Middle East, and North Africa, 800–1800." *Review of Economics and Statistics* 95, no. 4: 1418–37.

Bossy, John. 1985. *Christianity in the West: 1400–1700*. Oxford: Oxford University Press.

Bosworth, Clifford. 1996. *The New Islamic Dynasties*. New York: Columbia University Press.

Boucoyannis, Deborah. 2015. "No Taxation of Elites, No Representation: State Capacity and the Origins of Representation." *Politics & Society* 43, no. 3: 303–32.

Boucoyannis, Deborah. 2021. *Kings as Judges: Power, Justice, and the Origins of Parliaments*. Cambridge: Cambridge University Press.

Brand, Paul. 1992. *The Making of the Common Law*. London: Hambledon Press.

Brand, Paul. 2007. "Henry II and the Creation of English Common Law." In *Henry II: New Interpretations*, edited by Christopher Harper-Bill and Nicholas Vincent. Woodbridge: The Boydell Press, 215–41.

Brecke, Peter. 2012. *Conflict Catalog (Violent Conflicts 1400 AD to the Present in Different Regions of the World)*. Utrecht, Netherlands: Centre for Global Economic History at Utrecht University.

Brewer, John. 1989. *The Sinews of Power: War, Money and the English State, 1688–1783*. New York: Alfred A. Knopf.

Brooke, Z.N. (1931) 1981. *The English Church and the Papacy*. Cambridge: Cambridge University Press.

Brooke, Z.N. 1938. *A History of Europe from 911 to 1198*. London: Methuen & Co.

Brooke, Z.N. 1978. "The Issue of Law: Conflict of Churches." In *The Investiture Controversy*, edited by Karl F. Morrison. Huntington, New York: Robert F. Krieger Publishing Company, 6–11.

Brundage, James A. 2008. *The Medieval Origins of the Legal Profession: Canonists, Civilians, and Courts*. Chicago: Chicago University Press.

Brundage, James. 2009. *Law, Sex, and Christianity in Medieval Europe*. Chicago: University of Chicago Press.

Cammett, Melani, and Pauline Jones. 2022. "Politics in Muslim Societies: What's Religion Got to Do with It?" In *The Oxford Handbook of Politics in Muslim Societies*, edited by Melani Cammett and Pauline Jones. Oxford: Oxford University Press.

Campbell, James. 1986. *Essays in Anglo-Saxon History*. London: Hambledon Continuum.

Canning, Joseph. 1983. "Ideas of the State in Thirteenth and Fourteenth-Century Commentators on the Roman Law." *Transactions of the Royal Historical Society* 33:1–27.

Canning, Joseph. 2011. *Ideas of Power in the Late Middle Ages: 1296–1417*. Cambridge: Cambridge University Press.

Cantoni, Davide, and Noam Yuchtman. 2014. "Medieval Universities, Legal Institutions, and the Commercial Revolution." *Quarterly Journal of Economics* 129, no. 2: 823–87.

Cantor, Norman. 1958. *Church, Kingship, and Lay Investiture in England 1089–1135*. Princeton: Princeton University Press.

Carocci, Sandro. 2016. "Popes as Princes? The Papal States (1000–1300)." In *A Companion to the Medieval Papacy*, edited by Keith Sisson and Atria Larson. Leiden, NL: E.J. Brill: 66–84.

Carruthers, Bruce. 1990. "Politics, Popery, and Property: A Comment on North and Weingast." *The Journal of Economic History* 50, no. 3: 693–8.

Carsten, Francis. 1959. *Princes and Parliaments in Germany, from the Fifteenth to the Eighteenth Century*. Oxford: Clarendon Press.

Cavanaugh, William. 2009. *The Myth of Religious Violence*. Oxford: Oxford University Press.

Cazel, Fred. 1989. "Financing the Crusades." In *The History of the Crusades*. Vol. 6, *The Impact of the Crusades on Europe*, edited by Harry Hazard and Norman Zacour. Madison: University of Wisconsin Press, 116–49.

Centeno, Miguel. 2002. *Blood and Debt: War and the Nation-State in Latin America*. University Park, PA: Penn State University Press.

Chambers, David S. 2006. *Popes, Cardinals, and War*. London: I.B. Tauris.

Charron, Nicholas, Carl Dahlström, and Victor Lapuente. 2012. "No Law Without a State." *Journal of Comparative Economics* 40: 176–93.

Cheyette, Frederic. 1973. "The Invention of the State." In *Essays on Medieval Civilization: The Walter Prescott Webb Memorial Lectures*, edited by Bede Karl Lackner and Kenneth Roy Philip. Arlington: University of Texas Press, 143–78.

Chibnall, Marjorie. 2004. "England and Normandy, 1042–1137." In *The New Cambridge Medieval History*, Vol. 4, edited by David Luscombe and Jonathan Riley-Smith. Cambridge: Cambridge University Press, 191–216.

Chrimes, Stanley Bertram. 1952. *An Introduction to the Administrative History of Mediaeval England*. Oxford: Basil Blackwell.

Ciepley, David. 2017. "Is the US Government a Corporation? The Corporate Origins of Modern Constitutionalism." *American Political Science Review* 111, no. 2: 418–35.

Cipolla, Carlo. (1993) 2004. *Before the Industrial Revolution: European Society and Economy 1000-1700.* London: Routledge.

Clark, David. 1986. "The Medieval Origins of Modern Legal Education: Between Church and State." *American Journal of Comparative Law* 35: 653–719.

Coleman, David. 2000. "Spain." In *The Reformation World*, edited by Andrew Pettegree. London and New York: Routledge, 296–305.

Coleman, Edward. 1999. "The Italian Communes. Recent Work and Current Trends." *Journal of Medieval History* 25, no. 4: 373–97.

Connolly, Serena. 2009. "Petitioning in the Ancient World." In *Medieval Petitions: Grace and Grievance*, edited by W. Mark Ormrod, Gwilym Dodd, and Anthony Musson. York: York Medieval Press, 47–63.

Conran, James, and Kathleen Thelen. 2016. "Institutional Change." In *The Oxford Handbook of Historical Institutionalism*, edited by Orfeo Fioretos, Tulia G. Falleti, and Adam Sheingate. Oxford: Oxford University Press, 51–70.

Costa Lopez, Julia. 2020. "Political Authority in International Relations: Revisiting the Medieval Debate." *International Organization* 74, Spring: 222–52.

Costa Lopez, Julia, Benjamin De Carvalho, Andrew Latham, Ayse Zarakol, Jens Bartelson, and Minda Holm. 2018. "In the Beginning There Was No Word (For It): Terms, Concepts, and Early Sovereignty." *International Studies Review* 20, no. 3: 489–519.

Cox, Gary W. 2012. Was the Glorious Revolution a Constitutional Watershed? *Journal of Economic History* 72, no. 3: 567–600.

Cox, Gary W., and Barry R. Weingast. 2017. "Executive Constraint, Political Stability, and Economic Growth." *Comparative Political Studies* 51, no. 3: 279–303.

Cowdrey, Herbert Edward John. 1998. *Pope Gregory VII, 1073-1085.* Oxford: Oxford University Press.

Cowdrey, Herbert. 2004. "The Structure of the Church, 1024–1073." In *The New Cambridge Medieval History*, Vol. 4, edited by David Luscombe and Jonathan Riley-Smith. Cambridge: Cambridge University Press, 229–67.

Dagron, Gilbert. 2003. *Emperor and Priest: The Imperial Office in Byzantium.* Cambridge: Cambridge University Press.

Davies, Rees. 2003. "The Medieval State: The Tyranny of a Concept?" *Journal of Historical Sociology* 16, no. 2: 1–21.

D'Avray, David. 2010. *Medieval Religious Rationalities.* Cambridge: Cambridge University Press.

D'Avray, David. 2017. "Stages of Papal Law." *Journal of the British Academy* 5: 37–59.

Daniel, William. 2009. "The Power of Governance Enjoyed by the Supreme Tribunal of the Apostolic Signatura with Historical Antecedents." *Ius Ecclesiae* 21: 631–52.

Dębiński, Antoni. 2010. *Church and Roman Law.* Lublin, Poland: KUL.

de Carvalho, Benjamin, Halvard Leira and John Hobson. 2011. "The Big Bangs of IR: The Myths That Your Teachers Still Tell You about 1648 and 1919." *Millennium* 39, no. 3: 735–58.

de Mesquita, Bruce Bueno. 2000. "Popes, Kings, and Endogenous Institutions: The Concordat of Worms and the Origins of Sovereignty." *International Studies Review* 2, no. 2: 93–118.

de Mesquita, Bruce Bueno. 2022. *The Invention of Power.* New York: Public Affairs.

de Ridder-Symoens, Hilde. 2003. *A History of the University in Europe, Volume 1: Universities in the Middle Ages.* Cambridge: Cambridge University Press.

de Sousa, Armindo. 1998. "Portugal." In *The New Cambridge Medieval History*, Vol. 7, edited by Christopher Allmand. Cambridge: Cambridge University Press, 627–44.

Deanesly, Margaret. 1969. *History of the Medieval Church, 590-1500.* London: Methuen.

DeLong, Brad, and Andrei Shleifer. 1993. "Princes and Merchants: European City Growth before the Industrial Revolution." *Journal of Law and Economics* 36, no. 2: 671–702.

Demouy, Patrick. 1990. "Synodes diocésains et conciles provinciaux à Reims et en Belgique seconde aux XIe-XIIIe siècle." In *La Champagne et ses administrations,* edited by Georges Clause et al. Paris: La Manufacture, 93–112.

Denton, Jeffrey, and John Dooley. 1987. *Representatives of the Lower Clergy in Parliament 1295-1340.* London: Royal Historical Society Studies in History 50.

Dincecco, Mark, and Massimo Onorato. 2016. "Military Conflict and the Rise of Urban Europe." *Journal of Economic Growth* 21, no. 3: 259–82.

Dincecco, Mark, and Massimiliano Onorato. 2018. *From Warfare to Wealth.* Cambridge University Press.

Dincecco, Mark, and Yuhua Wang. 2018. "Violent Conflict and Political Development over the Long Run: China versus Europe." *Annual Review of Political Science* 21: 341–58.

Dittmar, Jeremiah E. 2011. "Information Technology and Economic Change: The Impact of the Printing Press." *Quarterly Journal of Economics* 126, no. 3: 1133–72.

Dixon, C. Scott. 2000. "The Princely Reformation in Germany." In *The Reformation World,* edited by Andrew Pettegree. London and New York: Routledge, 146–65.

Dodd, Gwilym. 2007. *Justice and Grace: Private Petitioning and the English Parliament in the Late Middle Ages.* Oxford: Oxford University Press.

Dodd, Gwilym. 2014. "Reason, Conscience, and Equity: Bishops as the King's Judges in Later Medieval England." *History* 99, no. 335: 213–39.

Donahue, Charles. 1974. "Roman Canon Law in the Medieval English Church: Stubbs vs. Maitland after 75 years in the Light of Some Records from the Church Courts." *Michigan Law Review* 74, no. 4: 647–716.

Donahue, Charles. 2016. "The Courts of the *Ius Commune.*" In *The History of Courts and Procedure in Medieval Canon Law,* edited by Wilfried Hartmann and Kenneth Pennington. Washington, DC: Catholic University of America Press.

Doner, Richard F., Bryan K. Ritchie, and Dan Slater. 2005. "Systemic Vulnerability and the Origins of Developmental States: Northeast and Southeast Asia in Comparative Perspective." *International Organization* 59, no. 2: 327–61.

Dorin, Rowan. 2015. *Banishing Usury: The Expulsion of Foreign Moneylenders in Medieval Europe, 1200-1450.* Doctoral Dissertation, Harvard University.

Dorin, Rowan. 2021. "The Bishop as Lawmaker in Late Medieval Europe." *Past & Present* 253: 45–82.

Doucette, Jonathan Stavnskær, and Jørgen Møller. 2021. "The Collapse of State Power, the Cluniac Reform Movement, and the Origins of Urban Self-Government in Medieval Europe." *International Organization* 75, no. 1: 204–23.

Downing, Brian. 1989. "Medieval Origins of Constitutional Government." *Theory and Society,* 18: 213–47.

Downing, Brian. 1992. *The Military Revolution and Political Change.* Princeton: Princeton University Press.

Doyle, William. 1997. "Secular Simony: The Clergy and Sale of Office in 18th Century France." In *Religious Change in Europe 1650-1914,* edited by Nigel Aston. Oxford: Clarendon Press, 135–48.

Duby, Georges. 1978. *The Three Orders.* Chicago: University of Chicago Press.

Duggan, Anne. 2010. "Roman, Canon and Common Law in Twelfth-Century England: The Council of Northampton (1164) Re-examined." *Historical Research* 83, no. 221: 379–408.

Dupuy, R. Ernest, and Trevor N. Dupuy. 1993. *The Harper Encyclopedia of Military History.* New York: HarperCollins.

Edelstein, Daniel. 2021. "Rousseau, Bodin, and the Medieval Corporatist Origins of Popular Sovereignty." *Political Theory* 50, no.1: 142–68.

Eire, Carlos. 2016. *Reformations: The Early Modern World, 1450–1650.* New Haven: Yale University Press.

Eisner, Manuel. 2011. "Killing Kings: Patterns of Regicide in Europe, AD 600–1800." *British Journal of Criminology* 51, no. 3: 556–77.

Ekelund, Robert B., Robert F. Hébert, and Robert D. Tollison. 1989. "An Economic Model of the Medieval Church." *Journal of Law, Economics, and Organization* 5, no. 2: 307–31.

Ekelund, Robert B., Robert F. Hébert, Robert D. Tollison, Gary M. Anderson, and Audrey B. Davison. 1996. *Sacred Trust: The Medieval Church as an Economic Firm.* Oxford: Oxford University Press.

Eldevik, John. 2011. "Bishops in the Medieval Empire: New Perspective on the Church, State, and Episcopal Office." *History Compass* 9, no. 10: 776–90.

Ergang, Robert. 1971. *Emergence of the National State.* New York: Van Nostrand Reinhold.

Ertman, Thomas. 1997. *Birth of the Leviathan: Building States and Regimes in Medieval and Early Modern Europe.* Cambridge: Cambridge University Press.

Ertman, Thomas. 2017. "Otto Hintze, Stein Rokkan, and Charles Tilly's Theory of European State-building." In *Does War Make States?: Investigations of Charles Tilly's Historical Sociology,* edited by Lars Bo Kaspersen and Jeppe Strandbjerg. New York: Cambridge University Press, 52–69.

Fawtier, Robert. 1963. *Capetian Kings of France: Monarchy and Nation, 987–1328.* Macmillan International Higher Education.

Fichtner, Paula. 1976. "Dynastic Marriage in Sixteenth-Century Habsburg Diplomacy and Statecraft: An Interdisciplinary Approach." *American Historical Review* 81, no. 2: 243–4.

Figgis, John. (1906) 1960. *Political Thought from Gerson to Grotius.* New York: Cambridge University Press.

Finer, Samuel. 1997. *The History of Government from the Earliest Times: The Intermediate Ages,* Vol. 2. New York: Oxford University Press.

Fischer, Markus. 1992. "Feudal Europe, 800–1300: Communal Discourse and Conflictual Practices." *International Organization* 46, no. 2: 427–66.

Fouquet, Roger, and Stephen Broadberry. 2015. "Seven Centuries of European Economic Growth and Decline." *Journal of Economic Perspectives.* 29, no. 4: 227–44.

Fried, Johannes. 2015. *The Middle Ages.* Cambridge: Harvard University Press.

Friedrichs, Jörg. 2001. "The Meaning of New Medievalism." *European Journal of International Relations* 7, no. 4: 475–501.

Fukuyama, Francis. 2011. *The Origins of Political Order: From Prehuman Times to the French Revolution.* New York: Farrar, Straus and Giroux.

Genet, Jean-Philippe. 1990. "L'état moderne: un modèle opératoire." In *L'état moderne. Genèse, bilans et perspectives,* edited by Jean-Philippe Genet. Paris: CNRS.

Genet, Jean-Philippe. 1992. "Introduction: Which State Rises?" *Historical Research,* 65, no. 157: 119–33.

Gieysztor, Aleksander. 1979. *History of Poland.* Warsaw: PWN.

Gieysztor, Aleksander. 1998. "The Kingdom of Poland and The Grand Duchy of Lithuania, 1370–1506." In *The New Cambridge Medieval History,* Vol. 7, edited by Christopher Allmand. Cambridge: Cambridge University Press, 727–47.

Gilchrist, John. 1969. *The Church and Economic Activity in the Middle Ages.* London: MacMillan.

Glete, Jan. 2002. *War and the State in Early Modern Europe: Spain, the Dutch Republic and Sweden as Fiscal-Military States, 1500–1660.* London: Routledge.

Goldstone, Jack. 2009. *Why Europe? The Rise of the West in World History 1500–1850*. McGraw-Hill Higher Education.

Goody, Jack. 1983. *The Development of Family and Marriage in Europe*. Cambridge: Cambridge University Press.

Goodman-Bacon, Andrew. 2021. "Difference-in-Differences with Variation in Treatment timing." *Journal of Econometrics* 225, issue 2: 254–77.

Gordon, Bruce. 2000. "Conciliarism in Late Medieval Europe." In *The Reformation World*, edited by Andrew Pettegree. London and New York: Routledge, 31–50.

Górecki, Piotr. 1993. *Parishes, Tithes and Society in Earlier Medieval Poland, ca 1100–1250*. Philadelphia: American Philosophical Society.

Górski, Karol, V. Raczyńska and C. Raczyńska. 1966. "The Origins of the Polish Sejm." *Slavonic and East European Review* 44, no. 102: 122–38.

Gorski, Philip. 2003. *The Disciplinary Revolution: Calvinism and the Rise of the State in Early Modern Europe*. Chicago: University of Chicago Press.

Gorski, Philip, and Vivek Sharma. 2017. "Beyond the Tilly Thesis 'Family Values' and State Formation in Latin Christendom." In *Does War Make States?: Investigations of Charles Tilly's Historical Sociology*, edited by Lars Bo Kaspersen and Jeppe Strandsbjerg. Cambridge: Cambridge University Press, 98–124.

Gottfried, Robert. 1983. *The Black Death: Natural and Human Disaster in Medieval Europe*. New York: MacMillan.

Green, Louis. 1999. "Florence." In *The New Cambridge Medieval History*, Vol. 5, edited by David Abulafia. Cambridge: Cambridge University Press, 479–96.

Greenfeld, Liah. 1996. "The Modern Religion?" *Critical Review* 10, no. 2: 169–91.

Greengrass, Mark. 2014. *Christendom Destroyed*. London: Penguin Books.

Greif, Avner. 2006. *Institutions and the Path to the Modern Economy*. Cambridge: Cambridge University Press.

Grell, Ole Peter. 2000. "Scandinavia." In *The Reformation World*, edited by Andrew Pettegree. London and New York: Routledge, 257–76.

Grzymala-Busse, Anna. 2015. *Nations Under God: How Churches Use Moral Authority to Influence Policy*. Princeton: Princeton University Press.

Grzymala-Busse, Anna. 2020. "The Medieval and Religious Roots of the European State." *Annual Review of Political Science* 12: 19–36.

Guenée, Bernard. 1985. *States and Rulers in Later Medieval Europe*. Oxford: Basil Blackwell.

Hall, Rodney, and Friedrich V. Kratochwil. 1993. "Medieval Tales: Neorealist 'Science' and the Abuse of History." *International Organization* 47, no. 3: 479–91.

Hamre, Lars. 2003. "Church and Clergy." In *The Cambridge History of Scandinavia*, Vol. 1, edited by Knut Helle. Cambridge: Cambridge University Press, 653–76.

Harding, Alan 2002. *Medieval Law and the Foundations of the State*. Oxford: Oxford University Press.

Harriss, Gerald. 1975. *King, Parliament and Public Finance in Medieval England to 1369*. Oxford, UK: Oxford University Press.

Harriss, Gerald. 1993. "Political Society and the Growth of Government in Late Medieval England." *Past & Present* 138: 28–57.

Härter, Karl. 2011. "The Permanent Imperial Diet in European Context: 1663–1806." In *The Holy Roman Empire 1495–1806*, edited by R.J.W Evans, Michael Schaich, and Peter Wilson. London: Oxford University Press, 115–35.

Haskett, Timothy. 1996. "The Medieval English Court of Chancery." *Law and History Review*, 14, no. 2: 245–313.

Hay, Denys. 1995. *Europe in the Fourteenth and Fifteenth Centuries*. New York: Longman Publishing.

Held, David. 1995. *Democracy and the Global Order: From the Modern State to Cosmopolitan Governance*. Stanford: Stanford University Press.

Helle, Knut. 2003. "Towards Nationally Organised Systems of Government: Introductory Survey." In *The Cambridge History of Scandinavia*, Vol. 1, edited by Knut Helle. Cambridge: Cambridge University Press, 345–52.

Helmholz, Richard. 1987. *Canon Law and the Law of England*. Chicago: University of Chicago Press.

Helmholz, Richard. 1994. "Excommunication in Twelfth Century England." *Journal of Law and Religion* 11, no. 1: 235–53.

Helmholz, Richard. 2004. "Excommunication." In *The Oxford History of the Laws of England: The Canon Law and Ecclesiastical Jurisdiction from 597 to 1640s*. Oxford: Oxford University Press.

Helmholz, Richard. 2015. "Canon Law and Roman Law." In *Cambridge Companion to Roman Law*, edited by David Johnston. Cambridge: Cambridge University Press, 396–422.

Henrich, Joseph. 2020. *The WEIRDest People in the World*. New York: Farrar, Straus, and Giroux.

Herbst, Jeffrey. (2000) 2014. *States and Power in Africa*. Princeton: Princeton University Press.

Herde, Peter. 2000. "From Adolf of Nassau to Lewis of Bavaria, 1292–1347." In *The New Cambridge Medieval History*, Vol. 6, edited by Michael Jones. Cambridge: Cambridge University Press, 515–50.

Herzog, Tamar. 2018. *A Short History of European Law*. Cambridge: Harvard University Press.

Hilaire, Jean. 2011. *La Construction De L'état De Droit Dans Les Archives Judiciaires De La Cour De France Au XIIe Siècle*. Paris: Dalloz.

Hintze, Otto. (1905) 1975. *The Historical Essays of Otto Hintze*, edited by Felix Gilbert. New York: Oxford University Press.

Hoffman, Philip. 2015. *Why Did Europe Conquer the World?* Princeton: Princeton University Press.

Hoffman, Philip, and Jean-Laurent Rosenthal. 1997. "The Political Economy of Warfare and Taxation in Early Modern Europe: Historical Lessons for Economic Development." In the *Frontiers of Institutional Economics*, edited by John Drobak and Jon Nye. St. Louis, MO: Academic Press, 31–55.

Hollenbach, Florian, and Jan Pierskalla. 2022. "State-Building and the Origin of Universities in Europe, 800–1800." Manuscript.

Houghton, Robert. 2018. "Italian Bishops and Warfare during the Investiture Crisis: The Case of Parma." In *Between Sword and Prayer: Warfare and Medieval Clergy in Cultural Perspective*, edited by Radosław Kotecki, Jacek Maciejewski, and John S. Ott. Leiden, NL: Brill, 274–302.

Howe, John. 1988. "The Nobility's Reform of the Medieval Church." *The American Historical Review* 93, no. 2: 317–39.

Howe, John. 2016. *Before the Gregorian Reform: The Latin Church at the Turn of the First Millennium*. Ithaca: Cornell University Press.

Hsia, R. Po-Chia. 2005. *The World of Catholic Renewal, 1540–1770*. Cambridge: Cambridge University Press.

Huang, Chin-Hao, and David C. Kang. 2022. "State Formation in Korea and Japan, 400–800 CE: Emulation and Learning, Not Bellicist Competition." *International Organization* 76, no. 1: 1–31.

Hudson, John. 2001. "Henry I and Council." In *The Medieval State: Essays Presented to James Campbell*, edited by James Campbell, David Palliser, and John Maddicott. London: Hambledon Press, 109–26.

Hughes, Jane Frecknall, and Lynne Oats. 2007. "King John's Tax Innovations–Extortion, Resistance, and the Establishment of the Principle of Taxation by Consent." *Accounting Historians Journal* 34, no. 2: 75–107.

Hughes, Michael. 1992. *Early Modern Germany, 1477–1806.* London: Macmillan.

Hui, Victoria Tin-Bor. 2005. *War and State Formation in Ancient China and Early Modern Europe.* Cambridge: Cambridge University Press.

Hyde, John Kenneth. 1973. *Society and Politics in Medieval Italy: The Evolution of the Civil Life, 1000–1350.* New York: St. Martin's Press.

Imai, Kosuke, Luke Keele, and Dustin Tingley. 2010. "A General Approach to Causal Mediation Analysis." *Psychological Methods* 15, no. 4: 309–34.

Isenmann, Eberhard. 1999. "The Holy Roman Empire in the Middle Ages." In *The Rise of the Fiscal State in Europe, 1250–1815,* edited by Richard Bonney. Oxford: Oxford University Press, 243–80.

Jaeger, C. Stephen. 1987. "Cathedral Schools and Humanist Learning, 950–1150." *Deutsche Vierteljahrsschrift für Literaturwissenschaft und Geistesgeschichte* 61, no. 4: 569–616.

Jaeger, C. Stephen. 2013. *The Envy of Angels: Cathedral Schools and Social Ideals in Medieval Europe, 950–1200.* University of Pennsylvania Press.

Jedin, Hubert. 1993. *The Medieval and Reformation Church.* New York: Crossroad.

Johnson, Noel, and Mark Koyama. 2017. "States and Economic Growth: Capacity and Constraints." *Explorations in Economic History* 64: 1–20.

Jones, Eric. (1981) 2003. *The European Miracle: Environments, Economies and Geopolitics in the History of Europe and Asia.* Cambridge, UK: Cambridge University Press.

Jones, Michael John. 2009. "Origins of Medieval Exchequer Accounting." *Accounting, Business, and Financial History* 19, no. 3: 259–85.

Jones, Philip. 1997. *The Italian City-State: from Commune to Signoria.* Oxford: Oxford University Press.

Jordan, William Chester. 2001. *Europe in the High Middle Ages.* London: Penguin Books.

Jordan, William Chester. 2009. *A Tale of Two Monasteries: Westminster and Saint-Denis in the Thirteenth Century.* Princeton: Princeton University Press.

Jordan, William Chester. 2015. *Louis IX and the Challenge of the Crusade.* Princeton: Princeton University Press.

Joseph, Lisa. 2015. *Dynastic Marriage in England, Castile and Aragon, 11th–16th Centuries.* PhD Dissertation, University of Adelaide.

Kaeuper, Richard W. 1988. *War, Justice, and Public Order: England and France in the Later Middle Ages.* Oxford: Oxford University Press.

Kaeuper, Richard W. 2001. *Chivalry and Violence in Medieval Europe.* Oxford University Press on Demand.

Kagay, Donald J. 1981. *The Development of the Cortes in the Crown of Aragon, 1064–1327.* PhD Dissertation, Fordham University.

Kaminsky, Howard. 2000. "The Great Schism." In *The New Cambridge Medieval History,* edited by Michael Jones. Cambridge: Cambridge University Press, 674–96.

Kantorowicz, Ernst. (1957) 2016. *The King's Two Bodies.* Princeton: Princeton University Press.

Karaman, Kivanç, and Şevket Pamuk. 2013. "Different Paths to the Modern State in Europe: The Interaction between Warfare, Economic Structure, and Political Regime." *American Political Science Review* 107: 603–26.

Kay, Richard. 2002. *The Council of Bourges, 1225: A Documentary History.* New York: Routledge.

Kern, Fritz. (1948) 1985. *Kingship and Law,* translated by S.B. Chrimes. Westport, CT: Greenwood Press.

Kiernan, Victor G. 1965. "State and Nation in Western Europe." *Past & Present* 31: 20–38.

Kiernan, Victor. 1980. *State and Society in Europe 1550–1650.* Oxford: Basil Blackwell.

Kiser, Edgar, and Yoram Barzel. 1991. "The Origins of Democracy in England." *Rationality and Society* 3, no. 4: 396–422.

Kłoczowski, Jerzy. 2000. *A History of Polish Christianity*. Cambridge: Cambridge University Press.

Kokkonen, Andrej, and Anders Sundell. 2014. "Delivering Stability—Primogeniture and Autocratic Survival in European Monarchies 1000–1800." *American Political Science Review* 108, no. 2: 438–53.

Konrad, Kai, and Stergios Skaperdas. 2007. "Succession Rules and Leadership Rents." *Journal of Conflict Resolution* 51, no. 4: 622–45.

Konrad, Kai, and Stergios Skaperdas. 2012. "The Market for Protection and the Origin of the State." *Economic Theory* 50, no. 2: 417–43.

Kotecki, Radosław. 2018. "Lions and Lambs, Wolves and Pastors of the Flock: Portraying Military Activity of Bishops in Twelfth-Century Poland." In *Between Sword and Prayer: Warfare and Medieval Clergy in Cultural Perspective*, edited by Radosław Kotecki, Jacek Maciejewski, and John Ott. Leiden, Boston: Brill, 303–40.

Kotecki, Radosław, Jacek Maciejewski, and John Ott. 2018. *Between Sword and Prayer: Warfare and Medieval Clergy in Cultural Perspective*. Leiden, Boston: Brill.

Krasner, Stephen. 1993. "Westphalia and All That." In *Ideas and Foreign Policy*, edited by Judith Goldstein and Robert O. Keohane. Ithaca, NY: Cornell University Press, 235–64.

Kraus, Henry. 1979. *Gold Was the Mortar: The Economics of Cathedral Building*. London: Routledge & Kegan Paul.

Kroeschell, Karl. 1973. *Deutsche Rechtsgeschichte 2 (1250–1650)*. Hamburg: Rowohlt.

Kuran, Timur. 2011. *The Long Divergence*. Princeton: Princeton University Press.

Lal, Apoorva, Mac Lockhart, Yiqing Xu, and Ziwen Zu. 2021. "How Much Should We Trust Instrumental Variable Estimates in Political Science? Practical Advice Based on Over 60 Replicated Studies." Manuscript, Stanford University.

Landes, David. 1998. *The Wealth and Poverty of Nations*. New York: W. Norton.

Lange, Tyler. 2016. *Excommunication for Debt in Late Medieval France*. Cambridge: Cambridge University Press.

Lathan, Andrew. 2012. *Theorizing Medieval Geopolitics. War and World Order in the Age of the Crusades*. New York: Routledge.

Lawrence, Clifford Hugh. 2015. *Medieval Monasticism: Forms of Religious Life in Western Europe in the Middle Ages*. New York: Routledge.

Levi, Margaret. 1988. *Of Rule and Revenue*. Berkeley: University of California Press.

Leyser, Karl. 1994. *Communications and Power in Medieval Europe: The Carolingian and Ottonian Centuries*, Vol. 1. London: The Hambledon Press.

Linehan, Peter. 2000. "Castile, Portugal, and Navarre." In *The New Cambridge Medieval History*, Vol. 6, edited by Michael Jones. Cambridge: Cambridge University Press, 619–50.

Linehan, Peter. 2004. "Spain in the Twelfth Century." In *The New Cambridge Medieval History*, Vol. 4, edited by David Luscombe and Jonathan Riley-Smith. Cambridge: Cambridge University Press, 475–509.

Little, Richard, and Barry Buzan. 2002. "International Systems in World History: Remaking the Study of International Relations." In *Historical Sociology of International Relations* edited by Stephen Hobdon and John M. Hobson. Cambridge: Cambridge University Press, 200–22.

Loyn, Henry Royston. 1963. *Anglo-Saxon England and the Norman Conquest*. New York: St. Martin's Press.

Lunt, William E. 1926. *The Valuation of Norwich*. Oxford: Clarendon Press.

Lustick, Ian S. 1996. "History, Historiography, and Political Science: Multiple Historical Records and the Problem of Selection Bias." *American Political Science Review* 90, no. 3: 605–18.

Maddicott, John. 2010. *The Origins of the English Parliament 924-1327*. Oxford: Oxford University Press.

Magdalino, Paul. 1984. "Byzantine Snobbery." In *The Byzantine Aristocracy, IX to XIII Centuries*, edited by Michael Angold. Oxford: BAR Publishing, 58–78.

Magdalino, Paul. 1994. "Justice and Finance in the Byzantine State, Ninth to Twelfth Centuries." In *Law and Society in Byzantium, Ninth–Twelfth Centuries*, edited by Angeliki Laiou and Dieter Simon. Washington, DC: Dumbarton Oaks Research Library and Collection, 93–116.

Maitland, F.W. 1898. *Roman Canon Law in England*. London, Methuen.

Malegam, Jehangir Yezdi. 2013. *The Sleep of Behemoth: Disputing Peace and Violence in Medieval Europe, 1000–1200*. Ithaca, NY: Cornell University Press.

Mann, Michael. 1986. *The Sources of Social Power*. Cambridge: Cambridge University Press.

Mann, Michael. 1988. *States, War and Capitalism: Studies in Political Sociology*. Oxford: Blackwell.

Marongiu, Antonio. 1968. *Medieval Parliaments*, translated by S.J Woolf. London: Eyre and Spottswoode.

Marx, Anthony. 2003. *Faith in Nation*. New York: Oxford University Press.

Mazzuca, Sebastián. 2021. *Latecomer State Formation: Political Geography and Capacity Failure in Latin America*. New Haven: Yale University Press.

McIlwain, Charles. 1932. "Medieval Estates." In *The Cambridge Medieval History*, edited by J. B. Bury. New York: Macmillan, chapter 23.

McKee, Sally. 2010. *Uncommon Dominion: Venetian Crete and the Myth of Ethnic Purity*. Philadelphia: University of Pennsylvania Press.

McNeil, Kent. 2020. "Authority in Medieval Europe: Empire, Papacy and the Rights of Infidels." *History of Political Thought* 41, no. 2: 221–247.

McNeill, William. (1982) 2013. *The Pursuit of Power*. Chicago: University of Chicago Press.

McSweeney, Thomas. 2019. *Priests of the Law: Roman Law and the Making of Common Law's First Professionals*. Oxford: Oxford University Press.

Miller, Maureen. 2009. "The Crisis in the Investiture Crisis Narrative." *History Compass* 7, no. 6: 1570–80.

Millet, Hélène, ed. 2003. "Introduction." In *Suppliques Et Requêtes: Le Gouvernement Par La Grâce En Occident (XIIe-XVe Siècle)*. Rome: École française de Rome, 1–18.

Millet, Hélène, and Peter Moraw. 1996. "Clerics in the State." In *Power Elites and State Building*, edited by Wolfgang Reinhard. Oxford: Clarendon Press, 173–188.

Mitchell, Sydney. 1951. *Taxation in Medieval England*. New Haven: Yale University Press.

Mitteraurer, Michael. 2010. *Why Europe? The Medieval Origins of its Special Path*. Chicago: University of Chicago Press.

Mokyr, Joel. 2017. *A Culture of Growth*. Princeton: Princeton University Press.

Mokyr, Joel. 1990. *The Lever of Riches: Technological Creativity and Economic Progress*. Oxford, UK: Oxford University Press.

Møller, Jørgen. 2015. "The Medieval Roots of Democracy." *Journal of Democracy* 26, no.3: 110–23.

Møller, Jørgen. 2017. *State Formation, Regime Change, and Economic Development*. New York: Routledge.

Møller, Jørgen. 2017a. "Medieval Origins of the Rule of Law: The Gregorian Reforms as Critical Juncture?" *Hague Journal on the Rule of Law* 9, no. 2: 265–82.

Møller, Jørgen. 2018. "Medieval Roots of the Modern State: The Conditional Effects of Geopolitical Pressure on Early Modern State Building." *Social Science History* 42, no. 2: 295–316.

Møller, Jørgen. 2019. "Bringing the Church Back In: Ecclesiastical Influences on the Rise of Europe." *Politics and Religion* 12, no. 2: 213–26.

Møller, Jørgen. 2021. "Reading History Forward." *PS: Political Science & Politics* 54, no. 2: 249–53.

Møller, Jørgen, and Jonathan Stavnskær Doucette. 2021. *The Catholic Church and European State Formation, AD 1000–1500*. Manuscript, University of Aarhus.

Monahan, Arthur P. 1987. *Consent, Coercion, and Limit: The Medieval Origins of Parliamentary Democracy*. Leiden, NL: E.J. Brill.

Morby, John. 1989. *Dynasties of the World: A Chronological and Genealogical Handbook*. New York: Oxford University Press.

Morgenthau, Hans. 1985. *Politics among Nations*. New York: McGraw-Hill.

Morris, Colin. 1989. *The Papal Monarchy: The Western Church from 1050 to 1250*. Oxford: Oxford University Press.

Morris, Ian. 2014. *War! What Is It Good For?: Conflict and the Progress of Civilization from Primates to Robots*. New York: Farrar, Straus and Giroux.

Müller, Harald. 2016. "The Omnipresent Pope: Legates and Judges Delegate." In *A Companion to the Medieval Papacy*, edited by Keith Sisson and Atria Larson. Leiden, NL: E.J. Brill: 199–219.

Mundy, John. 2000. *Europe in the High Middle Ages 1150–1300*. Edinburgh: Longman.

Murdoch, Graeme. 2000. "Eastern Europe." In *The Reformation World*, edited by Andrew Pettegree. London and New York: Routledge, 190–210.

Nederman, Cary. 2009. "Hegel on the Medieval Foundations of the Modern State." in *Lineages of European Political Thought: Explorations along the Medieval/Modern Divide from John of Salisbury to Hegel*. Washington, DC: Catholic University of America Press, 323–42.

Nederman, Cary. 2021. "*Quod Omnes Tangit:* Constitutional Principle or Malleable Authority?" Paper Presented at the Annual Meeting of the American Political Science Association.

Nelson, Brian. 2006. *The Making of the Modern State*. New York: Palgrave MacMillan.

Nexon, Daniel. 2009. *The Struggle for Power in Early Modern Europe: Religious Conflict, Dynastic Empires, and International Change*. Princeton: Princeton University Press.

Norr, Knut Wolfgang. 1982. "Institutional Foundations of New Jurisprudence." In *Renaissance and Renewal in the Twelfth Century*, edited by Robert L. Benson and Giles Constable. Cambridge, MA: Harvard University Press, 324–38.

North, Douglass. 1981. *Structure and Change in Economic History*. New York: W.W. Norton.

North, Douglass. 1991. "Institutions." *Journal of Economic Perspectives* 5, no. 1: 97–112.

North, Douglass, and Barry Weingast. 1989. "Constitutions and Commitment: The Evolution of Institutions Governing Public Choice in Seventeenth-Century England." *The Journal of Economic History* 49, no. 4: 803–32.

North, Douglass, and Robert Thomas. 1973. *The Rise of the Western World*. Cambridge: Cambridge University Press.

North, Douglass, John Wallis, and Barry Weingast. 2009. *Violence and Social Orders: A Conceptual Framework for Interpreting Recorded Human History*. Cambridge: Cambridge University Press.

Nunn, Nathan. 2009. "The Importance of History for Economic Development." *Annual Review of Economics* 1: 65–92.

Oakley, Francis. 1972. "Conciliarism at the Fifth Lateran Council?" *Church History* 41, no. 4: 452–63.

Oakley, Francis. 2003. *The Conciliarist Tradition: Constitutionalism in the Catholic Church 1300–1870*. Oxford: Oxford University Press.

Oakley, Francis. 2010. *Empty Bottles of Gentilism: Kingship and the Divine in Late Antiquity and the Early Middle Ages (to 1050)*. New Haven, CT: Yale University Press.

Oakley, Francis. 2012. *The Mortgage of the Past: Reshaping the Ancient Political Inheritance (1050–1300)*. New Haven: Yale University Press.

Oakley, Francis. 2015. *The Watershed of Modern Politics: Law, Virtue, Kingship, and Consent (1300–1650)*. New Haven: Yale University Press.

Ober, Josiah. 2015. *The Rise and Fall of Classical Greece*. Princeton: Princeton University Press.

Obertyński, Zdzisław, and Bolesław Kumor. 1974. *Historia Kościoła w Polsce*. Poznań: Pallotinum.

Oldroyd, David. 1997. "Accounting in Anglo-Saxon England: Context and Evidence." *Accounting History* 2, no. 1: 7–34.

Ormrod, W. Mark. 1995. *Political Life in Medieval England, 1300–1450*. New York: St. Martin's Press.

Ormrod, W. Mark. 1999. "England in the Middle Ages." In *The Rise of the Fiscal State in Europe c. 1200–1815*, edited by Richard Bonney. Oxford: Oxford University Press: 19–52.

Ormrod, W. Mark. 2000. "England: Edward II and Edward III." In *The New Cambridge Medieval History*, Vol. 6, edited by Michael Jones. Cambridge: Cambridge University Press: 273–95.

Ormrod, W. Mark, Gwilym Dodd, and Anthony Musson, eds. 2009. *Medieval Petitions: Grace and Grievance*. Woodbridge: York Medieval Press.

Orrman, Eljas. 2003. "Church and Society." In *The Cambridge History of Scandinavia*, edited by Knut Helle. Cambridge: Cambridge University Press: 421–62.

Osiander, Andreas. 2001. "Sovereignty, International Relations, and the Westphalian Myth." *International Organization* 55, no. 2: 251–87.

Ott, John. 2015. *Bishops, Authority and Community in Northwestern Europe, c. 1050–1150*. Cambridge: Cambridge University Press.

Ozment, Steven. 1980. *The Age of Reform*. New Haven: Yale University Press.

Padgett, John, and Walter Powell. 2012. *The Emergence of Organizations and Markets*. Princeton: Princeton University Press.

Parish, Helen. 2000. "England." In *The Reformation World*, edited by Andrew Pettegree. London and New York: Routledge, 225–36.

Parker, Geoffrey. 1996. *The Military Revolution*. Cambridge: Cambridge University Press.

Partner, Peter. 1999: "The Papacy and the Papal States." In *The Rise of the Fiscal State in Europe, 1250–1815*, edited by Richard Bonney. Oxford: Oxford University Press, 359–80.

Peltzer, Jörg. 2008. *Canon Law, Careers and Conquest: Episcopal Elections in Normandy and Greater Anjou, c. 1140–c. 1230*. Cambridge: Cambridge University Press.

Pennington, Kenneth. (1984) 2018. *Pope and Bishops: The Papal Monarchy in the Twelfth and Thirteenth Centuries*. Philadelphia: University of Pennsylvania Press.

Pennington, Kenneth. 2012. "Roman Law at the Papal Curia in the Early Twelfth Century." In *Canon Law, Religion and Politics: Liber Amicorum*, edited by Uta-Renate Blumenthal, Anders Winroth, and Peter Landau. Washington, DC: The Catholic University Press, 233–52.

Pennington, Kenneth. 2016. "The Jurisprudence of Procedure." In *The History of Courts and Procedure in Medieval Canon Law*, edited by Wilfried Hartmann and Kenneth Pennington. Washington, DC: Catholic University of America Press, 125–59.

Pettegree, Andrew, ed. 2000. *The Reformation World*. London and New York: Routledge.

Philpott, Daniel. 2001. *Revolutions in Sovereignty: How Ideas Shaped Modern International Relations*. Princeton: Princeton University Press.

Pincus, Steven C.A., and James A. Robinson. 2011. *What Really Happened during the Glorious Revolution?* Working Paper No. 17206. National Bureau of Economic Research.

Pitz, Ernst. 1971. *Papstreskript und Kaiserreskript im Mittelalter*. Tübingen: Bibliothek des Deutschen Historischen Instituts in Rom, 36.

Poggi, Gianfranco. 1978. *The Development of the State*. Stanford: Stanford University Press.

Poggi, Gianfranco. 1990. *The State: Its Nature, Development, and Prospects*. Stanford: Stanford University Press.

Porter, Bruce. (1994) 2002. *War and the Rise of the State*. New York: The Free Press.

Post, Gaines. 1943. "Roman Law and Early Representation in Spain and Italy, 1150–1250." *Speculum* 18: 211–32.

Post, Gaines. 1964. *Studies in Medieval Legal Thought: Public Law and State 1100–1322*. Princeton: Princeton Legacy Library.

Rabb, Theodore. 2006. *The Last Days of the Renaissance*. New York: Basic Books.

Radding, Charles, and Antonio Ciaralli. 2007. *The Corpus Iuris Civilis in the Middle Ages*. Leiden, NL: E.J. Brill.

Rady, Martyn. 2000. *Nobility, Land and Service in Medieval Hungary*. Houndsmills, Basingstoke: Palgrave.

Reid, Jonathan. 2000. "France." In *The Reformation World*, edited by Andrew Pettegree. London and New York: Routledge, 211–24.

Reinhard, Wolfgang, ed. 1996. *Power Elites and State Building*. Oxford: Clarendon Press.

Rennie, Kriston R. 2007. "'Uproot and Destroy, Build and Plant': Legatine Authority under Pope Gregory VII." *Journal of Medieval History* 33, no. 2: 166–80.

Reuter, Timothy. 2011. "A Europe of Bishops." In *Patterns of Episcopal Power: Bishops in the Tenth and Eleventh Century Europe*. Berlin: Walter de Gruyten, 17–38.

Reynolds, Susan. 1996. *Fiefs and Vassals: The Medieval Evidence Reinterpreted*. Oxford: Oxford University Press.

Reynolds, Susan. 1997. *Kingdoms and Communities in Western Europe 900–1300*. Oxford: Oxford University Press.

Reynolds, Susan. 1997a. "The Historiography of the Medieval State." In *Companion to Historiography*, edited by Michael Bentley. New York: Routledge, 117–38.

Ribalta, Pere Molas. 1996. "The Impact of Central Institutions." In *Power Elites and State Building*, edited by Wolfgang Reinhard. Oxford: Clarendon Press, 19–39.

Richardson, Henry, and George Sayles. 1981. *The English Parliament in the Middle Ages*. London: Hambledon Press.

Rigaudiere, Albert. 1995. "The Theory and Practice of Government in the Western Europe in the Fourteenth Century." In *The New Cambridge Medieval History*, Vol. 6, edited by Timothy Reuter. Cambridge: Cambridge University Press, 17–41.

Riley-Smith, Jonathan. 2004. "The Crusades, 1095–1198." In *The New Cambridge Medieval History*, Vol. 4, edited by David Luscombe and Jonathan Riley-Smith. Cambridge: Cambridge University Press, 534–63.

Riley-Smith, Jonathan. 2005. *Crusades: A History*. New York: Continuum Books.

Ringer, Fritz. 2004. *Max Weber: An Intellectual Biography*. Chicago: University of Chicago Press.

Rist, Rebecca. 2016. "The Medieval Papacy, Crusading, and Heresy, 1095–1291." In *A Companion to the Medieval Papacy*, edited by Keith Sisson and Atria Larson. Leiden, NL: E.J. Brill, 309–32.

Robinson, Ian S. 1990. *The Papacy 1073–1198*. New York: Cambridge University Press.

Robinson, Ian S. 2004. "Reform and the Church, 1073–1122." In *The New Cambridge Medieval History*, Vol. 4, edited by David Luscombe and Jonathan Riley-Smith. Cambridge: Cambridge University Press, 268–334.

Robinson, Ian S. 2004a. "The Institutions of the Church, 1073–1216." In *The New Cambridge Medieval History*, Vol. 4, edited by David Luscombe and Jonathan Riley-Smith. Cambridge: Cambridge University Press, 368–460.

Robinson, Ian S. 2004b. "The Papacy, 1122–1198." In *The New Cambridge Medieval History*, Vol. 4, edited by David Luscombe and Jonathan Riley-Smith. Cambridge: Cambridge University Press, 317–83.

Rohan, Padraic. 2021. *Transforming Empire: The Genoese from the Mediterranean to the Atlantic, 1282–1492*. PhD dissertation, Department of History, Stanford University.

Rokkan, Stein. 1975. "Dimensions of State Formation and Nation Building: A Possible Paradigm for Research on Variations Within Europe." In *The Formation of National States in Western Europe*, edited by Charles Tilly. Princeton NJ: Princeton University Press, 562–600.

Rokkan, Stein. 1999. *State Formation, Nation-Building, and Mass Politics in Europe: The Theory of Stein Rokkan: Based on his collected works*. Oxford: Clarendon Press.

Rosenthal, Jean-Laurent, and Roy Bin Wong. 2011. *Before and Beyond Divergence*. Cambridge, MA: Harvard University Press.

Rowell, S.C. 2000. "Baltic Europe." In *The New Cambridge Medieval History*, Vol. 6, edited by Michael Jones. Cambridge: Cambridge University Press, 699–734.

Rubin, Jared. 2017. *Rulers, Religion, and Values: Why the West Got Rich and the Middle East Did Not*. Cambridge: Cambridge University Press.

Ruggie, John Gerard. 1998. "What Makes the World Hang Together? Neo-utilitarianism and the Social Constructivist Challenge." *International Organization* 52, no. 4: 855–85.

Ryder, Alan. 1976. *The Kingdom of Naples Under Alfonso the Magnanimous*. Oxford: Clarendon Press.

Ryder, Alan. 1998. "The Papal States and the Kingdom of Naples." In *The New Cambridge Medieval History*, Vol. 7, edited by Christopher Allmand. Cambridge: Cambridge University Press, 571–87.

Salonen, Kirsi. 2016. "The Curia: The Apostolic Penitentiary." In *A Companion to the Medieval Papacy*, edited by Keith Sisson and Atria Larson. Leiden, NL: E.J. Brill, 259–75.

Salonen, Kirsi. 2016a. "The Curia: The Sacra Romana Rota." *A Companion to the Medieval Papacy*, edited by Keith Sisson and Atria Larson. Leiden, NL: E.J. Brill, 276–88.

Salter, Alexander W., and Andrew T. Young. 2018. "Medieval Representative Assemblies: Collective Action and Antecedents of Limited Government." *Constitutional Political Economy* 29, no. 2: 1–22.

Sawyer, Peter. 2004. "Scandinavia in the Eleventh and Twelfth centuries." In *The New Cambridge Medieval History*, Vol. 4, edited by David Luscombe and Jonathan Riley-Smith. Cambridge: Cambridge University Press, 290–303.

Sayers, Jane. 1999. "The Influence of Papal Documents on English Documents before 1305." In *Papsturkunde und europäisches Urkundenwesen*, edited by Peter Herde and Herrmann Jakobs. Cologne: Böhlau Verlag, 161–200.

Sayles, George. (1961) 1988. *The Functions of the Medieval Parliament of England*. London: Hambledon Press.

Saylor, Ryan, and Nicholas Wheeler. 2017. "Paying for War and Building States: The Coalitional Politics of Debt Servicing and Tax Institutions." *World Politics* 69, no. 2: 366–408.

Schatz, Klaus. 1996. *Papal Primacy from Its Origins to the Present*. Collegeville, MN: The Liturgical Press.

Scheidel, Walter. 2019. *Escape from Rome*. Princeton: Princeton University Press.

Schubert, Ernst. 1997. "Der Mainzer Kurfürst als Erzkanzler im Spätmittelalter." In *Der Mainzer Kurfürst als Reichserzkanzler. Funktionen, Aktivitäten und Bedeutung des zweiten Mannes im alten Reich*, edited by Peter-Claus Hartmann. Wiesbaden: Steiner, 77–98.

Schulz, Jonathan. 2022. "Kin Networks and Institutional Development," *Economic Journal*, forthcoming.

Schumpeter, Joseph. (1918) 1991. "The Crisis of the Tax State." In *The Economics and Sociology of Capitalism*, edited by Richard Swedberg. Princeton, NJ: Princeton University Press, 99–140.

Schwarz, Brigide. 2016. "The Roman Curia (until about 1300)." In *The History of Courts and Procedure in Medieval Canon Law*, edited by Wilfried Hartmann and Kenneth Pennington. Washington, DC: Catholic University of America Press, 160–228.

Schwartzberg, Melissa. 2014. *Counting the Many: The Origins of Supermajority Rule*. Cambridge: Cambridge University Press.

Scott, Tom. 1998. "Germany and the Empire." In *The New Cambridge Medieval History*, vol. 7, edited by Christopher Allmand. Cambridge: Cambridge University Press, 337–66.

Sharma, Vivek S. 2015. "Kinship, Property, and Authority." *Politics & Society* 43, no. 2: 151–80.

Sharp, Sheila. 2001. "The West Saxon Tradition of Dynastic Marriage with Special Reference to the Family of Edward the Elder." In *Edward the Elder, 899–824*, edited by Nick Higham and David Hill. London: Routledge, 83–5.

Skinner, Quentin. 2009. "Hobbes and Republican Liberty." *Contemporary Political Theory* 8, 472–474.

Skinner, Quentin. 2018. "On the Person of the State." In *State Formations*, edited by John Brooke, Julia Strauss, and Greg Anderson. Cambridge: Cambridge University Press, 25–44.

Smith, Alistair L. 1964. *Church and State in the Middle Ages*. New York: Frank Cass.

Smith, Donald. 1970. *Religion and Political Development*. New York: Little, Brown.

Snow, Vernon F. 1963. "The Evolution of Proctorial Representation in Medieval England." *American Journal of Legal History* 7, no. 319–39.

Southern, Richard. 1970. *Western Society and the Church in the Middle Ages*. Harmondsworth, England: Penguin Books.

Spruyt, Hendrik. 1994. *The Sovereign State and Its Competitors*. Princeton: Princeton University Press.

Spruyt, Hendrik. 2002. "The Origins, Development, and Possible Decline of the Modern State." *Annual Review of Political Science* 5, no. 1: 127–49.

Spruyt, Hendrik. 2017. "War and State Formation: Amending the Bellicist Theory of State Making." In *Does War Make States?: Investigations of Charles Tilly's Historical Sociology*, edited by Lars Bo Kaspersen and Jeppe Strandsbjerg. Cambridge: Cambridge University Press, 73–97.

Strayer, Joseph. (1970) 1998. *On the Medieval Origins of the Modern State*. Princeton: Princeton University Press.

Stasavage, David. 2010. "When Distance Mattered: Geographic Scale and the Development of European Representative Assemblies." *American Political Science Review* 104, issue 4: 625–43.

Stasavage, David. 2002. "Credible Commitment in Early Modern Europe: North and Weingast Revisited." *Journal of Law, Economics, and Organization*, 18, no. 1: 155–86.

Stasavage, David. 2011. *States of Credit: Size, Power, and the Development of European Polities*. Princeton: Princeton University Press.

Stasavage, David. 2016. "Representation and Consent: Why They Arose in Europe and Not Elsewhere." *Annual Review of Political Science* 19: 145–62.

Stasavage, David. 2020. *The Decline and Rise of Democracy*. Princeton: Princeton University Press.

Stein, Peter. 1999. *Roman Law in European History*. Cambridge: Cambridge University Press.

Stollberg-Rilinger, Barbara. 2018. *The Holy Roman Empire*, translated by Yair Mintzker. Princeton: Princeton University Press.

Stone, Lawrence, ed. 1994. *An Imperial State at War: Britain from 1689 to 1815*. London: Routledge.

Storrs, Christopher, ed. 2009. *The Fiscal-Military State in Eighteenth-Century Europe.* Farnham, UK: Ashgate.

Sulovsky, Vedran. 2019. "The Concept of *Sacrum Imperium* in Historical Scholarship," *History Compass* 252, no. 4: 119–31.

Summerlin, Danica. 2016. "Papal Councils in the Middle Ages." In *A Companion to the Medieval Papacy*, edited by Keith Sisson and Atria Larson. Leiden, NL: E.J. Brill, 174–96.

Sussman, Nathan, and Yishay Yafeh. 2006. "Institutional Reforms, Financial Development and Sovereign Debt: Britain 1690–1790." *Journal of Economic History* 66, no. 4: 906–35.

Swanson, Robert Norman. 1989. *Church and Society in Late Medieval England.* Oxford: Blackwell.

Swanson, Robert Norman. 2000. "The Pre-Reformation Church." In *The Reformation World*, edited by Andrew Pettegree. London and New York: Routledge, 9–30.

Tabacco, Giovanni. 2004. "Northern and Central Italy in the Eleventh Century." In *The New Cambridge Medieval History*, Vol. 4, edited by David Luscombe and Jonathan Riley-Smith. Cambridge: Cambridge University Press, 72–93.

Tabacco, Giovanni. 2004a. "Northern and Central Italy in the Twelfth Century." In *The New Cambridge Medieval History*, Vol. 4, edited by David Luscombe and Jonathan Riley-Smith. Cambridge: Cambridge University Press, 422–40.

Taylor, Brian D., and Roxana Botea. 2008. "Tilly tally: War-making and State-making in the Contemporary Third World." *International Studies Review* 10, no. 1: 27–56.

Teschke, Benno. 2003. *The Myth of 1648: Class, Geopolitics, and the Making of Modern International Relations.* London: Verso.

Teschke, Benno. 2017. "After the Tilly Thesis: Social Conflict, Differential State-formation and Geopolitics in the Construction of the European System of States." In *Does War Make States?: Investigations of Charles Tilly's Historical Sociology*, edited by Lars Bo Kaspersen and Jeppe Strandsbjerg. Cambridge: Cambridge University Press, 25–51.

Thies, Cameron. 2005. "War, Rivalry, and State Building in Latin America." *American Journal of Political Science* 49, no. 3: 451–65.

Tierney, Brian. (1964) 1988. *The Crisis of Church and State 1050–1300.* Toronto: Mart 21.

Tierney, Brian. 1966. "Medieval Canon Law and Western Constitutionalism." *Catholic Historical Review* 52, no. 1: 1–17.

Tierney, Brian. 1982. *Religion, Law, and the Growth of Constitutional Thought 1150–1650.* Cambridge: Cambridge University Press.

Tilly, Charles. 1975. *The Formation of National States in Western Europe.* Princeton: Princeton University Press.

Tilly, Charles. 1985. "War Making and State Making as Organized Crime." In *Bringing the State Back In*, edited by Peter B. Evans, Dietrich Rueschemeyer, and Theda Skocpol. Cambridge: Cambridge University Press, 169–91.

Tilly, Charles. 1992. *Coercion, Capital, and European States, AD 990–1992.* Cambridge, MA: Blackwell Publishers.

Tilly, Charles, and Willem P. Blockmans, eds. 1994. *Cities and the Rise of States in Europe, AD 1000 to 1800.* Boulder: Westview Press.

Titone, Fabrizio. 2013. "Aragonese Sicily as a Model of Late Medieval State Building." *Viator* 44, no. 1: 217–50.

Toch, Michael. 1999. "Welfs, Hohenstaufen, and Habsburgs." In *The New Cambridge Medieval History*, Vol. 5, edited by David Abulafia. Cambridge: Cambridge University Press, 375–404.

Tuchman, Barbara. 1978. *A Distant Mirror: The Calamitous 14th Century.* New York: MacMillan.

Tucker, Penny. 2000. "The Early History of the Court of Chancery: A Comparative Study." *The English Historical Review* 115, no. 463: 791–811.

Tullberg, Jacob. 2020. *Kingdoms and Sultanates: The Formation of Regional Polities in Medieval Europe Seen from a Comparative Perspective*. Manuscript.

Ullmann, Walter. (1955) 1965. *The Growth of Papal Government in the Middle Ages*. London: Methuen & Co.

Ullmann, Walter. 1977. *Medieval Foundations of Renaissance Humanism*. London: Paul Elek.

Vauchez, André. 1999. "The Church and the Laity." In *The New Cambridge Medieval History*, Vol. 5, edited by David Abulafia. Cambridge: Cambridge University Press, 182–203.

Van Creveld, Martin. 1999. *The Rise and Decline of the State*. Cambridge: Cambridge University Press.

Van Zanden, Jan Luiten. 2009. *The Long Road to the Industrial Revolution: The European Economy in a Global Perspective, 1000–1800*. Leiden, NL: E.J. Brill.

Van Zanden, Jan Luiten, Eltjo Buringh, and Maarten Bosker. 2012. "The Rise and Decline of European Parliaments, 1188–1789." *Economic History Review* 65, no. 3: 835–61.

Verger, Jacques. 1998. "Schools and Universities." In *The New Cambridge Medieval History*, Vol. 7, edited by Christopher Allmand. Cambridge: Cambridge University, 220–42.

Verger, Jacques. 1999. "The Universities and Scholasticism." In *The New Cambridge Medieval History*, Vol. 5, edited by David Abulafia. Cambridge: Cambridge University Press, 256–78.

Verger, Jacques. 2003. "Universities." In *A History of the University in Europe: Volume 1, Universities in the Middle Ages*, edited by Hilde de Ridder-Symoens. Cambridge: Cambridge University Press, 66–81.

Voigtländer, Nico, and Hans Joachim Voth. 2013. "Gifts of Mars: Warfare and Europe's Early Rise to Riches." *Journal of Economic Perspectives* 27, no. 4: 165–86.

Vries, Peer. 2013. *Escaping Poverty*. Vienna: V &R unipress.

Wang, Yü-ch'üan. 1949. "An Outline of the Central Government of the Former Han Dynasty." *Harvard Journal of Asiatic Studies* 12, nos. 1/2: 134–87.

Wang, Yuhua. 2022. *The Rise and Fall of Imperial China*. Princeton: Princeton University Press.

Warren, W.L. 1992. *The Governance of Norman and Angevin England 1086–1272*. London: Edward Arnold.

Watt, John. 1999. "The Papacy." In *The New Cambridge Medieval History*, edited by David Abulafia. Cambridge: Cambridge University, 107–63.

Watts, John. 2009. *The Making of Polities: Europe, 1300–1500*. Cambridge: Cambridge University Press.

Watson, Adam. 1992. *The Evolution of International Society*. London: Routledge.

Wayno, Jeffrey. 2018. "Rethinking the Fourth Lateran Council of 1215." *Speculum* 93, no. 3: 611–37.

Weber, Max. 1958. *The City*. New York: Free Press.

Weingast, Barry. 1997. "The Political Foundations of Democracy and the Rule of the Law." *American Political Science Review* 91, no. 2: 245–63.

Weingast, Barry. 2021. "Adam Smith's Industrial Organization of Religion: Explaining the Medieval Church's Monopoly and its Breakdown in the Reformation." Manuscript, Stanford University.

Weiß, Stefan. 2016. "The Curia: Camera." In *A Companion to the Medieval Papacy*, edited by Keith Sisson and Atria Larson. Leiden, NL: E.J. Brill, 220–38.

Wendt, Alexander. 1999. *Social Theory of International Politics*. Cambridge: Cambridge University Press.

Whalen, Brett. 2019. *The Two Powers*. Philadelphia: University of Pennsylvania Press.

Wickham, Chris. 1984. "The Other Transition: From the Ancient World to Feudalism." *Past & Present* 103: 3–36.

Wickham, Christopher. 2009. *The Inheritance of Rome: A History of Europe from 400 to 1000*. London: Penguin UK.

Wickham, Chris. 2015. *Sleepwalking into a New World: The Emergence of Italian City Communes in the Twelfth Century*. Princeton: Princeton University Press.

Wickham, Chris. 2016. *Medieval Europe*. New Haven: Yale University Press.

Wieacker, Franz. 1995. *A History of Private Law in Europe with Particular Reference to Germany*, translated by Tony Weir. Oxford: Oxford University Press.

Wiedemann, Benedict. 2018. "The Character of Papal Finance at the Turn of the Twelfth Century." *English Historical Review* 133, no. 562: 503–32.

Wieruszowski, Hélène. 1966. *The Medieval University: Masters, Students, Learning*. Princeton, N.J.: Van Nostrand.

Wilks, Michael. 1963. *The Problem of Sovereignty in the Middle Ages*. Cambridge: Cambridge University Press.

Wilson, Peter H. 2016. *Heart of Europe: A History of the Holy Roman Empire*. Cambridge: Harvard University Press.

Winroth, Anders. 2000. *The Making of Gratian's Decretum*. Cambridge: Cambridge University Press.

Winroth, Anders. 2008. "Recent Work on the Making of Gratian's Decretum." *Bulletin of Medieval Canon Law* 26: 1–29.

Witt, Ronald. 2012. *The Two Latin Cultures and the Foundation of Renaissance Humanism in Medieval Italy*. Cambridge: Cambridge University Press.

Witte, John. 2018. "Law and the Protestant Reformation." In *Oxford Handbook of European Legal History*, edited by Heikki Pihlajamäki, Markus Dubber, and Mark Godfrey. Oxford: Oxford University Press, 583–610.

Wolfe, Martin. 1972. *The Fiscal System of Renaissance France*. New Haven, CT: Yale University Press.

Wyrozumski, Jerzy. 2004. "Poland in the Eleventh and Twelfth Centuries." In *The New Cambridge Medieval History*, Vol. 4, edited by David Luscombe and Jonathan Riley-Smith. Cambridge: Cambridge University Press, 277–89.

Zacour, Norman. 1976. *An Introduction to Medieval Institutions*. New York: St. Martin's Press.

Zema, Demetrius. 1944. "The Houses of Tuscany and of Pierleone in the Crisis of Rome in the Eleventh Century." *Traditio* 2: 155–75.

Ziblatt, Daniel. 2006. *Structuring the State*. Princeton University Press.

Zimmerman, Reinhard. 2015. *Cambridge Companion to Roman Law*. Cambridge: Cambridge University Press, 452–80.

Zutshi, Patrick. 1999. "The Papal Chancery and English Documents in the Fourteenth and Early Fifteenth Centuries." In *Papsturkunde und europäisches Urkundenwesen*, edited by Peter Herde and Herrmann Jakobs. Cologne: Böhlau Verlag, 201–18.

Zutshi, Patrick. 2000. "The Avignon Papacy." In *The New Cambridge Medieval History*, Vol. 6, edited by Michael Jones. Cambridge: Cambridge University Press, 651–73.

Zutshi, Patrick. 2003. "Innocent III and the Reform of the Papal Chancery." In *Innocenzo III: Urbis et Orbis*, edited by Andrea Sommerlechner. Atti del Congresso. Internazionale, Roma, 9–15 settembre 1998. Rome: Istituto storico italiano per il Medio Evo, 84–101.

Zutshi, Patrick. 2007. "Petitioners, Popes, Proctors: The Development of Curial Institutions, c. 1150–1250." In *Pensiero e sperimentazioni istituzionali nella 'Societas Christiana' (1046-1250)*. Milan: Vita e Pensiero, 265–93.

Zutshi, Patrick. 2009. "Petitions to the Pope in the Fourteenth Century." In *Medieval Petitions: Grace and Grievance*, edited by W. Mark Ormrod, Gwilym Dodd, and Anthony Musson. York: University of York Press, 82–98.

INDEX

Abramson, Scott, 55n20

absolutism, 10–11, 146, 168, 173–76

Accursius, 18n27, 117

administration. *See* governing institutions

Adrian VI (pope), 175n41

Al-Andus, 22, 24

Albigensian Crusade, 50n10

Alexander III (pope): canon law and, 123; civil law, prohibition of studying, 140; Frederick I, conflict with, 28; judicial procedure, insistence on, 131; Lombard League, alliance with, 48; papal justice under, 104; on papal nepotism, 102n37; plea to aid the Holy Land, 93; support for England, 44; universities and, 138, 140–41

Alexander IV (pope), 50

Alexander V (claimant to the papacy), 72

Alexander VI (pope), 105n42

Alfonso VI (king of Léon and Castile), 29

Alfonso VIII (king of Castile), 95

Alfonso IX (king of Léon), 153

Alfonso X (king of Castile), 131

Aragon: absolutism, 174; appeals to Rome forbidden, 173; Chancery, 90; the medieval parliament, 146; proctorial representation, 165; royal succession, 156; taxation, 98, 157n13; union with Castile, 65n26

Archbishop of Cologne, 108n46

Archbishop of Mainz, 81, 108

Archbishop of Trier, 108n46

Aristotle, 128, 141

assize: of Clarendon, 29; as court, 106; of Northampton, 119

Austria, 65n26, 108n47

Avignon papacy, 39–40, 72, 84, 99–100, 142

Azo of Bologna, 166

Baltic Crusades, 50

Batou, Jean, 64, 168

Bean, Richard, 9

Becket, Thomas, 44, 89n17, 126, 127n18, 134, 140

Béla III (king of Hungary), 90, 154n11

Benedict XIII (claimant to the papacy), 72

benefices, 17n26, 22, 92, 102, 111; as payment in lieu of salary, 83, 86, 89. *See also* sale of clerical office

Berman, Harold, 131

Bernard of Clairvaux, 161

Bireley, Robert, 112n52

bishops: appointment, 3, 152n8; as church administrators, 86; collection of taxes, 91; as a conduit of church influence, 5–6, 31–35, 178; consultation in Scandinavia and Poland, 146n1; dioceses in Europe by 1250, 33; as a double-edged sword for the church, 111; election, 151n6; the Investiture Conflict and, 51–52 (*see also* Investiture Conflict); as judges, 34–35, 122, 129–32; as local magnates, 33–34; medieval parliaments, association with, 168–70; as papal deputies, 15, 32; "prince bishops," 33–34; as secular administrators 15, 31–35, 77; revolt against Gregory VII, 83n8; as royal chancellors, 6, 89–90, 126; synods/council/assemblies, participation in, 149–50, 167–70

Black Death/Plague, 40n36, 101

Blaydes, Lisa, 44–45

Bodin, Jean, 69

Bohemia, 147n2, 176

Bolesław I (duke of Poland), 31n20

Bolesław the Bold (king of Poland), 53n15

Boniface VIII (pope): *Clericis Laicos,* 38; Crusade against enemies in the papal states, 50; excommunications, 44; majority principle confirmed, 152; papal authority, assertion of, 27, 72; Philip IV and Edward I, conflict with, 37–39, 70–71, 127, 150, 181; *Unam Sanctam,* 39

Boniface IX (pope), 101

Borghese, Camilo, 102n36

Borghese, Orazio, 102n36

Bosker, Maarten, 12n16

England (*continued*)
  Great Schism, 72; the judiciary, 106,
  129, 160n21; King's Bench 106, 129,
  160fn21; land holdings by the church,
  2; legal development, 115, 117, 119, 129,
  131n24, 139n30; Magna Carta, 30;
  parliament, 146–47, 158–60, 166, 173;
  parliament as high court, 154; papal
  influence, efforts to limit, 53, 72, 100n34;
  petitions, 154, 166; pipe rolls, 96, 98n32;
  Protestant Reformation, 174–75; *Quod
  omnes tangit* principle, 162; representation, 157–58, 165; royal councils,
  147; royal justice, 129n20; shire courts,
  29n18; state-building kings, 29–30;
  taxation, 93–99; taxation and consent,
  156–59
Ertman, Thomas, 9n9, 10
Eugenius III (pope), 129–30, 164
Eugenius IV (pope), 72, 172
Europe: in 1000, 1300, and 1648, 59–61;
  fragmentation, 55–61, 177–78; papal
  conflict and territorial fragmentation,
  61–67
excommunication, 44–47

Ferdinand I (king of Léon and Castile), 30
Ferdinand II (king of Aragon), 65n26, 72
Ferdinand III (king of Léon and Castile), 29
Flanders, 146
Foliot, Gilbert, 139
fragmentation: of Europe, 55–61, 177–78;
  the Great Schism and, 72 (*see also*
  Great Schism); of the Holy Roman
  Empire, 54–55, 177–78; papal conflict
  and territorial, 61–67; rise of communes and, 67–69
France (i.e., the territory that became
  France): absolutism, 174; administrative development, 24, 57, 80; Avignon
  papacy, 39–40, 48, 71, 84, 85n10,
  99–100, 151n6; bishops/clergy in government, 35, 89–90, 111, 167; Capetian
  dynasty, 22–23; centralization of
  power, 56–7; Chancery, 89–90; church
  influence on state formation, 57, 107,
  102–3; conflict with papacy, 37–8,
  70, 89; control over church, 38–40,
  72, 94, 106–7, 175; decentralized rule
  in, 24; English governing institutions
  and, differences between, 97–98, 115,

118–19, 159; the Great Schism, 72–73;
  investiture, 53; the judiciary, 106–7;
  law, 115, 119, 131n24; parliament, 146,
  159–60; nobility exempt from taxation,
  157n13, 159; papal influence, efforts
  to limit, 72; parliament as high court,
  154; proctorial representation, 165;
  the Protestant Reformation, 175; *Quod
  omnes tangit* principle, 162; regional
  assemblies, taxation and, 160; sale of
  offices, 102–3; state-building kings,
  29–30; taxation, 94, 97, 99, 159; unit
  of representation, 158n15; the University of Paris, 134
Franciscans, 38n32, 111, 141n32
Francis I (king of France), 173n36
Frederick I Barbarossa (Holy Roman
  Emperor): Italy, attempt to control,
  26, 28, 48; legal argumentation
  employed by, 115, 126; Lombard League
  and, 68; proctors summoned, 165;
  Roman law, usage of, 118, 125–26;
  University at Bologna, chartering of,
  136
Frederick II (Holy Roman Emperor):
  chancery in Sicily, 90; Constitutions of
  Melfi, 128; death, 58; excommunication,
  46; Gregory IX, battle against, 48, 50,
  68; Innocent III, conflict with, 28;
  Innocent IV, conflict with, 126; Italy,
  attempt to control, 26, 42–43; legal
  argumentation by, 115; parliaments
  summoned, 146; *Privilegium*, 146;
  proctors summoned, 165; *Quod omnes
  tangit* principle, 161–62; Sicily, control
  of, 29; University of Naples, founding
  of, 137
Frederick III (Holy Roman Emperor),
  53n16
Frederick the Fair, 54n17

Gaudry (bishop of Laon), 67n29
Gediminas (king of Lithuania), 49
Gelnhausen, Conrad of, 171
Genet, Jean-Philippe, 12n15
Germany (i.e., the territory that became
  Germany): fragmentation, 29, 59–60,
  177; Holy Roman Empire established,
  22–23; unification of, 187. *See also*
  Bohemia; Brandenburg; Holy Roman
  Empire; Prussia

A NOTE ON THE TYPE

THIS BOOK has been composed in Miller, a Scotch Roman typeface designed by Matthew Carter and first released by Font Bureau in 1997. It resembles Monticello, the typeface developed for The Papers of Thomas Jefferson in the 1940s by C. H. Griffith and P. J. Conkwright and reinterpreted in digital form by Carter in 2003.

Pleasant Jefferson ("P. J.") Conkwright (1905–1986) was Typographer at Princeton University Press from 1939 to 1970. He was an acclaimed book designer and AIGA Medalist.

The ornament used throughout this book was designed by Pierre Simon Fournier (1712–1768) and was a favorite of Conkwright's, used in his design of the *Princeton University Library Chronicle*.